Indians of California

INDIANS
OF CALIFORNIA

THE CHANGING IMAGE

By James J. Rawls

UNIVERSITY OF OKLAHOMA PRESS : NORMAN AND LONDON

BY JAMES J. RAWLS

Dan De Quille of the Big Bonanza (ed.) (San Francisco, 1980)
California: An Interpretive History (with Walton Bean) (New York, 1983)
Indians of California: The Changing Image (Norman, 1984)
Land of Liberty: A United States History (with Philip Weeks) (New York,1985)

Library of Congress Cataloging-in-Publication Data

Rawls, James J.
  Indians of California.

  Bibliography: p. 257
  Includes index.
  1. Indians of North America—California—Public opinion—History.
2. Public opinion—California—History. 3. California—Ethnic relations.
4. California—History. I. Title.
E78.C15R35   1984   979.4   83–21710
ISBN–0–8061–2020–7

  5   6   7   8   9   10   11   12   13   14   15   16   17   18   19   20   21

For my father and mother

Contents

Illustrations

Maps

xi

Preface

THROUGHOUT recorded history the California Indians have suffered from what today we call a negative stereotype. From the time of the first white contacts observers judged the Indians of California to be exceedingly primitive and viewed their cultures with boundless disdain and contempt. Even today gross misrepresentations and demeaning distortions continue, but, thanks to the researches of modern anthropologists, we also have an appreciation of the complexity and beauty of the lost world of the California Indian civilizations.

What is not so well understood, even today, is that white attitudes toward the Indians of California have also been complex. We have come to accept the generalization that whites on the California frontier regarded the Indians, whom they called "diggers," as utterly primitive people without redeeming value. Yet white attitudes were never so simple nor static. White observers consistently described the California Indians as primitive people, but their attitudes toward the "primitives" changed dramatically over the generations of contact.

When Anglo-Americans first visited California in the early nineteenth century, the future state was a remote province of the Spanish empire. Most of the native peoples whom the Americans encountered were clustered around the coastal missions between San Diego and San Francisco. The early visitors from the United States, reflecting a tradition of denigration as old as the Spanish empire itself, described the Indians of California as primitive victims of Hispanic mistreatment and "enslavement." They agreed that the Indians were surely primitive, but asked whether they did not even so have a right to liberty. Later, as Anglo-Americans began to settle permanently in California and to set themselves up in the manner of Mexican rancheros, they came to view the Indians as a primitive but useful class of laborers. They believed the Indians' aboriginal way of life only made them more docile, tractable, and readily exploitable. During the gold rush, as hundreds of thousands of new immigrants flooded into California, hostilities between whites and Indians rapidly accelerated. White miners, ranchers, and farmers came to see the Indians as threats to their prosperity and security. The dominant image of the California Indians came to be that of an obstacle blocking white progress. The whites believed that the Indians were indeed primitive and therefore that they were all the more repulsive and expendable.

The engine in this evolution of attitudes and images was the changing needs of the white observers. Needing to discredit Hispanic claims in California, American observers saw the Indians as victims; needing to acquire a cheap labor force, they viewed the Indians as a useful class; needing to gain unimpeded access to the resources of the Golden State, they regarded the Indians as obstacles to be eliminated.

The images of the California Indians contained in this book reveal very little about the realities of California Indian culture. The quotations from the historical sources are exact, yet the images of the Indians are often distorted by the overriding self-interest of the observers. Specialists in California ethnology—exercising the greatest caution—may use the primary accounts from which the images are derived to reconstruct the life of aboriginal California, and indeed such pioneers in the field as Stephen Powers and Alfred Kroeber have done precisely that. My purpose is not to duplicate their work. I intend to use these images of the California Indians not as a lens through which to see Indian culture but as a mirror in which to see the creators of the images and to understand the relations that they established with the Indians. Our focus will be on white attitudes, but we shall also look at the customs, practices, laws, and institutions that resulted from those attitudes. The major conclusion of this book is that these nineteenth-century American images of California Indians, while often distorted and inaccurate in their portrayal of the native people, reflected most accurately and consistently the needs of the white observers. If there is a larger truth here, it is that these images tell us more about the image makers than about their subjects.

Acknowledgments

ACKNOWLEDGMENTS are
due many individuals for their advice and counsel in the preparation
of this book. I am especially grateful to three who have guided my
research and have read earlier drafts of the work. My greatest debt
is to the late Walton Bean, Professor of History at the University
of California, Berkeley, who gave each chapter careful scholarly
criticism and who was the source of never-failing goodwill and en-
couragement. Likewise, Professor James D. Hart, Director of the
Bancroft Library, has supported this enterprise with a personal
warmth and enthusiasm that has been sustaining. His criticism has
directed me to greater clarity of expression and precision in the use
of language. Winthrop D. Jordan, formerly Professor of History in
the University of California, Berkeley, and now Professor of History
in the University of Mississippi, asked difficult questions and helped
make the book tighter in composition and logic. From his work I
have derived the basic model for much of my own.

I am also grateful to Professor George H. Phillips of the Department of History at the University of Colorado. He has read
the complete manuscript twice and made many valuable comments
and suggestions. His guidance has been especially helpful in the
final stages of preparing the manuscript for publication.

I am indebted to several others who have read portions of the
manuscript and been generous with their suggestions for improve-
ment: Sherburne F. Cook; Richard Frost; Maynard Geiger; Elsa
Gippo; Robert Ryal Miller; Norris Pope, Jr.; John N. Shumway;
Kevin Starr; and Marilyn Ziebarth. I also wish to acknowledge
William F. Strobridge, Chief of Historical Services in the United
States Army Center of Military History, for his help in locating
materials in the National Archives. To the staff of the Bancroft
Library I shall always be thankful for their kindly assistance and

comfortable accommodations. All of the illustrations in this book are courtesy of the Bancroft Library.

A portion of Chapter 5 appeared in the *California Historical Quarterly*, and to its editors I am grateful for permission to use here a revised version of that material.

On a more personal note, I acknowledge Linda, Benjamin, and Elizabeth, without whose patience and understanding this book could never have been completed; and my parents, without whose values it would never have been begun.

Indians of California

WHY do the nations so furiously rage together,
why do the people imagine a vain thing?

Psalm 2:1

Prologue

CALIFORNIA represents the high-water mark of Spanish expansion in North America: it was the last and the northernmost settlement of Spain on the continent. Its discovery occurred in 1542 during the early decades of European enthusiasm for such elusive fantasies as El Dorado, the Seven Cities of Gold, and the mythical northwest passage to the Orient, the Strait of Anian. More than two centuries passed between the European discovery of California and its settlement by Spanish Franciscan missionaries in 1769. By that time Spain had come to realize that the native peoples of the New World were its most enduring source of wealth; it was upon this resource that Spain had erected its Latin-American empire.

The most striking quality of the Spanish empire was its commitment to the preservation, conversion, and exploitation of the native population—in short, their inclusion within the empire. From its beginning on the islands of the West Indies the American empire of Spain had depended upon American Indians for much of its food production and almost all its labor. As the conquest was extended on the mainland, the Indian population continued to be the basis of the imperial economy and society.[1]

In the centuries before the settlement of California a bewildering variety of Spanish institutions evolved for the exploitation of Indian labor—*encomienda, repartimiento, hacienda*—but this variety should not obscure the fundamental similarity in the status of all conquered Indian groups. They made up a lower class sharply and permanently different from that of their European masters. The most important of the early institutions was encomienda, under which Spaniards were granted groups of Indians from whom they were entitled to receive both tribute payments and labor. Later encomienda was replaced by repartimiento, and Indian villages were required to send out a quota of their male population to work for a fixed num-

3

ber of weeks, in rotation, throughout the year. In practice, a person wishing a repartimiento would file a petition stating that he needed the services of Indian laborers and that he would promise to treat them well. If his petition was approved by colonial officials, the grant of Indian workers would be made. In 1633 the viceroy of New Spain decreed the end of repartimiento, but by that time it had already been replaced in large measure by the more efficient labor institution of debt peonage and the hacienda. Under the new system Indians either established permanent residence on a hacienda or lived within an Indian community and hired themselves out to the hacienda. This system was less coercive than either encomienda or repartimiento, for in theory the Indians were free to choose their employers. This freedom, however, was severely restricted by the extension of credit from employer to employee. In one way or another, Indian laborers soon found themselves enmeshed in a debtor-creditor relationship with their employers, a relationship from which they rarely escaped. The hacienda culminated the evolution of Indian labor relations in the Spanish empire, and debt peonage came to be the dominant form of labor control throughout the eighteenth century.[2]

One of the crudest methods of Spanish labor exploitation was the outright enslavement of Indians, but Indian slavery was never the dominant form of labor relationship in the empire. In virtually every royal pronouncement on the subject the crown maintained that the Indians of the New World were free men.[3] At the heart of Spanish Indian policy was a moral and economic dilemma: Indians were free, yet their labor was essential to the empire's existence; not enough Indians were willing to volunteer their labor, yet to compel them to labor would be a violation of their liberty. The resolution, such as it was, of this dilemma lay in the Spanish definition of liberty. Indians were free to move about and own property and had access to the courts, but they were manifestly not free to be idle or to refuse to contribute to the general well-being of Spanish society. In this sense Indians were free to work, just as the hidalgo was free to govern and bear arms, and the priest to preach and pray. As J. H. Parry has noted, "The liberty of the Indian, in the sense in which Spanish legislators used the word, meant, *mutatis mutandis,* the kind of liberty which a legally free peasant enjoyed in Spain; liberty within the context of the whole society to which he belonged, and subject to discharging the appropriate obligations towards that society, as laid down by custom."[4]

4

Thus throughout Spanish colonial history the Indians remained in a kind of twilight zone between freedom and slavery. Compulsion was applied, under the law, in carefully prescribed ways; the Indians were forced to perform their obligations as "free" men. Most students of Hispanic-Indian relations agree that the ideal of Indian freedom was never realized, that the demand for Indian labor was unrelenting, and that compulsion was universal. Much of the legislation intended to regulate relations with Indians and protect their rights was ineffective, either because of local opposition or because of inadequate supervision. Abuses of the system were common. Whatever the law might say, in actual practice the distinction between slavery and "free compulsory labor" was often difficult to make.[5]

In considering the status of the Indian peoples in the Spanish empire, it is also important to remember that the various forms of compulsory labor were part of the larger "civilizing" or Hispanicizing purposes of Spain. From the beginning of Spanish contact with the New World, Spain sought justification for its conquest, dispossession, and exploitation of the Indians in the Christian duty of conversion. Spanish dominion, of course, was based on the famous bulls of Pope Alexander VI, which granted to Castile virtually all of the land of the Indies and obligated the conquerors to bring the natives to Christianity. A large part of the instructions to nearly every Spanish explorer and colonial governor was taken up with the matter of converting and "civilizing" Indians. Indeed, one of the distinctive aspects of the Spanish empire was the union of church and crown, each committed to conquest and expansion and each supporting the other in the extension of Spanish and Christian civilization.[6]

The church, that is, the missionary orders, bore the primary responsibility for the spiritual conquest. On the frontiers of Spanish America—from Paraguay and Chile to Texas and California—the Dominicans, Jesuits, and Franciscans established hundreds of missions and converted tens of thousands of native people. On the frontier the missions were the primary instrument for the cultural transformation of the Indians and for their inclusion within the empire.[7]

Thus it is hardly surprising that, when Spanish officials contemplated settling Upper, or Alta, California in the eighteenth century, they turned to a missionary order. At that time the Franciscans were the only group actively interested in California, though at the beginning of the seventeenth century the Jesuits had pushed the frontier of New Spain northward by establishing missions in modern-day Arizona and along the coastline of Baja California. After the expulsion of the Jesuits from the New World by Charles III in 1767, the Franciscans had taken over the Baja California missions, and they continued to press for expansion of the chain farther northward. When the order came for the settlement of Alta California, the Franciscans were chosen for the task. California was to be, in terms made familiar by Herbert Eugene Bolton, a mission borderland.

The Indians of Alta California who thus became subjects of the Spanish crown were remarkably diverse. Numbering perhaps 300,000, they were divided into more than 100 separate tribes or nations. Four of the major North American linguistic groups were present in California, plus one that is distinctly and solely Californian. Apparently, over the centuries representatives of the various North American language groups had migrated to California, perhaps attracted by the same qualities that have lured more recent immigrants. Once in California, they retained their distinctive languages. Native California contained speakers of over one hundred dialects, 70 percent of which were as mutually unintelligible as English and Chinese. No area of comparable size in North America, or perhaps in the world, contained a greater variety of native languages and cultures than did aboriginal California.[8] (See map 1.)

Alfred Kroeber has divided California into six major, geographically distinct "culture areas," within which residents shared common traits, such as dress, housing, manufacturing methods, routine activities, and economic pursuits.[9] Four of these areas—the southern, central, northwestern, and northeastern—are considered to be part of the larger "California culture area"; while the remaining two regions, the Great Basin and the Colorado River areas, are linked to California only by the accident of modern political boundaries.

The twenty or so tribes of the southern California culture area were among the first to be inducted into the Spanish missions. Here, along the southern coast, were some of the most populous tribes in California. The Chumash Indians, of the area between present-day San Luis Obispo and Ventura, lived in large villages, some of which had more than a thousand residents. Sustained by the great abundance of shellfish and other sea life, the Chumash were skilled as navigators and fishermen. Their oceangoing canoes, con-

CULTURE AREAS

S = Southern
C = Central
NW = Northwestern
NE = Northeastern
GB = Great Basin
CR = Colorado River

MAP 1. California Tribal Territories and Culture Areas. Based on maps in Robert F. Heizer, ed., *California,* vol. 8 of William C. Sturtevant, ed., *Handbook of North American Indians,* and Robert F. Heizer and Albert B. Elsasser, *The Natural World of the California Indians.*

structed of planks lashed together and caulked with asphaltum, permitted extensive travel between the coast and the numerous offshore islands.[10] They also produced some of the most colorful and spectacular rock paintings in North America. The extant paintings, found on caves and rock outcroppings throughout southern California, are almost always abstract in design; even when life forms are depicted they are highly stylized and imaginative. Campbell Grant, the foremost authority on California rock art, has concluded that the extraordinarily fanciful quality of many of these paintings suggests that the artists may have been under the influence of the hallucinogenic drug *toloache*.[11]

The use of this powerful drug, prepared from the jimsonweed *(Datura stramonium)*, probably originated among the Gabrielino Indians (so named because they were brought by the Spaniards to the San Gabriel mission). The drug then spread north to the San Joaquin Valley and south to San Diego. Its use was part of a complex initiation ritual, the central feature of which was the ingestion by adolescent boys of a solution of *toloache*. While under the drug's influence, the boys not only would experience hallucinations but also would be subjected to long sermons by the guiding shamans, or priests, of the cult. Among the Gabrielinos and the Juaneños (who were native to the area around San Juan Capistrano) the cult was much elaborated and was related to belief in a deity called Chinigchinich. In general, however, the rituals and costumes of the southern tribes were simple and rather somber, taking on what Kroeber has called a "specifically inward character" in marked contrast to the outward-directed affairs of other tribes in California.[12]

The central California culture area covered about half the present territory of the state, and within it were eighteen major tribes. About three-fifths of all the natives of Alta California lived in this vast area. Along the central coast and throughout the Sacramento and San Joaquin valleys the climate was mild, and plant and animal life was abundant. Famine was unknown, for the oaks of the rich valley plains and rolling foothills produced acorns—the staple of the Indians' diet—in greater quantities than could be consumed. Likewise, berries, seeds, fish, deer, elk, and waterfowl were available in bountiful supply. Tribal dress and housing reflected the mild climate, and both were often minimal. Women generally wore a short skirt of skins or plant fibers, while men often wore nothing at all. Ceremonial dress included brightly colored headdresses of plumes and sticks covered with feathers. Housing varied from the

Costanoans with feathered headdresses at San Francisco. Drawn in 1816 by the Russian-born artist Louis Choris, a member of the Otto Kotzebue expedition to California.

reed-thatched shelters along the coast to the semisubterranean homes of the interior valleys, which were banked with earth for insulation. Each village also had an earth-covered temescal, or sweathouse, used daily by men as a ritually purifying act. Following their hot air "bath," the men would plunge into a nearby lake or stream. Material-culture items, such as weapons and tools, were generally simple and unornamented, but in basketry the California natives exceeded all others in skill and accomplishment.

The basic unit of political organization was the village community, or tribelet, comprising several small villages within an area of two hundred to three hundred square miles. The acknowledged leader or chief of a tribelet customarily resided in the community's principal village. Lacking the power of life and death over other members of the group, a leader's authority rested on the trust that the tribelet placed in him. There was a strong sense of territoriality among the various tribes of central California, and trespassing was

Interior of a temescal, or sweathouse, in central California. From a drawing by William Smythe in the first English-language book devoted wholly to California, Alexander Forbes's *California: A History of Upper and Lower California*, published in 1839.

often met by forceful opposition. Generally, however, the native peoples were peaceful and sedentary. Individuals often had very few contacts outside their own homeland, and village sites remained occupied by generation after generation. Warfare was rare and usually limited to petty conflicts with few casualties.

Shamans within each group were skilled in the arts of healing, treating sprains, torn ligaments, and other injuries. They also cured disease by elaborate rituals and by sucking out the "pain." Overhanging all their activities was what Theodora Kroeber has called "the gossamer curtain of religion," the substance of which was a creation myth. The Creator Gods had made the earth and retreated from it, leaving the world for the human beings who came after them. From their gods the people "inherited, as it were, the old brooding nostalgic love of the land, of the Way as it was anciently set. And this determined the direction, the force, and the temper of

10

their religious understanding and practice and emotion, hence their values and what they would and would not do and be."[13]

The northwestern California culture area included fourteen separate tribes who were part of the larger North Pacific Coast culture that extended from California to Alaska. One of the distinctive features of this regional culture was the great value placed upon the accumulation of material wealth. Private ownership of resources, such as the exclusive right to gather acorns from a particular oak grove or to fish for salmon from a particular pool, was carried further here than anywhere else in California. A man's social status was determined by the possession of conspicuous objects of wealth, such as woodpecker scalps, large obsidian blades, white deerskins, or strips of the tubular mollusk shells known as dentalia. As one might expect, the northwestern people also took great care in the manufacture and elaboration of tools and implements. The simple dress of the central area was augmented here by twined basket caps for the women decorated with intricate geometric designs.

The emphasis on wealth also found expression in religious beliefs and practices in the Northwest. The shaman, who was generally a woman, would remove pains from her patient, but always for a fee. If her first treatment was unsuccessful, she would return to try again and would be paid again. In the World Renewal Cult such ceremonies as the Jumping Dance and the White Deerskin Dance not only served to renew or maintain the natural world, perpetuating abundant acorn crops and salmon runs, but also provided an opportunity for men of substantial means to display their accumulated wealth.

Political organizations in the Northwest were even weaker than the loose collections of villages in central California. The northwestern tribes did enjoy, however, a highly developed system of law. Precise values were set on material goods, and injuries or trespasses were settled by just compensation through adjudication by third parties. Leadership rested among the richest men, who surrounded themselves with their relatives. Thus in the Northwest the individual and his own private collection of wealth and privileges took precedence over the affairs of the group.[14]

The tribes of northeastern California subsisted at a relatively simple cultural level. Because food was scarce in this desolate area, the people spent a larger portion of their time hunting small game and gathering seeds and roots. As a consequence they had neither the time nor the resources to indulge in the complex rituals and

11

ceremonies characteristic of their neighbors in the northwest. Also, in contrast to the densely populated heartland of California, the northeastern corner of the state was only thinly settled.[15] Likewise, the tribes of the Great Basin, living along the present-day eastern border of the state and in the eastern deserts of southern California, had to accommodate themselves to a difficult environment. Food and even water were scarce here; famines were frequent. To sustain themselves, these tribes had constantly to move in search of such game as desert rats and rabbits. Their material possessions were limited, consisting of little more than clothing, baskets, bows and arrows, and rabbit-catching nets. California anthropologist Robert F. Heizer has observed: "Where the majority of California Indians were generally well off, and in some areas unusually favored as regards food, the desert areas were characterized by want and poverty and hunger—indeed, no American Indians were less materialistic and displayed a simpler culture than is found in the Great Basin area."[16]

Farther south, along the Colorado River, conditions were somewhat more hospitable to human habitation. The fertile floodplain of the Colorado provided a perfect environment for the cultivation of corn, beans, and pumpkins, and thus the tribes of this area could supplement their hunting and gathering with a rudimentary agriculture. Some farming was practiced elsewhere in California—tobacco crops, for example, were ubiquitous, and the Cahuillas of the south-central area also were agriculturalists—but nowhere else did a people depend as much upon planting and harvesting as in the Colorado region. The Colorado River tribes also regarded themselves more as national entities, unlike the village- or tribelet-oriented people elsewhere in the state, and they acted as political units when engaged in aggressive or defensive war. Along the Colorado warfare had a strong mystical value; courage in mortal combat was prized above all other virtues. In nearly every other part of the state warfare had a wholly negative value and was far less technically advanced. Finally, in contrast to the parochialism of most California natives, the people of the Colorado River traveled extensively outside their own territory, carrying trade goods to the coast and into the southern San Joaquin Valley.[17]

As we conclude this briefest of surveys of California Indian cultures, we cannot help but be struck by the unsatisfactoriness of the term "California Indian." Obviously this convenient abstraction makes little sense unless many qualifying specifications are appended to it. The problem is really a local variation of the more general problem of using the term "Indian" to refer to the two thousand or more cultures and societies that flourished in the Western Hemisphere before the arrival of Europeans. The concept of the California Indian is a white invention. It was created for the purposes of description and analysis, but it was also useful as a stereotype for whites overwhelmed by the diversity of the peoples encountered in the area.[18] The literature of white contacts with the California tribes is filled with references to "California Indian characteristics" or "the traits of the California Indian." The culture of one tribelet is taken as an illustration of all of California Indian culture, or, conversely, it is assumed that some broad generalization will explain the behavior of any given community of California Indians. Thus we find a disappointing lack of discrimination among many whites who set out to record their impressions of the natives of the state.

As we shall see, when white observers distinguished between the California Indians, the most important and most common standard they applied was the nature of the Indians' relationship to white civilization. Thus we have "mission" and "gentile" Indians, "tame" and "wild" Indians, "useful" and "hostile" Indians. Of course, many whites did attempt conscientiously to record finer distinctions among Indians. For example, the names that they gave the natives reflect their sense of geography. Thus we have the Diegueños of San Diego, the Nicoleños of San Nicolas Island, and the Mill Creeks of Tehama County. It is worth repeating, however, that the subdivisions generally did not controvert the broader assumption that the California Indians were a distinct entity and that individual Indians, tribes, and tribelets differed mainly in the nature of their relationship with whites.

In 1769, José de Gálvez, *visitador-general* in New Spain, selected the *presidente* of the Baja California missions, Junípero Serra, to lead a group of missionaries on an expedition to Alta California. Accompanying Serra was a body of Spanish military forces under Captain Gaspar de Portolá. This Portolá-Serra expedition, known in the annals of California history as the "Sacred Expedition," marks the beginning of permanent European settlement in California. Over the next half century the Franciscans established twenty-one mis-

13

sions along the Pacific Coast from San Diego to San Francisco Bay. These coastal missions formed the core of Hispanic California. (See map 2.)

The missions of Alta California, like those on other Spanish frontiers, were more than just religious institutions. They illustrate well the unique blend of church and crown, of secular and spiritual matters, in the Spanish empire. The royal treasury, for example, provided an annual stipend for each missionary and a grant of about $1,000 for the founding of each mission. In addition, a garrison of a half dozen or more soldiers was provided for each mission to protect the priests and to assist them in enforcing discipline. In return for this secular aid, the missions fulfilled some important political functions. They were designed to settle and defend the lands over which Spain claimed dominion; built like military fortresses, they were arranged in the shape of a quadrangle with adobe walls six to eight feet thick. The missions also countered foreign influence among the Indians on the frontier and deterred other nations from molesting Spanish settlements (if they had any intention of doing so). Furthermore, the missionaries benefited the empire by providing detailed information on new lands and by encouraging migration of Spaniards to the empire's frontiers.[19]

The principal concern of the missionaries was the conversion of the Indians to Christianity, and the success of their enterprise is indicated by the record of nearly 54,000 baptisms in California during the mission period.[20] Virtually all of the Indians along the California coast south of San Francisco were converted as neophytes under the direction of the Franciscans. (The term "neophyte" was the Spanish designation for an Indian who had been baptized. An unconverted Indian was a "gentile.") Religious conversion, however, was not the sole concern of the missionaries. The Franciscans also recognized that effective Christianization could not be separated from the larger process of acculturation. Their aim was to bring about a rapid and thoroughgoing transformation of the natives. The Indians were to be Hispanicized not only in religion but also in social organization, language, dress, work habits, and virtually every other aspect of their lives. To bring about such fundamental changes, the Indians first had to be concentrated, by force if necessary, so that the missionaries could closely regulate their activities.[21]

The missions established in California were *reducción* or *congregación* missions, of the kind developed in the late sixteenth century for use where Indian populations were not already densely concen-

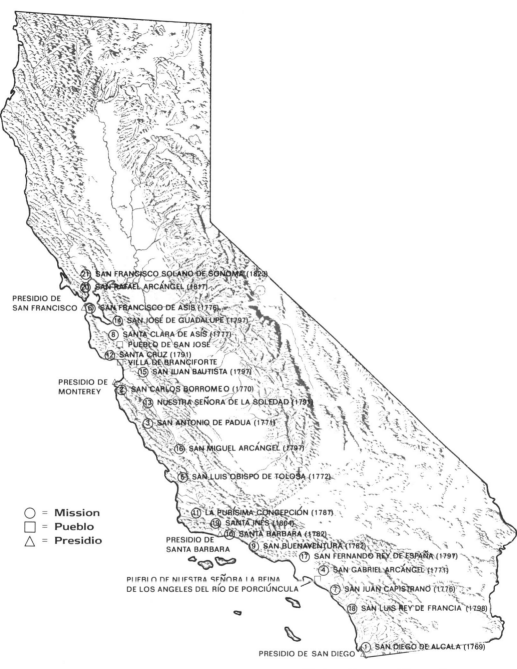

○ = **Mission**
□ = **Pueblo**
△ = **Presidio**

㉑ SAN FRANCISCO SOLANO DE SONOMA (1823)
⑳ SAN RAFAEL ARCÁNGEL (1817)

PRESIDIO DE
SAN FRANCISCO △⑥ SAN FRANCISCO DE ASÍS (1776)

⑭ SAN JOSÉ DE GUADALUPE (1797)

⑧ SANTA CLARA DE ASÍS (1777)
□ PUEBLO DE SAN JOSÉ
⑫ SANTA CRUZ (1791)
▱ VILLA DE BRANCIFORTE
⑮ SAN JUAN BAUTISTA (1797)

PRESIDIO DE △② SAN CARLOS BORROMEO (1770)
MONTEREY
⑬ NUESTRA SEÑORA DE LA SOLEDAD (1791)

③ SAN ANTONIO DE PADUA (1771)

⑯ SAN MIGUEL ARCÁNGEL (1797)

⑤ SAN LUIS OBISPO DE TOLOSA (1772)

⑪ LA PURÍSIMA CONCEPCIÓN (1787)
⑲ SANTA INÉS (1804)
△⑩ SANTA BARBARA (1782)
PRESIDIO DE
SANTA BARBARA ⑨ SAN BUENAVENTURA (1782)
⑰ SAN FERNANDO REY DE ESPAÑA (1797)
④ SAN GABRIEL ARCÁNGEL (1771)
PUEBLO DE NUESTRA SEÑORA LA REINA
DE LOS ANGELES DEL RÍO DE PORCIÚNCULA □ ⑦ SAN JUAN CAPISTRANO (1776)
⑱ SAN LUIS REY DE FRANCIA (1798)

① SAN DIEGO DE ALCALA (1769)
PRESIDIO DE SAN DIEGO △

MAP 2. Hispanic California. Based on a map in Walton Bean and James J.
Rawls, *California: An Interpretive History.*

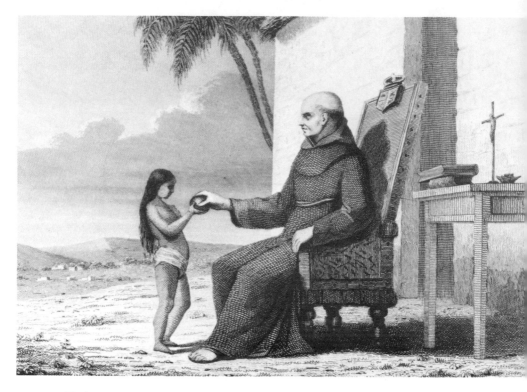

Father Narcisco Durán and an Indian child, probably at Mission San José.
From a lithograph in the published account of Eugène Duflot de Mofras's
visit to California in 1841 and 1842.

trated in native pueblos. By various means the Indians were con-
gregated around the missions, where they were "reduced" from
their "free, undisciplined" state to become regulated and disciplined
members of colonial society.[22] Inside the missions the priests exercised an absolute authority over the neophytes in matters both spiritual
and temporal. Resistance to this authority was met with reproof
and, when it continued, with the lash, stocks, irons, and other means
of punishment. Soldiers garrisoned at the missions or at one of the
nearby presidios assisted in the enforcement of discipline and in the
recapture of runaway Indians (once an Indian became a neophyte,
he was considered no longer free to reject his vows and return to
his former lands or way of life). Although resistance to the Spaniards
was greater than has sometimes been recognized, the missions ul-

Indian workers under guard at the Presidio of San Francisco. From an 1816 drawing by Louis Choris.

timately succeeded in transforming the coastal population of California.[23]

By the end of the Spanish mission period in 1821 the Indians between San Diego and San Francisco had been removed from their native villages and relocated in and around the missions. Acculturation had proceeded to a remarkable degree, and the mission Indians had learned to perform a variety of new tasks: weaving, tanning, and blacksmithing; the making of bricks, tiles, pottery, shoes, saddles, wine, candles, and soap; the herding of horses, cattle, sheep, goats, and other livestock; and the planting, irrigating, and harvesting of vegetables and grains. The construction and decoration of mission buildings were accomplished almost entirely with native labor. About ten thousand acres around the missions were cultivated by Indian farm workers, and Indian herdsmen tended nearly 400,000 cattle, more than 60,000 horses, and over 300,000 hogs, sheep, and goats.[24]

In addition to transforming the way of life of the California Indians, the missions also inadvertently contributed to their destruction. During the mission period the native population between San Francisco and San Diego fell from 72,000 to 18,000, a decline of over 75 percent. Most of this decline was caused by the introduction of new diseases, especially those of a nonepidemic and venereal variety, for which the Indians lacked immunity. The missions increased the incidence of disease because of the aggregations of Indians at the mission compounds, the changes in the Indians' diets and resulting dietary deficiencies, increased intercommunication among Indian groups, the poor sanitation at the missions, and the lack of medical care. The social environment of the missions—the unfamiliar labor, the new system of crime and punishment, the suppression of familiar patterns of behavior—further contributed to the decline.[25] As Alfred Kroeber once remarked: "It must have caused many of the Fathers a severe pang to realize, as they could not but do daily, that they were saving souls only at the inevitable cost of lives. And yet such was the overwhelming fact. The brute upshot of missionization, in spite of its kindly flavor and humanitarian root, was only one thing, death."[26]

By the time the California mission system had reached maturity, around 1800, the neophytes constituted the economic base of the Spanish colony. Their labor produced the buildings, food, manufactured items, and the colony's few exportable goods. That labor, however, was not always freely given. Sherburne F. Cook in a seminal study, *The Conflict Between the California Indian and White Civilization* (1943), has concluded that the California missions were built upon a system of forced labor. Because the labor required in the missions was so different from that to which the Indians had been accustomed before missionization, Cook argued, "the church administrators were obliged to exercise a coercion which rapidly induced the development of a full-scale forced-labor system." Cook was careful to point out, however, that the missionaries did not personally benefit from this arrangement. Neither the mission produce nor any income derived from it belonged to the Franciscans: "Furthermore, in theory always, and in practice usually, the fruit of Indian labor was devoted to the welfare and improvement of the Indian himself. Any selfish enrichment of the missionary was incidental and contrary to the tenets of the Church." Thus, while a system of forced labor existed in the missions, Cook maintained, the economic relationship between priest and Indian could best be described as "communal."[27]

The missions of California, like those elsewhere, were designed as temporary institutions. When the work of Christianization and civilization was done, the missionaries were expected to move on to new frontiers. The missions were to be turned over to the secular clergy, and the common mission lands distributed among the former neophytes. In theory, the period from founding to secularization of each mission was to be ten years, but in California the period of tutelage was much longer. Although the missionaries did not intend it, one of the results of their work was that the Indians under their direction were made exploitable — exploitable, that is, by persons other than missionaries and in arrangements other than communal. Before the establishment of the missions the Indians of California had not been of much use to Europeans. Scattered in small bands, for the most part, the natives had neither the skills nor the discipline that would make them useful. The missions changed all that, however, by concentrating the Indians, training them in valuable skills, and inculcating in them the discipline of regular labor as the Spaniards saw it. Although the missionaries intended to prepare the Indians for self-sufficiency within the colonial society, in fact, they prepared them for severe and extensive exploitation once the missions were disbanded. As the missions neared their end, the released neophytes were much sought after by Mexican rancheros, who viewed them as a potentially valuable supply of labor.

Although the Spanish government had attempted to secularize the frontier missions as early as 1749, it was not until after Mexican independence in 1821 that the Franciscans were finally replaced by secular priests and the California missions converted to parish churches. For the Indians secularization meant that they were no longer compelled to remain at the missions. Under the secularization decree of 1834 half of the mission lands were to be reserved for those Indians who wished to remain at the missions; few Indians, however, were able to retain their property for long. Most of the former mission lands, as well as other tracts along the coast and in the valleys of California, were granted to private citizens by the new Mexican government. Under Mexico's liberal colonization policy individuals could obtain rancho grants in California of up to 50,000 acres. During the entire Spanish period only twenty private land grants had been made, whereas 500 ranchos were created by the Mexican government.

A California rancho might employ as few as twenty or as many as several hundred Indian workers. The Indian work force totaled perhaps four thousand in all, including both former mission Indians and new recruits gathered by the rancheros. Some of the former neophytes stayed on briefly at the missions, while others deserted to the interior or to the centers of civilian Mexican settlement. Most of the former mission Indians, however, were taken over by the rancheros and continued to work without interruption for their new masters. The important difference between work at the rancho and at the mission was that on the rancho the communal relationship was lacking: the profits of Indian labor were appropriated almost entirely by the ranchero.[28]

The rancho economy, like that of the missions, was based on the cultivation of grain and huge herds of cattle. The rancheros traded hides and tallow for manufactured goods from foreign traders along the coast. As at the missions, the work of herding, slaughtering, hide tanning, and tallow rendering and all the other manual tasks were performed by Indian workers. In return for their labor the Indians usually received nothing more than shelter, food, and clothing. The rancheros were in absolute control over their workers and used several means of coercion—persuasion, economic pressure, violent force—to recruit and maintain their labor supply. "In short," Sherburne Cook has concluded, "the hacienda-peon society was introduced without much modification from Mexico to California and was impressed thoroughly upon the social thought of the state."[29]

While one must distinguish carefully the communal quality of the missions from the earlier forms of Indian labor exploitation in the

Spanish colonies, such caution is not necessary when describing the ranchos. Here the system of Indian labor exploitation was virtually identical to that which prevailed throughout New Spain in the eighteenth century and in regions of Mexico at the time of independence. The Indians were nominally free, but in practice they were bound to the service of the ranchero as long as he cared to hold them. As on the great haciendas of Mexico, the rancho Indians could not leave their employers if they were in debt to them, and it was commonplace for the rancheros to keep their laborers constantly in debt. Under this system of peonage the Indians' freedom was restricted in many ways. The Indians were prohibited, for instance, from moving from place to place without having a properly signed discharge from their last employer showing that they were not in debt to him. Fines of five dollars could be levied on employers who acquired Indian workers without such a discharge. Thus the rancho society of Mexican California was essentially a feudal society. The rancheros ruled as lords on their great landed estates, and the Indian workers who tended the fields and herds were their serfs.[30]

The status of the Indians in Hispanic California, in sum, was not much different from the status of Indians throughout Spanish America. The Franciscan missionaries had demonstrated that under strong discipline and training the California Indians could perform similar labor and work under similar conditions as Indians elsewhere in the empire. The rancheros in the Mexican period abandoned the padres' interest in conversion and their communal model of economic organization but expanded the practice of forced labor, bringing California into rough conformity with the dominant form of Indian labor control in eighteenth-century Latin America, the institution of hacienda and Indian peonage. The division of California society into an elite of Hispanos and a mass of Indian laborers thus reflected a tradition that reached back to the founding of the Spanish empire.

PART I

Victims

IN a word, everything reminded us of a habitation in Saint Domingo, or any other West India colony. The men and women are assembled by the sound of the bell, one of the religious conducts them to their work, to church, and to all other exercises. We mention it with pain, the resemblance is so perfect, that we saw men and women loaded with irons, others in the stocks; and at length the noise of the strokes of a whip struck our ears.—Jean François Galaup de La Pérouse, *A Voyage Round the World in the Years 1785, 1786, 1787, and 1788*

DESTITUTE of industry themselves, [the Californians] compel the poor Indian to labor for them, affording him a bare savage existence for his toil, upon their plantations and the fields of the Missions. In a word, the Californians are an imbecile, pusillanimus race of men, and unfit to control the destinies of that beautiful country.—Thomas Jefferson Farnham, *Life and Adventures in California, and Scenes in the Pacific Ocean*

1

Prophetic Patterns

THE first views we have of the California Indians are in the journals of the several voyages of European exploration made along the west coast of North America in the sixteenth century. Unfortunately, the information contained in these accounts is not very great. We have, for example, some brief descriptions and place-names of California Indians from Juan Rodríguez Cabrillo's voyage of discovery in 1542. The people Cabrillo observed along the southern coast and at Monterey appeared friendly, but, since they exhibited no wealth, their presence did little to encourage further European contact. "They were dressed in skins," Cabrillo wrote of the Eastern Coastal Chumash, "and wore their hair very long and tied up with long strings interwoven with the hair, there being attached to the strings many gewgaws of flint, bone, and wood."[1]

The landing of Francis Drake somewhere near San Francisco Bay in 1579 produced the second European description of California Indians. The official log of the Drake voyage has never been found, but the notes of Drake's chaplain and diarist contain some notice of the Coast Miwoks whom the Englishmen encountered. "Their men for the most part goe naked," the chaplain observed, "the women take a kinde of bulrushes, and kembing it after the manner of hempe, make themselues thereof a loose garment, which being knitte about their middles, hanges downe about their hippes, and so affordes to them a couering of that, which nature teaches should be hidden: about their shoulders, they weare also the skin of a deere, with the haire upon it."[2] Subsequent landings by Spanish voyagers, such as Sebastián Rodríguez Cermeño and Sebastián Vizcaíno, yielded more fascinating glimpses of the natives of California, but the record of observations remained slight.[3]

With the coming of the Franciscans in the eighteenth century the opportunities for a fuller account of aboriginal California increased

25

greatly. With few exceptions, however, the priests wrote little of the culture of the Indians in their charge. "The Franciscan missionaries," Robert F. Heizer has concluded, "were not concerned with recording the 'heathenish customs' of their 'gentile' (that is, unbaptized) wards, whom they generally classed as ignorant and stupid savages."[4] The exceptions to this lack of interest consist mainly of the linguistic studies of Fray Felipe Arroyo de la Cuesta and Fray Buenaventura Sitjar, the replies of eighteen California missionaries to an official Spanish inquiry in 1812, and Fray Gerónimo Boscana's account of Juaneño religion, "Chinigchinich," written in the early nineteenth century. Boscana, a Mallorcan priest who spent much of his missionary life at San Juan Capistrano, characterized native religious customs and beliefs as "horrible," "ludicrous," and "ridiculous" and concluded that the "Indians of California may be compared to a species of monkey."[5]

Partly because other early sources of information on the California Indians are of such limited value, the accounts of foreign visitors to Hispanic California after 1769 have assumed great importance. During the years when California was a Spanish and Mexican province the area was visited by geographers, diplomats, sea captains, and traders from England, France, Russia, and other European nations. These observers were often highly literate and acute, and they produced an impressive body of travel literature describing California and its inhabitants. It is to this literature that we must turn for our first fully rounded images of California Indians. The images of Indians in this European travel literature are also important because we find in them the initiation of a pattern of perception and description that was later shared by Anglo-American visitors to California. To a remarkable extent the early visitors to California from the United States ordered their impressions along the lines established by their European predecessors.

When Jean François Galaup de La Pérouse and the crews of the *Boussole* and *Astrolabe* anchored their ships in Monterey Bay in September, 1786, they became the first foreign visitors to call on the Spanish frontier outposts in Alta California. Even before disembarking, La Pérouse, the leader of this official round-the-world voyage of exploration and discovery, was impressed by the abundance of life in California. He recorded in his journal that the ships were surrounded by a herd of spouting whales and that the surface of the bay was covered with cavorting pelicans. After putting in to Monterey for several weeks, La Pérouse cataloged the extraordinary abundance of California wildlife: seals, hares, rabbits, stags, bears, foxes, wolves, wildcats, partridges, woodpeckers, sparrows and titmice. Conditions in California seemed ideal for the flourishing of living things: "There is not any country in the world, which more abounds in fish and game of every description," La Pérouse observed.[6] The abundance of flourishing wildlife, the unusually salubrious climate, the "inexpressible fertility," and the breathtaking natural beauty, seemed to La Pérouse (and later to a host of others) the outstanding characteristics of California.[7]

Reflecting growing international interest in California, such descriptions were often followed by remarks on the apparent failure or inability of the Spanish-speaking colonists properly to appreciate or exploit the natural riches of California. As if the implications of such comments were not clear enough, some visitors went on to note the vulnerability of California, its sparse population, and its weak defenses.[8] "At first one is astonished," wrote Captain Cyrille Pierre La Place, of the frigate *l'Artémise*, in 1837, "that this . . . country, so beautiful, so fertile and at the same time so easy to take, has not yet become the prey of the great nations of the Old World." The present owners of the area he viewed with disgust as both ignorant and lazy.[9] A few years later another Frenchman, Captain Joseph de Rosamel of the warship *Danaïde*, noted, "Upper California is a very fertile land and it is ideally suited for raising animals, grains and vines." Rosamel then postulated that, if only it had been colonized by a hard-working industrious people able to develop its potential it would be a prosperous and thriving land. Instead, "inhabited by a people for whom life's supreme happiness consists of horseback-riding and sleeping, what can you expect from her? Nothing, except conquest by the first people who take the trouble to seize her!"[10] Likewise, British visitors, such as George Vancouver and Frederick Beechey, found it incredible that a land of such beauty, fertility, good climate, and capacious harbors should be allowed to lie fallow. The remarks of Francis Simpkinson, a midshipman aboard the *HMS Sulphur*, were typical: "In possession of a beautiful and fertile country where anything might be produced, and blessed with a climate like that of Italy, the Californians might if they pleased soon raise themselves to wealth and importance, but that unfortunate spirit of indolence which alike pervades all classes completely destroys these blessings."[11]

27

Nothing was more striking to these early visitors than the contrast between the land of California and its unworthy, indolent population. California, with all its abundance, fertility, natural beauty, and potential for wealth, required a population worthy of developing it. These early visitors might disagree over who among them was worthy of this land, but most could agree that the present colonizers were inadequate.

What of the California Indians? What place do they occupy in these early accounts of life in California? Almost invariably the natives of California were described in these early travel accounts as exceedingly primitive in comparison not only with Europeans but also with other Indian cultures. The familiar (and often incorrect) contrasts were made between the wandering and nonagrarian nature of Indian "savagery" and European sedentary and agrarian "civilization." What stands out, however, is the degree of primitiveness attributed to the California Indians.

Many of the early visitors to California came as participants in worldwide commercial or scientific voyages. The natives of California were among many aboriginal groups whom they observed in the course of their travels, and naturally, when they composed their reports and reminiscences, comparisons came to mind. La Pérouse, for example, commented that the California Indians, in comparison with other North American Indians he had observed, were small, weak, dependent, and lacking in arts and industry.[12] Captain George Vancouver, who led several English naval expeditions that visited California, compared the California Indians with other aboriginal peoples whom he had observed around the world and concluded that with few exceptions the California tribes were the most primitive. In spite of all the laudable efforts of the Spanish missionaries, Vancouver commented, the Indians at Mission San Francisco remained "in the most abject state of uncivilization; and if we expect the inhabitants of Tierra del Fuego, and those of Van Dieman's land, they are certainly a race of the most miserable beings, possessing the faculty of human reason, I ever saw."[13]

Several elements of aboriginal culture were repeatedly cited by these early visitors as evidence of the extreme primitiveness of the California Indians. The near nudity of the natives, for example, frequently elicited comparisons between Indians and other "wild beasts" of the forest.[14] The conical reed houses and tule-reed boats

28

that were common along the central California coast were considered evidence of the Indians' inability to fashion more sophisticated structures. Captain Vancouver, for example, upon sighting tule boats on San Francisco Bay, commented that they were without exception "the most rude and sorry contrivances" that he had ever seen.[15] La Pérouse described the native houses around Monterey—made of long poles stuck in the earth and pulled together to form arches and covered with bundles of thatch—as "the most miserable that are to be met with among any people."[16] The Indians' watertight cooking baskets, feathered arrows, and headdresses evoked more positive comments, but such items were usually regarded as impressive exceptions to the general barrenness of Indian culture.[17] "However dull and heavy, however filthy, ugly, and disgusting, these people appear," wrote Georg Heinrich von Langsdorff in his narrative of the California voyage of Count Nikolai Petrovich Rezanov in 1806, "yet they show a great fondness for ornaments and sports."[18]

Many of the early European visitors viewed the complexion, physiognomy, and stature of the California Indians as the most damning evidence of their extreme "brutishness" and "stupidity."[19] During his visit to San Francisco in 1817, Lieutenant Camille de Roquefeuil stated that the Indians of California were short and squat with neither grace nor vigor and that "their faces bear the imprint of apathy and stupidity."[20] Abel Du Petit-Thouars, captain of the *Venus* on a voyage of scientific and commercial exploration in the 1830s saw the Costanoans at Mission San Carlos Borromeo as having unusually dark skin, black hair, large mouths and "a stupid air which in general corresponds to their intelligence, not much higher than that of animals."[21] Langsdorff likewise described the Indians of San Francisco as badly proportioned with a dull, heavy, and neglected appearance. Neither he nor the crew could recall having seen "the human race on such a low level."[22]

These early visitors often wondered how to account for the presence of peoples whom they considered to be among the world's most primitive in a country possessing such an ideal climate, rich abundant wildlife, and fertile soil. Although outside observers regarded the Spanish and Mexican populations as unworthy of such a land, the Hispanos were, after all, relatively recent arrivals in California. It was contemptible that they had failed to develop California or appreciably to benefit from its landscape, but it was not nearly as puzzling as the supposed anomaly of the California Indians. The Europeans wondered how it was that they after hundreds of generations had

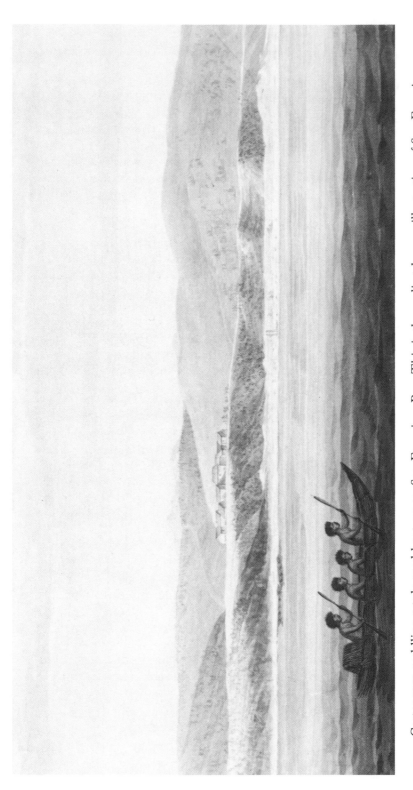

Costanoans paddling a tule reed boat across San Francisco Bay. This is the earliest known illustration of San Francisco and its native inhabitants. From a drawing probably made by the German-born physician, Georg Heinrich von Langsdorff, during the 1806 visit of Count Nikolai Petrovich Rezanov.

Northern Valley Yokuts on the shores of San Francisco Bay with bow, arrows, and animal-skin quivers. Note especially their nudity, dark complexion, and distinctive physiognomy. From a lithograph based on an original 1816 watercolor by Louis Choris.

not benefited more from their environment. This question—or, more broadly, the problem of accounting for the extreme primitiveness of most of the California tribes—was the prime intellectual problem posed by the Indians of California in the minds of their early European observers. It was stated most clearly by the German born physician Georg Heinrich von Langsdorff. After his stay in San Francisco in the spring of 1806, during which he had time for considerable observation and comment on the local Indian population, Langsdorff was left puzzled:

> Although it must be allowed generally, as facts incontestible, that a
> moderate climate is the most favorable to the human species, and that

31

the mild regions of the globe are those which nature points out to man as the most friendly for his habitation, yet here we find a most striking exception to the general rule.

Here, on this western coast of North America, in the thirty-eighth degree of north latitude, where the aborigines live in a very moderate and equable climate, where there is no lack of food and no care about habitations or clothing . . . where an abundance of roots, seeds, fruits, and the products of the sea, in many varieties are at their hands,— these people are, notwithstanding, small, ugly, and of bad proportion in their persons, and heavy and dull in their minds. . . . I frankly acknowledge that the phenomenon of these Californian pigmies, in such a mild climate, and with an abundance of food, is to me a puzzle.[23]

Two separate solutions were suggested to this problem, one of which may be termed environmental, and the other historical. The environmentalists argued that the primitiveness of California Indians was a natural product of their idyllic environment. This was an interesting local expression of the larger controversy during the late eighteenth and early nineteenth centuries over the origins of the diversity of mankind. As the horizons of European knowledge had expanded, the multiplicity of new plants, animals, and human beings had created an acute problem for the natural scientists of the Enlightenment. The preferred explanation for the diversity came to be environmental: different climates and physical landscapes were believed to be responsible for different forms of life and different human cultures. Specifically, the environment of North America was responsible for the peculiar flora, fauna, and people of the New World.

Further debate raged, however, over the nature of that environment and the quality of the life that it had produced. The great French naturalist Comte Georges de Buffon argued that the insalubrious physical environment of the Western Hemisphere was responsible for the deficiencies both of American wildlife and of the American Indian. Thomas Jefferson denied that analysis and argued for the superiority of the American environment and of its natural products, human and otherwise.[24] There was a curious twist to the dispute in California, in that the European visitors argued that the *superior* natural environment of California had somehow created an *inferior* people. They argued that the abundance of wildlife and the temperate climate of the area had made life too easy for the California Indians.[25]

32

Claude François Lambert, for example, praised the region's fertility, abundance, and climate. The soil was so rich, he noted, and the seasons were so perfect that plants bore three times a year instead of just once. In all its natural products California was flourishing; Lambert even stated that in the spring a "kind of manna" fell that was as sweet as sugar. Yet in this ideal setting the California Indians remained primitive. Lambert found the explanation in the natural abundance of California: "Tho' heaven has been so bountiful to the [California Indians], and tho' their soil spontaneously produces what does not grow elsewhere without a great deal of trouble and pains, yet they have no regard to the riches and abundance of their life, they are little solicitous about everything else." In such a setting only the most primitive devices were necessary to survive. Weapons remained simple; clothing was unnecessary; housing was of only casual concern. "The trees defend them from the heat of the sun by day," Lambert observed, "and of the branches and leaves they make a kind of bower, to screen themselves from the injuries of the nocturnal air."[26]

The environmental solution to Langsdorff's puzzle found its fullest development in the memoirs of Russian visitor Kirill Timofeevich Khlebnikov. Seeking to account for the primitiveness of the California Indians, whom he acknowledged were often described as stupid, Khlebnikov argued that their circumstances did not require them to be intelligent. Among the circumstances that he described were the "climate and environment" of California, which so readily supplied the natives with food: "The oak produces acorns, which comprise the chief provision; in many places wild rye grows, the grain of which is gathered by the Indians. In the ground they find many hamsters, Siberian marmots, mice, frogs, etc., which make up their diet." Khlebnikov then proceeded to describe the abundance of larger game as well—geese, ducks, mountain sheep, goats, and deer. Furthermore, since the climate was so mild, the natives had no need of elaborate shelters and thus could "find refuge in the hollows of big trees, in mountain clefts or in tents made of twigs." Likewise, Khlebnikov observed, "The climate does not compel them to dress in skins or textile fabrics. Men and women go around nude." After cataloguing these and other examples, Khlebnikov concluded:

Since the native in his primitive condition readily finds his chief needs, food and shelter, everywhere, there is consequently no reason for exerting his intellectual capacities in improving his state; he thinks that of all the inhabitants of the entire world, those of neighboring territories or territories rumored of, he is the happiest. Perhaps it is this mode of life that is responsible for his deep ignorance.[27]

In contrast to Khlebnikov, other visitors to California speculated that the condition of the California tribes was caused more by historical than by environmental factors. Visitors often noted the contrasts between the "heavy and dull" mission neophytes and the more "lively" unconverted Indians.[28] Captain Du Petit-Thouars, for example, was struck by the difference between "the entirely independent Indians who live far from the missions" and the "dull and unintelligent" mission neophytes. "One cannot help thinking," he concluded, "that perhaps the state of idiocy in which they are found may be due to the cloistered life and to the slavery to which they have been bound since infancy."[29] Where others had found in the natural conditions an explanation for the primitiveness that they perceived in the California Indians, Du Petit-Thouars speculated that the explanation lay in that "unnatural" feature of the landscape the mission.

Beginning with La Pérouse in 1786, a description of the missions and a judgment on their effectiveness was de rigueur for early visitors to California. For better or worse, the early image of the California Indians and that of the California missions were intimately joined. There was always disagreement over the nature of the missions, but most observers viewed them critically and expressed a considerable degree of sympathy for the Indians. In this critical view the California Indians figured as victims of an oppressive institution, as slaves who possessed rights that were violated and whose limited potential was not being developed. The Indians' natural rights to private property and to liberty were denied; their daily lives were made miserable by frequent and harsh corporal punishment. Some observers charged that not only were the Indians held to the missions by force but also many had been originally recruited by force. In spite of the often-noted productivity of the missions, critics maintained that the mission Indians were receiving inadequate instruction in practical skills and that their religious instruction was shallow and ineffective. Later visitors concluded that the rapid depopulation of coastal California was a direct result of Spanish efforts at missionization.

La Pérouse's *Voyage Round the World,* published in 1797, was the first account of Hispanic California by an outsider, and accurately foreshadowed the sensibilities of many subsequent visitors. In a familiar passage La Pérouse described the scene at Mission San Carlos Borromeo, which reminded him of a slave plantation in the West Indies: "The men and women are assembled by the sound of the bell, one of the religious conducts them to their work, to church, and to all other exercises. We mention it with pain, the resemblance is so perfect, that we saw men and women loaded with irons, others in the stocks; and at length the noise of the strokes of a whip struck our ears." La Pérouse, however, was careful to distinguish between the missionaries who were "individually humane and good" and the institution of the mission, which he regarded as reprehensible. What most disturbed him was the delegation to the missionaries of absolute temporal and spiritual power over the neophytes, which he judged to be a violation of the Enlightenment ideals of equality and "the rights of man." He condemned the missions for inflicting corporal punishments for acts that were not considered criminal offenses in Europe and for not allowing the neophytes to renounce their vows and freely return to their native villages. Those who attempted to leave the mission, he noted, were forced to return by squads of soldiers and then publicly flogged. Even within the mission the neophytes' freedom was restricted. For example, the single men and women were locked in separate dormitories at night.[30]

La Pérouse questioned whether the authoritarian structure of the missions, the corporal punishments, and the denial of freedom were necessarily the most effective means to deal with the Indians. He argued that "even these" backward people perhaps had a sense of justice, which, when violated, rendered all efforts to "civilize" them a failure. He asked whether it would be possible to convince at least some of the Indians of "the advantages of a society founded on the rights of the people." La Pérouse suggested that perhaps the missionaries were underestimating the potential of the California Indians. Their efforts at "civilizing" the natives were undercut by their own prejudice: persuaded that "the reason of these men is never clear," the padres considered themselves justified in treating the Indians like children. As they were constituted, La Pérouse concluded, the California missions were "by no means calculated" to free the Indians from their "state of ignorance."[31]

That La Pérouse was not alone in his criticisms of the missions should be clear to anyone who reads through the subsequent Euro-

Neophytes at Mission San Carlos Borromeo in Carmel, lined up in rigid formation for the visit of Jean François Galaup de La Pérouse in 1786. From a watercolor copy, painted in 1791, of the lost original painted at the occasion by Gaspard Duché de Vancy.

pean travel literature of the late eighteenth and early nineteenth centuries.[32] For example, the narrative of Auguste Bernard Duhaut-Cilly's voyage in the 1820s contains an extensive critique of the mission system. Duhaut-Cilly asked, "What do the padres demand from the Indians of Upper California?" and replied, "A little labor in exchange for abundant nourishment, good clothing and the benefits of civilization." He concluded, "In spite of these evident advantages the instinct of liberty is there crying to them to prefer to this quiet, though monotonous, state, the poor and uncertain life of their woods and their marshes." Duhaut-Cilly pictured the California Indians as engaged in a heroic struggle against the mission system. When asked by Mexican authorities to transport three Indians who were charged with some unspecified crime, Duhaut-Cilly reluctantly agreed but then allowed them to escape. While on board the *Héros*, Duhaut-Cilly reported proudly, the Indians were given their freedom—for France had no slavery, and they were then on French soil. He noted that they "at no time failed to conduct themselves most exemplarily; but they knew that, in a few days they should again find their fetters and their tyrants." Duhaut-Cilly described several instances in which Indians had escaped from "bad treatment" in the missions and had been pursued and punished by their "oppressors." The expeditions to recover mission runaways were condemned by Duhaut-Cilly as an "atrocious system."[33]

Duhaut-Cilly's belief that the California Indians were victims of a system of oppression is most clearly revealed in his description of Pomponio, an escaped Costanoan from Mission Dolores. In this remarkable passage a California Indian emerges as a truly heroic figure.

Among the Indians, of whom the larger part seem to be so submissive, there are some who know the prize of liberty, and who seek to gain it by flight. They easily succeed in escaping, but they are often retaken by emissaries sent in their pursuit by the missionaries and the commandants of the soldiers; and without considering that these men have done nothing but make use of the most natural right, they are generally treated as criminals, and pitilessly put in irons.

One of these unfortunate creatures, after several attempts to flee from his oppressors, had at last been condemned to die in irons by the commandant of San Francisco. It is true Pomponio, so he was called, had added to the offense of his numerous desertions, thefts and even murders of some of those appointed to bring him back to his prison. He bore upon each leg an enormous iron ring, riveted on in such a way as to leave him no hope of freeing himself from it; but this man, gifted with an energy and a courage proof against the most frightful tortures, conceives yet once more the plan of freeing himself, and he carries it out. When all his watchers are plunged in sleep, he sharpens a knife, cuts off his heel and slips off one of his fetters; thus, without uttering the least sigh, he mutilates himself in a nervous and sensitive part. But imagine what strength of mind he needs to begin again this cruel operation; for he has yet gained only half of his freedom! He hesitates not; he takes off the other heel and flees, without fearing the acute pain which each step adds to his sufferings: it is by his bloody tracks that his escape is discovered the next day.[34]

Like La Pérouse forty years earlier, Duhaut-Cilly wondered whether a more humane method of dealing with the Indians might not be possible.[35]

Other elements of La Pérouse's critique can be seen throughout the subsequent travel literature. Some observers, for example, criticized the use of military force to recruit or capture neophytes and the use of corporal punishment within the missions.[36] The criticism was sometimes mild, sometimes scathing. Dr. John Coulter, a British visitor, reported the possibility of forced recruitment or "kidnapping" of Indians for the missions and described in a tone of bemused indifference the whipping of neophytes who were late for mass.[37] In contrast, the Russian otter hunter Vassilli Petrovitch Tarakanoff described similar scenes—and worse—with suppressed horror. Tarakanoff had been captured by the Spaniards at San Pedro and held captive for over a year at Santa Barbara or San Fernando. His narrative of that experience includes scenes of vicious torture and cruelty: "From all I saw," he wrote, "I must say the Spaniards are bad men." At one point he described a group of neophytes who had left the mission and were being brought back by soldiers and priests:

> They were all bound with rawhide ropes and some were bleeding from wounds and some children were tied to their mothers.
>
> The next day we saw some terrible things.
>
> Some of the run-away men were tied on sticks and beaten with straps. One chief was taken out to the open field and a young calf which had just died was skinned and the chief was sewed into the skin while it was yet warm. He was kept tied to a stake all day, but he died soon and they kept his corpse tied up.[38]

La Pérouse's judgment that the missions were ill-designed to develop whatever potential the Indians possessed was also echoed by later observers.[39] Adelbert von Chamisso, a French-born botanist aboard the Russian ship *Rurik* on its 1816 visit to California, thought

38

it most unfortunate that the missionaries had such contempt for the neophytes' abilities: "None of them appear to have troubled themselves about their history, customs, religions or languages: 'They are irrational savages, and nothing more can be said of them. Who would trouble himself with their stupidity? Who would spend his time upon it?'"[40] And Captain Beechey argued that the missionaries' system of education was not well designed to bring out what intellectual powers the Indians had, and he suggested that they should make greater effort to learn the Indian languages. The padres in general, he complained, had "a lamentable contempt for the intellect of these simple people, and think them incapable of improvement beyond a certain point."[41]

Perhaps the most serious charge made against the missions was that they were responsible for ill health and death among the Indians of California.[42] Du Petit-Thouars, for example, described the "cruel ravages" of fevers, smallpox, measles, and dysentery among the neophyte populations. "The state of ill health does not extend to the uncivilized Indians," observed Beechey, and Du Petit-Thouars also noted that the "independent Indians" were "less subject to disease than those who live at the missions."[43] The poor health, disease, and high mortality rate among the neophytes led some visitors to speculate whether it was possible for the Indians to survive the process of being "civilized" at the missions: Would the ultimate result of the missions be Indian "civilization" or Indian extinction?[44]

Before leaving this consideration of early European views of the California Indians, we should note that not all comment on the missionary enterprise in Alta California was hostile. The missions had their defenders and, after secularization, a long line of eulogizers. In this more positive view the Indians were pictured not as exploited victims but rather as beneficiaries of the blessings of Hispanic civilization. The emphasis was on uplift and amelioration. The major concerns of mission defenders were either to demonstrate that the California Indians had in fact benefited from the missions or, less frequently, to explain why they had not much benefited. In either case the aboriginal cultures of the natives were described almost wholly in negative terms. On the one hand, the missions were to be admired for their success in substituting an obviously superior culture for an inferior one, yet, on the other hand, any failure to accomplish their noble enterprise was no fault of the missionaries but due instead to the hopeless primitiveness of the California Indians. Thus the defenders of the missions might deny that the Cali-

39

Costanoans fighting a mounted Spanish soldier armed with a lance. Note the conical reed, or thatch, house and the dress of the natives. From a pencil drawing probably by Tomás de Suria in 1791.

fornia Indians were victims, but they shared the view of the mission critics that the natives of California were indeed primitive.

Shortly after La Pérouse's visit in 1786, California welcomed one of the mission system's most enthusiastic defenders, Captain Alejandro Malaspina. Malaspina's voyage of scientific discovery, including his visit to California in 1791, has been described as "probably Spain's greatest exploratory contribution to the age of enlightenment."[45] Although both Malaspina and La Pérouse may be considered products of the Enlightenment, their reactions to the mission system were considerably different. In describing Alta California, Malaspina felt compelled to refute the "ridiculous inventions of many foreign authors, who confusing at times the system with the abuses, and ignoring always the primary object of such establishments, have painted all our missions in America as horrible and oppressive." There was no question in Malaspina's mind that the missionaries had accomplished a great good. The Spanish priests had brought to the Indians, "without the slightest shedding of blood, the end of a thousand local wars that were destroying them, social beginnings, a pure and holy religion, [and] safe and healthy foods." He considered these accomplishments even more impressive because of the extreme backwardness of the local Indians, whom he described as "certainly little ready for rapid progress in civilization." He reported that with the exception of the Chumash of Santa Barbara the natives of California demonstrated an incredible ineptitude in learning the simplest tasks taught them by the missionaries. In his view, the missionaries' work was so difficult and their accomplishment so remarkable because the California Indian was so nearly a beast—the subject of "animal instincts" which "degrade him, make him stupid, and almost convert his life into a living picture of that of irrational beings."[46]

This same theme appeared in the writings of several other early visitors. Lieutenant Edmond Le Netrel was favorably impressed by the missions' accomplishments and thought them especially noteworthy in light of the limited capacity of the Indian population. "It is astonishing," wrote Le Netrel, after listening to the neophyte orchestra and choir at Mission San José, "that one man had the patience and perseverance to teach such stupid beings as the Indians of Upper California to read music and play different instruments."[47] Likewise, Captain Joseph de Rosamel, who visited Monterey in June, 1840, praised the "beautiful missions" as fitting monuments to the men who "had civilized this vast and wild country." Secularization he regarded as a cruel and incompetent policy that was plunging the Indians back into "that savage state from which they had been dragged with so much difficulty."[48]

The early chroniclers of Hispanic California inevitably focused their attention on the relations between the Indians and the Spanish-speaking colonists, and generally their sympathies lay with the former rather than the latter. Many of these early visitors judged the Spaniards and Mexicans as unworthy of California and vigorously criticized the most conspicuous institution of their colonization, the mission. The dominant image of California Indians in this early travel literature is of primitive people who were victims of Hispanic mistreatment and exploitation.

How are we to account for that image? Part of the explanation is that the missions of California were indeed paternalistic and authoritarian institutions. Outside observers, bringing with them values shaped by the Enlightenment, judged the missions to be incompatible with their ideals of equality, liberty, and justice. The image, however, was also a clear reflection of the self-interest of the observers.

Long before settlement of Alta California the imperial rivals of Spain had been condemning Spaniards elsewhere for their mistreatment of the Indians of the Americas. The unflattering comments of La Pérouse and the other critics of Hispanic California are latter-day manifestations of a tradition of criticism of Spanish colonialism that began in the sixteenth century. In 1552, Bartolomé de Las Casas had published his scathing indictment of his countrymen's relations with the Indians of the New World. Although Las Casas hoped that his book would influence the Spanish crown to provide effective protection for the Indians, its most lasting result was to supply the enemies of Spain with ammunition in their verbal assaults on the Spanish empire. French, Dutch, and English propagandists over the next two and a half centuries produced a considerable literature, inevitably citing Las Casas as one of their sources, which described in bloody detail the horrors of Spanish mistreatment of the Indians. Collectively this literature formed a part of what came to be known as "La Leyenda Negra," or "the Black Legend," in which the Spaniards stood accused of gross misconduct in their relations with the Indians.[49]

The Black Legend, which had its roots in European rivalries that existed even before the discovery of America, flourished as the imperial competitors of Spain sought to establish their own claims to the New World. Because Spain was the earliest European power to lay claim to the hemisphere, it was incumbent upon later arrivals to discredit in some fashion the Spanish presence. The Black Legend thrived among those who needed a rationale to challenge or evict Spaniards from their possessions. The argument was plain enough: because the Spaniards had demonstrated such unconscionable cruelty and exploitation in their dealings with the native peoples of the New World, their claims should be invalidated, and more humane colonizers should take over, rescue the Indians, and develop the land in a proper way. By the late sixteenth century, with the growing ideological division of Europe into Protestant and Catholic, the anti-Hispanicism of the Black Legend had become heavily mixed with anti-Catholicism. Thus the church within the Spanish empire came under particular attack for either permitting or perpetuating cruelties toward the Indians.

Of course, not all visitors to Latin America came away with a negative impression of the Spaniards and their treatment of the native peoples. As we have seen in California, observers disagreed among themselves in evaluating Spanish intentions and accomplishments. The positive view of Spanish-Indian relations became part of a so-called White Legend, in which Spaniards were pictured as especially humane, just, enlightened, and energetic. One finds, however, that during times of conflict between Spain and its rivals images in the tradition of the Black Legend predominated. Such conflicts were particularly common during the early years of colonization, but Black Legend propaganda flourished as late as the mid-eighteenth century.[50]

The early European criticisms of the Hispanic enterprise in California and the image of California Indians as the victims of oppression are best understood when placed in the larger context of the Black Legend tradition. The expeditions initiated by La Pérouse in 1786 demonstrated the growing international interest in California, and the image of the mistreated and exploited California natives proved useful to those who wished to discredit the Spanish or Mexican presence in California.

2

The Vanguard

FRANKLIN Walker once commented that three animals brought Americans to California in the first half of the nineteenth century: the sea otter, the beaver, and the long-horned mission cattle.[1] While one might mention the role occasionally played by the mammoth Pacific gray and humpback whales, Walker is certainly correct to stress the importance of those first three animals in the history of Anglo-American contact with Hispanic California. The Americans who came in pursuit of otter and beaver pelts and the black hides of the mission cattle were not of one mind about California, but we can see in their scant writings a pattern of description and judgment that is already familiar to us from the writings of the European travelers who described California as an abundant land rich in unrealized potential. To the Americans the California Indians were extraordinarily primitive people, generally peacefully disposed but not of much use or interest, who had fallen as victims to Hispanic exploitation. Like the European travelers earlier, the early Anglo-American visitors to California often expressed more sympathy for the Indians whom they encountered than for their Hispanic hosts.

The first visitors from the United States actually to see California Indians were men engaged in hunting sea otter along the western coast of North America. The sea-otter hunters came following the publication in 1784 of Captain James Cook's narrative of his Pacific explorations. Cook revealed how, almost by accident, members of his crew gathered otter pelts along the Northwest Coast and then sold them at a tremendous profit in the Orient. Soon ships from the United States, England, Russia, Spain, and, to a lesser extent, France and Portugal were plying the coastal waters in search of these fur-bearing marine mammals. Sea otters could be found at many points along the coast from the Aleutians to Baja California, and some of the greatest concentrations were along the coast and in the bays and channels of Alta California.[2]

It is difficult to learn much about these earliest American contacts with California. Little is known of most of the early otter ships other than the fact of their presence in California waters and the number of otter skins that they carried away. We have few records of the impressions that California Indians may have made on these Americans.[3] Even if adequate records were available, however, it is unlikely that they would contain much notice of the California natives. For, unlike the Indians of the Northwest Coast, most of the natives of the warmer California coast had not developed techniques for hunting the otter, and as a consequence the Americans and Europeans did not establish any extensive trade with the California natives or frequently use them as hunters.[4]

It is true that, as early as 1780, California Indians had brought otter pelts to the Spanish missionaries or soldiers for trade. Likewise, by 1800, American traders had begun a small and, because of Spanish mercantile restrictions, illegal trade with the California Indians. Throughout the Spanish period, however, such contacts remained limited. As the historian of the trade, Adele Ogden, concluded: ". . . The number of otter skins which might be obtained by bartering were few. California Indians did not naturally take to hunting on a large scale, and the mission fathers . . . did not especially encourage them to do so."[5] After 1821, Spanish mercantile prohibitions had been removed, and, in response to the growing demand in California for manufactured goods, neophytes were encouraged by padres and Mexican officials to hunt the sea otter. The Indians were instructed to build more seaworthy craft and to shoot and capture the otters in more efficient ways.[6] Nevertheless, it is probably fair to conclude that most American otter hunters viewed the California tribes as only marginally useful in the trade—perhaps as more trouble than they were worth.[7]

The native population of the Far Northwest coast was a much more valuable source of labor for the otter hunters. Aleuts, Kodiaks, and other natives of the North were taken to California by American and Russian traders. These northwestern Indians and their white employers gained notoriety as aggressive and violent interlopers in California.[8] In an attempt to monopolize hunting around the Santa Barbara channel islands, American otter hunter George Nidever complained, the northwestern Indians would land and attack "the almost defenseless natives, killing many of them, as piles of human bones on these Islands . . . abundantly testify."⁹ Another early American otter hunter, William Dane Phelps, commented that when the Indians of the missions and the Kodiaks met in a "scrimmage" generally the Kodiaks emerged as the victors.¹⁰ In the tradition of Vancouver and La Pérouse, the American hunters compared the California Indians with other North American natives, and, predictably, the Californians emerged as inferior. In the estimation of the American otter hunters, the California Indians not only were of limited economic value but also were the somewhat pitiful victims of the more aggressive Indians on the north.

Our most important source for understanding the views of the sea-otter hunters is the journal of Captain William Shaler, published in the *American Register* in 1808. As Hubert Howe Bancroft noted, Shaler's narrative was the first extended account of California published in the United States.¹¹ Little is known of Shaler's early life, but probably he was of a prosperous New England commercial background. As captain of the *Lelia Byrd* of Salem, Shaler made several commercial voyages to California. The first, and probably the best-known, trip was made in 1803. It was described years later by the *Lelia Byrd*'s first mate, Richard J. Cleveland, in a book published in 1842. On this voyage the so-called Battle of San Diego was fought with Spanish authorities, during which several crewmen who had been arrested by the Spaniards were rescued by Cleveland and Shaler in a spectacular fashion.¹² Shaler himself described the less exciting second voyage made the following year.

Sailing down the northern Pacific Coast in 1804, Shaler recorded his impressions of the "wild beauties" of the countryside. The mountains and the forests, he wrote, "offer a view grand and sublime in the highest degree." An essential part of this romantic wilderness vision was the people who inhabited the woods. To Shaler they seemed scarcely differentiated from the rest of the wildlife: "Here nature reigns undisturbed. The slow progress of the savages toward cultivation has hardly raised them above the condition of brutes: except the human form and the use of language, there is little to distinguish them from the four-footed inhabitants of their forests." Although the wilderness evoked from Shaler expressions of sublimity and grandeur, it would be a mistake to regard him as a primitivist. The Indians whom he glimpsed in the forests along the northern coast were not "noble savages." Instead, he described them as "wretched brutes" who inhabited "wretched hovels" without the "least idea of culture" and whose language was barely adequate to express the most

46

common of ideas. While granting them some skill in the manufacture of "tolerable leather," watertight baskets, and sinew-backed hunting bows, Shaler generally pitied them for their extreme primitiveness.[13]

When the *Lelia Byrd* put in for water and furs at Trinidad Bay, Shaler attempted to elicit the good will of the local Yurok villagers. He became exasperated, however, when the Yuroks demanded payment for water that the crew had taken from the village water supply. Significantly, this resistance evoked from Shaler more pity than anger. He restrained his men from attacking the village, ordering instead the temporary seizure of several of the Indians and the discharge of the ship's four-pound cannon to intimidate the rest. This put an end to overt native hostility and allowed Shaler to correct a mistaken impression: "At first, I attributed [their] temerity to natural bravery; but I afterwards found it was rather stupid ignorance." The ease with which these California Indians were subdued contrasted greatly with the difficulties that the otter hunters regularly encountered with the natives of the far-northern coast.[14]

Echoing the judgment of George Vancouver forty years earlier, Shaler conceded that several Yurok men and women at Trinidad Bay, "if divested of their filth, might pass for handsome." The women were dressed with modesty, and Shaler was impressed that they rejected all the sexual advances made by his sailors. As the *Lelia Byrd* moved down the coast, Shaler began to generalize about the Indians of California. He concluded, "Indians of this country differ very little among each other in their persons, genius and manners: they are a dull, stupid people, of the ordinary stature, and far from comely." Only after observing the culture of the Chumash did Shaler grant an exception to that general picture. "The Indians that inhabit the shores and islands of the canal of Santa Barbara," he noted, "seem to be a race of people quite distinct from the other aboriginals of the country." Their intelligence, beauty, ingenuity, arts, canoes, wicker, and stone work all evoked praise from Shaler. The reason for their relative superiority, he speculated, might be found in a native legend that a race of white men had long ago been shipwrecked along the coast.[15]

Richard Cleveland's description of Shaler's earlier visit to California, *A Narrative of Voyages and Commercial Enterprises,* took little notice of the California Indians. He did comment, however, on the Gabrielinos of the southernmost channel island. In March, 1803, the *Lelia Byrd* had been becalmed near San Clemente Island. Upon landing, the crew discovered eleven men, women, and children in a cave, all of them "in a state of perfect nudity." In contrast to Shaler's praise for the Chumash of the northern islands, Cleveland wrote of these Gabrielinos: "I had been familiar with the Indians inhabiting the various parts of the western coast of America, but never saw any so miserable, so abject, so spiritless, so nearly allied to the brute."[16] This particular incident was the first published account of contact between Anglo-Americans and California Indians. The image that Cleveland produced was to be prophetic of later attitudes.

On November 26, 1826, Jedediah Strong Smith, leader of an expedition of American beaver trappers, reached Mission San Gabriel after an arduous crossing of the Mojave Desert and the San Bernardino Mountains. Smith and his men were the first white men from the United States to cross overland to California, and they effectively opened the fur trade of the far Southwest. Over the next decade hundreds of Americans engaged in this trade—trapping and trading from Taos and Santa Fe along the Humboldt, Gila, and Colorado rivers into California's Central Valley and along the coast to Los Angeles, San Diego, and other Mexican outposts.[17] To these beaver trappers, like the sea otter hunters on the coast, the California Indians were not significant. With the exception of the Mohaves along the Colorado River, the trappers did not consider the Indians of California to be as aggressive and potentially dangerous as the Indians whom they had encountered in the Southwest and on the Great Plains. Although the trappers took the usual precautions to pacify the Indians—making an occasional display of force and distributing gifts—they generally did not view the California Indians as serious threats to their operations. Nor did the California natives engage in any extensive trade with the fur trappers.[18] Elsewhere, of course, Indians were important suppliers of pelts, but in California the fur companies had to rely almost entirely on their own trapping.

For several reasons trappers commonly professed to admire and respect certain qualities of Indian life, and frequently they idealized Indians in their writings. Clearly they did so at least partly out of self-interest. By idealizing Indians as "natural men" who ought to be kept free from the corrupting influences of the settlers' civilization, the trappers were preserving them in their "natural" state as fur suppliers. Lewis O. Saum has argued that the image of "the Noble Savage appears far more universally than one might expect" in the writings of fur trappers.[19] It is difficult to find much support for Saum's generalization, however, in the literature of the California fur trade. Perhaps because the California Indians were thought to be less aggressive, or because they were less valuable to the trappers than were other Indians, the writings by or about the trappers of California do not contain images of noble savages. Instead they describe extraordinarily primitive people whom the trappers called "Diggers."

The label "Digger" later took on several meanings and eventually was applied to a multitude of cultural and linguistic groups in California and elsewhere. Usually it was pejorative, a term of denigration. It provided the Anglo-Americans with a handy rubric to suggest all the qualities of extreme primitiveness that European travelers had for decades attributed to California Indians. The word was first applied by the fur trappers to various peoples in the Great Basin culture area: the Shoshonis, the Paiutes, the Bannocks, Northern Paiutes, and Utes. Like the term "Indian" itself, "Digger" was applied so universally and indiscriminately that it became virtually meaningless. Initially, however, it was reserved for the Western Shoshonis, or Shoshokos. These people were distinguished in their aboriginal state by a lack of organized bands; a subsistence diet of seeds, roots, and small game; and simple or temporary housing structures. "Their most useful possession," according to a recent study, "was their pointed stick, with which they pried roots and native vegetables from the ground. This caused them to be known by the vague term 'Digger,' a name which they shared with the other Shoshoneans on a similar subsistence level."[20]

The Western Shoshonis lived as far north as Idaho, but the ones most frequently encountered by fur trappers heading for California were those who inhabited the barren plains and deserts of Nevada and Utah. As one observer pointed out in 1844, the Indians in that region were regarded by the trappers as "the most degraded and least intellectual Indians" they knew.[21] When Jedediah Smith's party of trappers passed through this country in 1827, Smith recorded in his journal that the region was inhabited by "Indians who appeared the most miserable of the human race having nothing to subsist on (nor any clothing) except grass seeds, grasshoppers, etc." That people as primitive as these should inhabit such a desolate waste seemed appropriate to Smith and other observers.[22] George Yount, a member of a later band of California trappers led by William Wolfskill, commented that the Indians who lived in the barren country of central Utah "well corresponded" with the region where they dwelt. Yount described a band of Paiutes as "a group of the lowest and most degraded of all the savage hords [*sic*] of the west . . . apparently the lowest species of humanity, approaching the monky [*sic*]—Nothing but their upright form entitles them to the name of man." He rendered the name of this group as "*Piuch,* a corruption of the word in the Eutau tongue which means Rootdiggers."[23]

The same qualities that the trappers attributed to the Western Shoshonis and Paiutes they subsequently attributed to the California Indians. For example, Jedediah Smith noted while traveling north through the Sacramento Valley: "[A] great many of these indians appear to be the lowest intermediate link between man and the Brute creation. In the construction of houses they are either from indolence or from a deficiency of genius inferior to the Beaver and many of them live without anything in the shape of a house and rise from their bed of earth in the morning like the animals around them and rove about in search of food." He described the valley itself, however, as having a fertile soil, a plentiful supply of game, and a pleasant climate. Here we find Smith confronted with the same puzzling situation that had confounded Langsdorff twenty years earlier: how to account for an extremely primitive people in a rich land. It made sense to Smith that the Indians in the Nevada deserts were primitive, but, according to that same line of reasoning, the California Indians ought to be possessed of a superior culture. "Degraded ignorant as these indians must be and miserable as the life appears which they lead," wrote Smith, "it is made more apparent by a contrast with the country in which they are placed, a country one would think rather calculated to expand than restrain the energies of man, a country where the creator has scattered a more than ordinary Share of his bounties."[24]

Not all trappers were as puzzled as Smith, but they continued to describe the California Indians in almost identical terms.[25] Zenas Leonard, a member of the Joseph Reddeford Walker expedition of 1833, described the Yokuts of the San Joaquin Valley as inferior to the Indians of the plains. Their housing was primitive, and their clothing was nonexistent. Their subsistence diet of acorns, he believed, left them "very delicate and feeble." At San Francisco Bay, Leonard concluded that "most all of the natives we met with since crossing the last mountain seem to belong to the same nation, as they were about the same colour and size—spoke the same language . . . and all appeared equally ignorant and dillatory [*sic*]—and most of them entirely naked." Traveling south to Monterey among the Costanoans, Leonard wrote, "All these Indians still seem to be very ignorant and stupid." As the Walker party left California, Leonard described the Indians in the foothills of the Sierra as living poorly and "equally as indolent as any of those we had met with in the Spanish dominions. They are generally small in stature, complexion quite dark. . . . Their principle diet during this season of the year consists of roots and weeds . . . all of which they eat raw."[26] In Leonard's narrative, written in 1835, the composite image of the California "Digger" was complete.

Although the beaver trappers regarded the California Indians as extremely primitive people, relations between the two groups were generally friendly. The pattern was one of caution and limited contact: gifts were exchanged, and occasionally trappers traded cloth and trinkets for food, but only rarely did they obtain significant quantities of beaver pelts through trade with the California natives. With the occasional exception of Mohaves along the Colorado River, the Indians of California were pictured in the fur-trade literature as generally passive and inoffensive.[27] The journals of the Smith expeditions of 1826 to 1828, for example, contain many images of peaceful, friendly, and even generous California Indians.[28] Both trappers and Indians seemed eager to avoid conflict or violence. Throughout his travels in California, Jedediah Smith conscientiously tried to maintain harmonious relations with the Indians. He reprimanded his men for any depredations against them and also dealt justly with offended or offending natives. As the Smith party moved through the interior of California, the Indians whom they encountered reacted with fright and then curiosity. Often the trappers' camp was filled with Indian men, women, and children. Smith and his chronicler, Harrison Rogers, often commented on the numbers and inoffensive nature of the primitive California tribes. The trappers liberally distributed gifts among the Indians, for they had found that California's Central Valley contained an abundant supply of beaver, and they needed the natives' friendship or tacit consent for their trapping activities.[29]

After leaving the area, Jedediah Smith shared with other trappers the story of his successful hunting in California. George Yount later recalled that Smith's party had "reported California to be the finest country in the world—having a charming Italian climate & a soil remarkably productive—They said the valleys swarmed with Indians, peacefully disposed, & the hills, mountains & streams with a profusion of game of every kind—that the Sacramento & San Joaquin abounded with Salmon & that Beaver were abundant in all the

Creeks & Rivers."[30] Not only was California a land of abundant game, but also the Indian population was "peacefully disposed." What more could a trapper want?

During the years when the beaver trappers were crossing the mountains and deserts of the Southwest to reach California, other Americans were arriving along the coast in trading ships from New England. By the 1820s the sea otter had been more or less hunted out, but as a result of the relaxation of commercial restrictions following the Mexican Revolution of 1821, American trade with California expanded. As Franklin Walker would have it, Americans were brought to California no longer by the sea otter and beaver alone but also by the long-horned black mission cattle.

Beginning in the 1820s, there developed an extensive trade of California cowhides and bags of rendered tallow for a great variety of foreign manufactured goods. First on the scene were British traders, specifically the firm of McCullough, Hartnell and Company, which monopolized the trade for several years. It was only after the dissolution of that firm in 1828 that American traders came to play a significant part in California commerce. As Adele Ogden has commented, "For the next two decades Yankee goods were the style, and Yankee traders always welcome."[31] One of the earliest successful American commercial voyages was that of the *Brookline*, which arrived in Monterey Bay in February, 1829. The vessel represented the Boston trading firm Bryant and Sturgis, which, after the demise of McCullough and Hartnell, came to dominate the trade.

The hide-and-tallow trade was significant not only for its immediate economic effects but also because the writings of several men engaged in the trade greatly heightened American interest in California. Aboard the *Brookline*, for example, was a young clerk from Boston, Alfred Robinson, who later produced a classic narrative, *Life in California*, published in 1846. In 1835 a second vessel of the Bryant and Sturgis firm, the *Pilgrim*, brought another young Bostonian to California, Harvard undergraduate Richard Henry Dana, who later wrote the most popular of all accounts of Mexican California. In *Two Years Before the Mast*, published in 1840, Dana described for his countrymen in precise detail the beauties of the California landscape, its capacious harbors, abundant wildlife, and salubrious climate "than which there can be no better in the world."

The Yankee traders' contact with the California Indians was usually limited to the neophytes in the missions and, after secularization, the

Indian workers on the ranchos. The hide traders paid little attention to the Indians whom they encountered, for the Indians proved of no greater use to the traders than they had been to the otter and beaver hunters. Richard Henry Dana's exasperation with the Indians at San Pedro typified the sentiments of these itinerant traders. At one point Dana had attempted to elicit the aid of a group of Gabrielinos to help him transport a load of hides, but these "lazy Indians," he reported, remained "squatting down on their hams, looking on, doing nothing . . . only shaking their heads, or drawling out 'no quiero.'"[32] Like earlier visitors to California, the traders compared the California Indians with other native peoples and found them "inferior." As others before them had done, they cited various aspects of the Indians' culture, appearance, and language as evidence of their extreme primitiveness. Dana, for instance, judged the rude straw huts and clothing of the natives at San Diego to be extremely primitive. "The language of these people," he added, "which is spoken by all the Indians of California, is the most brutish and inhuman language, without any exception, that I ever heard of, or that could well be conceived of. It is a complete *slabber*."[33]

Dana's perceptions were echoed in the writings of Faxon Dean Atherton, a young man who like Dana had come to California from Massachusetts as a clerk aboard a vessel engaged in the hide-and-tallow trade. In the diary of his California experiences Atherton contrasted the California Indians with the Shawnee and Delaware Indians of the East. He observed that in a battle between the Indians of the two coasts the westerners would suffer a quick defeat.[34] Atherton also contrasted the Indians of California with his preconceived notions of Indian nobility. After visiting the village around Mission San José, Atherton commented, "There is a certain some thing which I admire in the Indian character, *when at a distance*, but a close inspection of their habits and manners disgusts and destroys the illusion."[35]

In something of the same spirit as Atherton, William Henry Thomes, another young "hide drogher" from the East, described his days in California. Thomes had come to California in 1843, inspired by a reading of Dana's book. "I desired to see the same ports he had visited," Thomes later recalled," to get wet in the same surf, to gaze at the same pretty Mexican ladies, the same indolent Mexican caballeros, the same shiftless Indians, and the same skillful horse-riding rancheros."[36] Although he did not let Dana's images determine his own response to California, Thomes certainly came to the coast with Dana's words in mind, and, at least in the case of the Indians, he ordered his impressions on the model Dana had provided. For in spite of their other differences Thomes, Dana, and Atherton were consistent in the images of California Indians that they produced. Thomes described the Indians he saw at the missions and on the ranchos as a pitiable lot of unintelligent and "shiftless" people whose way of life he judged to be exceedingly primitive.[37]

While the hide traders found little to admire in the Indians of California, they also found little to fear. Thomes and his companions, for example, amused themselves while in Monterey by throwing firecrackers at the local Costanoans. On one occasion they tricked a "big Indian, half drunk," into accepting a firecracker as a cigarette. "The Indian sucked away with drunken complacency," Thomes later recalled, "but when the fuse fizzled he appeared a little surprised, and was still more astonished when the explosion occurred."[38] Obviously such people, fit subjects for practical jokes, were not a threat.

The image of California that emerges from the accounts of such men as William Shaler, Jedediah Smith, and Richard Henry Dana is that of a land of abundant wildlife, fertile soils, great harbors, and an unsurpassed climate. The Indians of California, while not occupying a prominent position in these accounts, appear almost universally as an inoffensive and extremely primitive people. Their primitiveness was a matter of some curiosity, and visitors responded with a mixture of pity and disgust. The early American visitors to California did not regard the Indians whom they encountered as of any particular use or value. Occasionally the otter hunters employed Indians as auxiliaries, but their utility was minimal. The beaver trappers received gifts of food and shelter from the Indians, but they did not engage in any extensive trade for pelts with them. While the Indians were the primary labor force on the missions and ranchos, they offered little assistance to the Anglo-Americans engaged in the hide-and-tallow trade. Yet it is important to remember that, although the natives did little to advance the interests of the early Anglo-American visitors, neither did they do anything to retard them. The peaceful, inoffensive nature of these Indians, often remarked upon, was a welcome contrast to the violent opposition that the otter hunters had encountered among the coastal Indians farther north. Similarly, the beaver trappers had had difficult relations with natives on the east.

In the literature of early Anglo-Americans in California the most common image of the Indian is as a victim of Hispanic mistreatment and exploitation. The American visitors reported that the Indians of California were held as serfs or slaves by their Spanish-speaking masters and subjected to acts of injustice and cruelty. The Hispanos, rather than working to develop the rich potential of California, were living a life of ease, dependent upon the labor of the inoffensive native population. These images suggest a remarkable continuity with the judgments of the earlier European visitors—and in a larger sense with the tenets of the Black Legend. California, the beautiful and abundant land, required an enterprising population to develop it. The Hispanos had proved themselves unworthy, and they ought to be replaced by a people more fit for the task. These sentiments underlay much of the early American reporting on California and remind us of the tremendous surge of American expansionism in the first half of the nineteenth century. We shall see that this image of California Indians unmistakably reflected the expansionist enthusiasms of these earliest visitors from the United States.

Sea-otter hunters Richard Cleveland and William Shaler, for example, were generally critical of the California Hispanos and their relations with the Indians. Cleveland described the missionaries as generally amiable though very ignorant, intolerant, and bigoted. He cited one padre in Baja California who boasted that he "had rendered God service by killing many of the Indians, who obstinately refused to be converted."[39] Shaler speculated in more depth about the impact of the missions on the California natives. Noting that Sebastián Vizcaíno and other early explorers had reported great numbers of people along the coast, Shaler was puzzled by the "extraordinary depopulation" of the area. He speculated that European diseases—especially venereal disease—and the Spaniards' lack of medical knowledge and practice were responsible for the deaths. The mission Indians he described as the "miserable remains" of the once-flourishing coastal population. He feared that in a few more years disease would "entirely exterminate them." Perhaps drawing directly upon La Pérouse, Shaler criticized the authoritarian structure of the missions. The Franciscans, he noted, ruled as "kings and pontiffs" and denied the Indians even such basic rights as that of private property.[40]

Shaler concluded his description of California with an appeal for American annexation, describing even the military tactics that he would recommend to accomplish that goal. "The conquest of this country would be absolutely nothing," Shaler assured his readers.

"In a word, it would be as easy to keep California in spite of the Spaniards, as it would be to wrest it from them in the first instance." Like the earlier European observers, Shaler praised the natural advantages of California and noted how inadequate the Spanish colonists were to develop the land's potential. He dismissed the Spanish population of California as a "mixed breed . . . of an indolent, harmless disposition, and fond of spiritous liquors." He noted, for example, that, although the countryside abounded in materials and excellent sites for wind and water mills, the Spaniards through a lack of industriousness had failed to construct a single mill. California had a great potential for wealth and importance; all it lacked was a worthy population and the proper government.[41]

Similar and even more forceful criticisms of the Hispanos can be found in the records of the beaver trappers who went overland to California in the succeeding decades. In contrast to the trappers' generally friendly relations with the Indians of California, their contact with the region's Hispanic colonists was often marked by a spirit of enmity. The trappers regarded their Mexican hosts with unbridled contempt, while the Mexicans viewed the American interlopers with considerable suspicion. Jedediah Smith, for example, was suspected of being a spy and was ordered out of California by Mexican Governor José María Echeandía in December, 1826. On his return trip in 1827 he was arrested by Father Narcisco Durán at Mission San José for his illegal entry into California and was again ordered out of the state by the governor.[42] The experiences of James Ohio Pattie in the Mexican Southwest were likewise unpleasant. Before the members of the Pattie expedition reached California, the governor of New Mexico had charged them with trapping without a license and confiscated all their furs. In Baja California, Pattie and his men were arrested and sent under guard to San Diego, where Governor Echeandía ordered the party jailed. Pattie won their release, he later claimed, only because he had happened to bring with him a supply of smallpox vaccine, which the Mexicans believed would be useful in controlling an epidemic that was ravaging the northern missions. In any event, Pattie and his men were released, but not before Pattie's father, Sylvester, died in the San Diego jail.[43]

Perhaps predictably, the images of the Mexican population in the fur-trade literature were none too friendly. One American trapper, commenting on the misadventures of the Pattie expedition, wrote: "The pusillanimity and insignificance of the Mexican nation is all that has saved them from that punishment which they so richly deserve, and which will sooner or later most assuredly overtake them. Their cruel treatment and murdering of foreigners is such as to bring down on them the most inveterate hatred of all civilized nations."[44] Like their European and American predecessors along the coast, the beaver trappers were often struck by the contrast between the abundant, fertile, beautiful California landscape and its Spanish-speaking inhabitants, whom they regarded as indolent and unworthy. Zenas Leonard, for example, described California as bounteous: "The soil is very productive—the timber is immensely large and plenty, and game, such as deer, elk, grizzly bear and antelopes are remarkably plenty." Yet the Mexican Californians, he observed, "generally, are very ignorant and much more indolent— have little or no ingenuity."[45] Washington Irving, in describing the experiences of the Bonneville-Walker expedition, also noted that California was a rich region with great potential. "Its inhabitants, themselves," added Irving, in reference to the Californios, "are but little aware of its real riches; they have not enterprise sufficient to acquaint themselves with a vast interior that lies almost a terra incognita; nor have they the skill and industry to cultivate properly the fertile tracts along the coast; nor to prosecute that foreign commerce which brings all the resources of a country into profitable action."[46]

Pattie's *Personal Narrative,* published in 1831, was the first full-scale description of California by an American. Pattie likewise praised all the natural advantages of California and contrasted those advantages with the Mexican population, whom he regarded as despicable. California, he wrote, "is no less remarkable for uniting the advantages of healthfulness, a good soil, a temperate climate, and yet one of exceeding mildness, a happy mixture of level and elevated ground, and vicinity to the sea. Its inhabitants are equally calculated to excite dislike, and even the stronger feelings of disgust and hatred. The priests are omnipotent, and all things are subject to their power." The Indians, he explained, were subject to "rigid and unremitting supervision" in the missions. "No bondage can be more complete, than that under which they live." Their labor was exacted through physical coercion, and the products of that labor were appropriated by the priests. "The greater part of these Indians were brought from their native mountains against their own inclinations, and by compulsion," Pattie concluded, "and then baptised; which act was as little voluntary on their part, as the former had been. After these preliminaries, they had been put to work, as converted Indians."

With a scarcely concealed note of admiration Pattie added that these conditions had led the neophytes "at times to rebel, and endeavor to escape from their yoke."[47]

The journals of the Smith expedition contain similar images of the neophytes. Harrison Rogers, a staunch Presbyterian, made it clear in his journal and in his conversations with California priests that he disagreed with Roman Catholic doctrine. He said, however, of the missionaries at Mission San Gabriel, "Although they are Catholicks by profession, they allow us liberty of conscience." This, combined with the generous hospitality that the trappers received at San Gabriel, led Rogers to call the resident padre, Father José Bernardo Sánchez, "the greatest friend that I ever met with in all my travels."[48] This personal regard for individual missionaries and appreciation for individual acts of hospitality did not, however, deter Rogers from noting the very different treatment that the Indians received at the missions. In 1786, La Pérouse had made a distinction between missionaries who were "individually humane and good" and the mission institution, which he regarded as oppressive.[49] Rogers noted the great activity at Mission San Gabriel—the blacksmithing, carpentry, ploughing, spinning, and weaving—but he believed that the Indians engaged in those tasks out of fear and the threat of physical punishment: "They are kept in great fear; for the least offense they are corrected; they are compleat slaves in every sense of the word." This impression of slavery was confirmed for Rogers, as it had been for La Pérouse, when he observed the use of whips, stocks, and hobbles on the neophytes. Rogers described a group of five or six Indians being whipped at San Gabriel. He noted that one who "did not like to submit to the lash was knocked down by the commandant, tied and severely whiped, then chained by the leg to another Indian." The armaments at the mission were mute testimony, Rogers commented, to the hostility that the Indians felt and that the missionaries feared.[50]

The Hispanos' use of armed force to recapture escaped mission neophytes seemed to many Anglo-American trappers the clearest evidence of Mexican brutality. In the winter of 1833–34, for example, a group of neophytes escaped from Mission San Juan Bautista, taking with them about three hundred horses. The local Mexican authorities invited Joseph Reddeford Walker's party of beaver trappers to join an expedition to recapture the runaways, promising them half the horses that might be captured. Thus Walker's men rode with the Mexicans to the camp of the escapees in the San Joaquin Valley.

The camp was found nearly deserted; the horses were mostly killed, and their meat was stretched to dry. The only people to be found were "a few old and feeble Indians" and several women and children. "The disappointment of the Spaniards now exceeded all bounds," wrote one of Walker's men, "and gave our men some evidence of the depravity of the Spanish character." Zenas Leonard described the scene:

> By way of revenge, after they found that there was no use in following the Indians into the mountain, the Spaniards fell to massacreing indiscriminately, those helpless creatures who were found in the wigwams with the meat, and cutting off their ears. Some of them were driven into a wigwam, when the door was barricaded, and a large quantity of combustible matter thrown on and around the hut, for the purpose of setting fire to it, and burning them all together. This barbarous treatment our men would not permit and they went and released the prisoners, when the Spaniards fell to work and dispatched them as if they were dogs. . . . On their arrival at our camp, the Spaniards told me that their object in taking off the ears, was to show the Priests and Alcaldes, that they had used every effort to regain the stolen property.[51]

In a somewhat garbled account of the same scene, Washington Irving commented that the Mexicans were guilty of "infamous barbarities" against the Indians. They seemed to compete with each other in seeing who could inflict the greatest outrage against the "poor Root Diggers." He described the Mexicans hunting "the poor Indians like wild beasts, and killing them without mercy." In this "savage sport" the Mexicans chased their victims at full speed, noosed them around the neck with their lassos, and then dragged them to their death.[52] James D. Hart has commented that "a people so depraved as those Irving depicts were naturally enough unable to take proper advantage of the land that was theirs."[53]

The American trappers also censured the Mexican rancheros for their armed raids on Indian villages to gather laborers.[54] Albert Morris described one such raid against the natives of the Clear Lake region, and his description was identical in tone with Zenas Leonard's condemnation of the earlier raid against the escaped San Juan neophytes. Both Leonard and Morris regarded the raids as part of a general pattern of Mexican cruelty and barbarity. In both trappers' descriptions the slaughter of Indians follows such scenes as Mexicans engaging in bull and bear fighting or Mexicans slaughtering cattle and seeming "to feast upon their agony" or Mexicans riding horses

59

until they dropped from exhaustion and then stabbing them to death.[55] The implication of Leonard's and Morris's images of these assorted "barbarisms" is clear: again to paraphrase Hart, so depraved a people as these were obviously unworthy of a land such as California. Morris, for example, showed no restraint in his criticism of the Mexicans' operations at Clear Lake. As the raiding party was returning with its captives to Sonoma, the young Indian children grew tired and fell behind. Morris wrote of the leader of the expedition, "On arriving at a little brook the fiend in human flesh, this unfeeling and black hearted commander dismounted from his horse, called the little children to him, baptized them one after another, and then dashed their brains out against the rocks." Morris continued:

> I could write pages of such and similar deeds, but I have said sufficient about their horrible and more than hellish deeds, and my heart sickens at the thoughts of them as I write them down, and I am forced to quit recording the heart sickening details of monsters in human flesh. Our countrymen know their characters and it is needless for me to say more.[56]

In the literature of the hide-and-tallow trade we find additional evidence of Anglo-American antipathy for Hispanos and sympathy for the California Indians. Richard Henry Dana and the other itinerant traders usually continued the tradition of La Pérouse and pictured the Indians as victims of Mexican "enslavement." Despite his exasperation with the "laziness" of the Indians at the San Pedro beach, Dana recognized that most of the work in California was done by Indians. He noted that the Franciscans had once owned all the cattle and kept the Indians as "their slaves, in tending their vast herds." After secularization the cattle and land had passed into the hands of the rancheros. "The change in the condition of the Indians," Dana continued, "was as may be supposed, only nominal: they are virtually slaves, as much as they ever were." Dana consistently described the Indians as occupying the bottom position of the social scale in Mexican California. Even the poorest of the Spanish-speaking residents, he noted, had an Indian to do their work. The only compensation due an Indian for his labor was a daily ration of food and occasionally some coarse clothing.[57]

Dana also described the unequal application of justice in California. He contrasted a case in which a local Californio had committed a murder and was not prosecuted for the crime with the case of an Indian who, in retaliation for the killing of his horse, had also committed a murder and was prosecuted, convicted, sentenced to death, and executed. Dana's image of the Indian murderer was sympathetic. "The poor wretch," he noted, was "sitting on the bare ground, in front of the calabozo, with his feet chained to a stake, and handcuffs about his wrists." Dana believed the Indian's sentence was unjust, for he had been sorely provoked and had committed the murder without premeditation; "yet he was an Indian, and that was enough." He cited the two cases, he said, "to give one a notion of the distribution of justice in California." Dana's discussion of the treatment of this Indian murderer was followed immediately by further comment on the general character of the Californios. The men, he wrote, were thriftless, proud, extravagant, and inveterate gamblers; the women, uneducated and of questionable morality.[58] Then, to emphasize the incongruity of these people and their land, Dana commented:

> Such are the people who inhabit a country embracing four or five hundred miles of sea-coast, with several good harbors; with fine forests in the north; the waters filled with fish, and the plains covered with thousands of herds of cattle; blessed with a climate, than which there can be no better in the world; free from all manner of diseases, whether epidemic or endemic; and with a soil in which corn yields from seventy to eighty fold. In the hands of an enterprising people, what a country this might be![59]

Other itinerant hide-and-tallow traders were even more forthright in their criticism of the treatment of the Indians in Mexican California. Faxon Dean Atherton, for instance, noted in his California diary that the major effect of the missions on the Indian population seemed to be the introduction of new disease. As a consequence the California Indians were "dying off like rotten sheep, literally, not figuratively." In conversation with the padre at San José, Atherton was surprised to learn that even the missionaries had accepted the impossibility of bettering the condition of the Indians and believed "that they must and will die off and disappear before the more morally educated white man." Like Dana, Atherton also commented on the injustice dealt the Indians in California. He noted that crimes were frequently blamed on Indians "who, poor devils, are probably as innocent of it as any of them, if not more so."[60]

Robert B. Forbes, the captain of a New England trading vessel in San Francisco in 1825, later recalled "the Christianizing Padres who at that time 'converted' the Indians by sending the guachos [*sic*] and rancheros into the field to catch them with the lasso, and mark them with the cross!" These alleged branding operations were ordered by "licentious priests" who compounded their cruelty by living in sin with "their *nieces* at the head of their households." The missionaries monopolized the trade, had many Indian servants, and exercised great control over the population. As a consequence of all this, Forbes concluded, they lived very well. In Forbes's description, like Dana's, the Indians and the missions appeared amid a celebration of the triumph of American civilization over California. Forbes returned to San Francisco about 1870 and was struck by the same contrasts that had impressed Dana upon his return to California in 1860. In 1825, California had been undeveloped by the Mexicans; only the coyote and the grizzly, the Indian and the cruel and licentious priest, had occupied the land. In 1870 the countryside was filled with railroads, steamers, fountains, orchards, and churches "bearing evidence of the good morals and respectable and enterprising population." Here Forbes was reporting the fulfillment of Dana's 1840 vision of California "in the hands of an enterprising people." Part of the evidence of the improvement of the land in American hands, Forbes made plain, was the elimination of such practices as lassoing Indians and branding them with the cross.[61]

The views of Dana, Atherton, and Forbes were confirmed by other Yankee visitors who, while not engaged in commerce, were in California at the same time as the hide traders and had experiences that paralleled those of the traders. Jonathan Green, for example, was a Protestant missionary sent to the Pacific Coast in 1829 by the American Board of Commissioners for Foreign Missions to report on the prospects there for Protestant missions. Green's report, published in November, 1830, contained an extensive description of the operations of the Catholic missions in California. Not surprisingly, Green judged the California missions to be a complete failure. After fifty years of effort the missions had succeeded only in degrading the Indians. Green proclaimed: "It is admitted by all with whom I have conversed on the coast, Catholic and Protestant, that these converted Indians, as they are called, are exceedingly degraded—much more so than their uncivilized neighbors. They are exceedingly uncleanly in their persons and habitations, are beastly drunkards, notorious gamesters, and are so many of them diseased in consequence of lewdness, that they are constantly dying off." Yet, though the Indians were "miserably deficient" in industry and skill, the Mexicans were even more so, and thus they forced the Indians to perform all the manual labor in California. If only the more enlightened

Protestant missionaries had reached California first, how different things might have been! But perhaps, argued Green, the situation could yet be saved if the United States extended its boundary at least as far as San Francisco Bay. Not only would that allow a more enterprising people access to a valuable port, but also it would permit Protestant missionaries to evangelize the coast and interior of California.[62]

The secular version of this expansionist argument was contained in the widely circulated report of Thomas Jefferson Farnham's visit to California in 1840. Farnham had mixed feelings about Spanish efforts at Christianization in California, but his image of the treatment of the neophytes was harsh. He noted, for example, that "every Indian, male and female, is obliged to attend worship; and if they lag behind, a large leathern thong, at the end of a heavy whip-staff, is applied to their naked backs." Once inside the church, Farnham continued, the man and women were separated by a broad aisle:

> In this aisle are stationed men with whips and goads to enforce order and silence, and keep them in a kneeling posture. By this arrangement, the untamed and vicious are generally made willing to comply with the forms of the service. In addition to these restraints, a guard of soldiers with fixed bayonets occupies one end of the church, who may suppress by their more powerful weapons any strong demonstrations against this comfortable mode of worshipping God.

Regarding the padres themselves, Farnham remained ambivalent. He wrote that "bating the objections which we have to the manner of conversion, and of sustaining them in the way of grace, no fault can be found with them." Although the priests were often misguided, they appeared to be sincere. Farnham, however, reserved his greatest criticism for the system of Indian labor exploitation. He excoriated the Mexicans as a "miserable people" who "sleep and smoke, and hum some tune of Castilian laziness; while surrounding nature is thus inviting them to the noblest and richest rewards of honest toil." He placed the Californios at the head of the human race in "cowardice, ignorance, pretension and dastardly tyranny." And how was that "dastardly tyranny" demonstrated?

> Destitute of industry themselves, they compel the poor Indian to labor for them, affording him a bare savage existence for his toil, upon their plantations and the fields of the Missions. In a word, the Californians are an imbecile, pusillanimous, race of men, and unfit to control the destinies of that beautiful country.[63]

Farnham's views of California, first published in 1844, represent a logical culmination of all the earlier Anglo-American accounts. His ambivalence toward the missionaries—many of whom at the time of his visit to California had already been removed from their posts by the Mexican government—reflects the difference of opinion that the California Franciscans always had evoked. His picture of the Californios as lazy and tyrannical recalls not only the earliest Anglo-American images but also the views of the earlier European visitors and, before them, the stock features of the Black Legend. Likewise, the image of California Indians as victims of Hispanic exploitation, as people compelled to labor for only the most meager compensation, had become by the 1840s the traditional view. The Hispanic Californians had revealed themselves unfit for California, not only by humming their "tune of Castilian laziness" and ignoring the imperative to develop California by "honest toil" but also by treating the Indians with such harshness and compulsion that their reign could only be described as a "dastardly tyranny."

In the first part of this chapter we saw that the Anglo-American visitors to Hispanic California described the California Indians as an extraordinarily primitive people who neither posed a threat nor were of much use or value. We have now seen that these visitors from the United States also described the Indians as victims of exploitation and cruelty and that such descriptions were part of a larger pattern of denigration of Hispanic California. Although the Indians themselves were not useful to the Anglo-Americans, the *image* of the Indian as a victim was very useful indeed. The Anglo-American visitors to Hispanic California needed some means of proving the Hispanos unworthy of such a rich land as California. The image of a valuable but undeveloped landscape satisfied this need. So too did the image of the Indians as victims, for in their exploitation of the Indians the Hispanos most clearly revealed their indolence and cruelty. This is not to argue that the image of the Indian occupied a central place in these early American reports of California, and certainly it is not to argue that the great stirrings of Manifest Destiny across the eastern half of the continent were stimulated by the image of long-suffering California Indians yearning to be free. What is suggested here is that the writings of the Anglo-American visitors were suffused with the expansionist sentiment of the day. They filled their reports with images of the valuable land that lay on the Pacific shore, criticized the Hispanos who occupied that land, and, in a tradition as old as the rivalry for American empire, described the Indians as victims of cruel exploitation at the hands of their Spanish-speaking masters.

PART II

A Useful Class

ABOUT San Bernardino the farm laborers are chiefly Indians. These people, of whom California has still several thousand, are a very useful class. They trim the vines; they plough; they do the household "chores;" they are shepherds, and trusty ones too, vaqueros, and helpers generally. Mostly, they live among the whites, and are their humble and, I judge, tolerably efficient ministers. . . . I found that it was thought a great advantage for a man to "have" Indians. — Charles Nordhoff, *California for Health, Pleasure and Residence: A Book for Travellers and Settlers*

3

Shifting Perspectives

AS early as 1818 citizens of the United States were taking up permanent residence in California. By the late 1830s the Anglo-American minority in Mexican California was sizable, including permanent representatives of New England trading firms, independent merchants, and successful cattle ranchers. To a remarkable degree, many of these early Anglo-Californians assimilated the Hispanic culture of their host country. Naturalized as Mexican citizens and baptized as Roman Catholics, they adopted Hispanicized names, married into local Californio families, and received grants of land from the Mexican government. In assessing the development of American attitudes toward the California Indians, this group of Hispanicized Anglo-Americans is important because in their writings we detect a movement away from the traditional view that the California Indians were victims of a cruel system of Hispanic exploitation. The traditional view had dominated the writings of American trappers and traders who had been only visitors to California, but in the accounts of the Americans who became permanent settlers in the future state that image began to erode. Anglo-Californians continued to describe the majority of California Indians as very primitive and generally inoffensive people, and they still acknowledged that many of the Indians had been held and trained against their will as laborers at the missions and ranchos, but they now began to see these matters in a rather different light.

The Anglo-Californians, in setting up their own enterprises, soon came to recognize the personal advantages of the Hispanic model of Indian labor exploitation, and along the coast and in the valleys of the interior they began to adopt this model as their own. The California Indians may have been primitive and exploited, but the Anglo-Californians began to accept the Indians' abject status as another of the advantages of life in California. Because the Indians were extremely primitive, they could be easily controlled, and they were the more easily controlled because so many had already been trained and disciplined by the Hispanos to become a "useful class" of laborers. We see the beginnings of this perspective among the Anglo-Californians of the 1830s. The same point of view was further developed by the overland American pioneers of the early 1840s and was shared by at least some of the Americans who came to California after its conquest by the United States in 1848.

One of the most prominent of the early Anglo-Californians was William Heath Davis, the Hawaiian-born son of a Boston ship-master. After several voyages to California in the 1830s, Davis decided in 1838 to settle there permanently. He acted as the San Francisco agent for a New England trading firm and later became a prominent independent merchant. Although unable to become a naturalized Mexican citizen, "Don Guillermo" was granted a permanent passport by the Mexican governor and later married María de Jesus Estudillo. As his biographer, Andrew F. Rolle, has remarked, "In his own person he came to represent a blending of California's Spanish and Anglo-Saxon culture."[1] In his memoirs of life in California in the 1830s, Davis was generally sympathetic to the operations of the missions and ranchos of California. The status of the Indians evoked from him no critical comments like those by Dana, Atherton, or Farnham. In the missions the neophytes were "kindly treated," Davis reported, "and soon became domesticated and ready and eager to adopt the habits of civilized life." The priests were "superior men in point of talent, education, morals and executive ability." After secularization, Davis observed, the "civilized Indians from the missions were scattered about the country, and many were to be found on the different ranchos. They were of peaceable disposition, were employed as vaqueros, and helped the rancheros at the planting seasons and at harvest time."[2] One such Californian who availed himself of this peaceably disposed labor supply was William Heath Davis.[3]

Another of the earliest English-speaking residents of California was William Edward Petty Hartnell, a native of Lancashire, England, who came to California in 1822 as an agent of the new commercial firm of McCullough, Hartnell and Company. Hartnell married a daughter of a prominent Californio family in 1825, was naturalized, and became a Roman Catholic in 1830. In the following year he was granted a large rancho near Monterey.[4] His main contacts with Indians were with the laborers on his and other ranchos. Like Dana, Hartnell was occasionally exasperated with "these enemies of work" and commented that, in dealing with them, "there is nothing else to do but have patience." But, unlike Dana, he had a greater opportunity for exercising patience in dealing with the Indian laborers. At his wedding to María Teresa de la Guerra, Hartnell was waited on by Indian servants, and on his rancho he adopted the local custom of adding a new servant to the household when each child was born. All the menial tasks on the ranch were performed by Indian laborers. For example, at the annual *matanza*, Mexican vaqueros were employed to kill the cattle, but the drudgery of slaughtering the beef was left to Hartnell's "servile Indians." The adobe bricks for his construction projects, like those of the missions, were all made by Indian labor. Hartnell even learned a local Salinan dialect better to direct the Indian workmen at the rancho.[5]

Thomas Oliver Larkin was one of the few Yankee traders who stayed in California and did not convert to Catholicism, take Mexican citizenship, or marry into a Californio family. Larkin came to Monterey from Boston in 1832 and prospered in a variety of commercial ventures, many of which involved the hide trade.[6] In 1844 he was appointed United States consul, and in that capacity he wrote "A Description of California" in 1846. This document makes only passing mention of the California Indians, and nowhere does it offer any criticism of Indian and white relations in Hispanic California. Larkin's only concern with the California Indians was to describe their role as useful laborers. He noted that before secularization the missions operated efficiently: the neophytes were taught many useful skills and were industriously employed in the workshops, gardens, and orchards and with the herds attached to the missions. Although the missions' herds had nearly all disappeared by 1846, and though many of the neophytes who had been taught the "Mechanical Arts" had died, the production of hides for export was still booming. "The baptized Indians now released by the demolishing of the Missions," Larkin assured his readers, "are engaged by the Inhabitants as Servants."[7]

Perhaps the man who most fully exemplified the assimilated American in California was Alfred Robinson. Robinson, resident agent of the Bryant and Sturgis company since 1829, was baptized as José María Alfredo in 1833 and was married to Ana María de la Guerra in 1836. He has been aptly labeled a "business and cultural middle man" between Mexican and American California; his relatively sympathetic views of Mexican California mark a turning point in American attitudes toward the land and its people.[8] He shared some of Dana's criticisms of Californio indolence and vice, but at the same time he was defensive of much of Latin culture. And, although he had become integrated into Mexican California like most of the Yankees there, he was a booster of American acquisition. In the journal of his first visit to California in 1829, he noted the extraordinary abundance of wildlife and the fertility of the soil in California and wrote that the country "only needs exertion to make it a promising situation."[9] Less ambiguously, he concluded his *Life in California*, published in 1846, by asking, "In this age of 'Annexation,' why not extend the 'area of freedom' by the annexation of California? Why not plant the banner of liberty there, in the fortress, at the entrance of the noble, the spacious bay of San Francisco?"[10]

Robinson's attitude toward the Indians under Spanish and Mexican domination was ambivalent. He presented a generally positive picture of mission operations, in which Indians learned and obediently performed their tasks as carpenters, masons, coopers, weavers, herdsmen, and so on. Yet he also remarked on an eccentric old padre at San Buenaventura who amused himself by thumping the heads of Indian boys with a long stick "and seemed delighted thus to gratify his singular propensities." More serious was Robinson's evident displeasure at the practice of the alcaldes at Mission San Luis Rey, who, he said, drove the neophytes to mass with whips: "The condition of these Indians is miserable indeed," he wrote, "and it is not to be wondered at that many attempt to escape from the severity of the religious discipline at the Mission." If the Indians escaped, Robinson continued, "they are pursued, and generally taken; when they are flogged, and an iron clog is fastened to their legs, serving as additional punishment, and a warning to others."[11] Yet Robinson's response to such practices was not always clear. In a revealing letter to the Bryant and Sturgis Company written in 1831, Robinson expressed his opposition to the "nonsensical plan" of releasing the Indians from the missions. Such an action, he told his employers, would mean the ruin of commerce in California.[12] In his *Life in California*, Robinson reported that secularization had not spelled the ruin of the hide trade after all. It only had redistributed the wealth in California and broken the monopoly of "the monastic institutions." Throughout his narrative, Robinson described his own dependence upon Indian laborers, and one senses here, as in the

Drawing of "An Indian Dressed in the 'Tobet'" by Alfred Robinson, author of *Life in California* (1846). Robinson based his drawing on information in Father Geronimo Boscana's account of Juaneno religion, "Chinigchinich."

accounts of his fellow Anglo-Californians, an unquestioning acceptance of the secular system of Indian labor exploitation.[13]

Keeping in mind the ambivalence of men like Alfred Robinson, one sees in the brief accounts of these Anglo-Californians the beginnings of a new pattern of perception. The temporary visitor to California—the French explorer, American beaver trapper, or Boston trader—freely criticized the Spanish missionary or Mexican ranchero for his treatment of the California Indians. Most of the itinerant Yankee traders, like their American and European predecessors, were critical of the "enslavement" of the California Indians. Then, as Anglo-Americans came to California to settle permanently and began to rely on the Indians for their labor supply, the flow of criticism began to diminish.

Beginning in 1841, California shared in the westward movement of overland migration that for several years had been directed farther north by the Oregon Trail. The rich alluvial soils of the Sacramento and San Joaquin valleys began to vie in popularity with the Willamette valley and the Columbia River basin. In 1841 the flow of overland pioneers began that after 1848 turned into a flood. The Americans who came in the 1840s were distinct in several ways from the earlier commercial group, and yet their attitudes toward California and its inhabitants were often similar. Ever since William Shaler's laconic remarks on the desirability of California and the ease with which it might be seized, American images of California had been laced with the notions of Manifest Destiny. The writings produced by the men who came to California in the 1840s, perhaps more than those of any other group, were also marked by expansionist sentiment. Indeed, some of their writings were consciously designed as tracts to encourage American settlement or American annexation of California. These pioneers from the United States were confident that at last this land of ideal climate, fertility, and natural abundance was being peopled by a worthy race. They were conscious of their role as the vanguard of Anglo-American settlers, and by their words and deeds they hoped to hasten the day when their fellow countrymen would join them in achieving the American destiny that manifestly lay in California.

One of the first important immigrants to reach California overland was John Marsh, a New Englander, who arrived in 1836 and soon purchased a large tract of land near Mount Diablo in Contra Costa County.[14] Marsh was an active proponent of American annexation of California, and on the suggestion of Thomas Larkin he wrote a widely publicized letter to Senator Lewis Cass of Michigan, dated January 20, 1846. In it Marsh described in superlatives the fertility, healthfulness, and climate of California. "As respects human health & comfort," he proclaimed, "the climate is incomparably better than that of any portion of the U. States. It is the most healthy country I have ever seen or have any knowledge of." He wrote approvingly that California "is rapidly peopling with emigrants from the U. States" and that "it cannot long remain in the hands of its present owners."[15]

The first overland expedition organized for the purpose of settlement in California was the Bidwell-Bartleson company of 1841. John Bidwell, the effective leader of the group, kept a record of the crossing to California and, upon arriving in California, sent his journal back east for publication. The resulting *Journey to California* (1842) showed Bidwell, like Marsh, to be an enthusiastic booster of California. He was greatly impressed with the variety and abundance of plant and animal life, and again and again in his journal he recorded species of California wildlife that "were growing in abundance." The agricultural possibilities were obviously great: "Of all places in the world," wrote Bidwell, "it appears to me, that none can be better adapted to the raising of cattle than California." Bidwell reported, however, that most of the "Spaniards" in California were lacking in ambition and spent only a few weeks of the year doing any work. "I know a few Spaniards who are industrious and enterprising," he conceded. "They have become immensely rich, this likewise is the case with the foreigners, who have used the least industry."[16] Bidwell assured potential immigrants to California from the United States that finding workers for their ranches and farms would not be any problem: "You can employ any number of Indians by giving them a lump of Beef every week, and paying them about one dollar for same time."[17] Similarly, Josiah Belden, another member of the Bidwell-Bartleson company, later explained that the California Indians were a primitive and inoffensive people who long ago had been brought from the mountains to the missions, where they were "somewhat Christianized and civilized," and later were employed by the ranchers. Through this process the "wild Indians" had been transformed into "very useful servants and laboring men for the rancheros and citizens." They performed all the labor in the province, wrote Belden without a hint of censure, "and were commonly docile and tractable."[18]

Fueled by such accounts as Bidwell's, expansionist sentiment in the United States intensified in the 1840s. At the same time the fundamental shift in attitudes toward the status of the Indians in Mexican California became more pronounced. The movement away from the traditionally critical view—a movement evident in the writings of the resident commercial group—accelerated. There was no less sense of the unworthiness of the indolent and degraded Mexicans for California. Indeed, such sentiments were at a peak in the 1840s. Yet the expansionist rationale that had been articulated by the trappers and traders underwent a significant alteration: the pioneer settlers came to view the Mexican policy of Indian exploitation not as an evil to be condemned but as a model worthy to be emulated. The primitiveness of the California Indians became less of an anomaly or a curiosity and more of an asset. The docile, tractable Indians joined the other features of California, such as its salubrious climate and fertile soil, which made the land so eminently desirable. The pioneer settlers came to realize that the primitiveness and inoffensiveness of the Indians, coupled with their years of "conditioning" at the missions and ranchos, made them a valuable natural resource. Recognition of the Indians' primitiveness and of the policies of the Mexicans were subsumed into a new attitude in which the primary consideration was the Indians' usefulness to the American settler.

John Marsh's attitudes are a prime example of the new point of view. Before coming to California, Marsh had served as an Indian subagent in Minnesota, and he probably had the Sioux in mind when he compared the California Indians with the "average tribes" east of the Rockies. He noted that the Californians' physiognomy—dark, with thick lips and a broad nose—contained "nothing of the proud & lofty bearing or of the haughtiness or ferocity so often seen east of the mountains."[19] The California Indians, Marsh stated, went about entirely naked and lived like beasts. These comments came in the midst of Marsh's glowing letter to Lewis Cass that described so enthusiastically the fertility and climate of California. Rather than citing the primitiveness of the Indians as an anomaly in an otherwise superior region, or puzzling over the reasons for their primitiveness, Marsh considered the Indians' condition as simply another aspect of California that he could recommend to prospective settlers. The Indians of California, he explained, "are easily domes-ticated, not averse to labor, [and] have a natural aptitude to learn mechanical trades." The missions, in their prime, had trained the Indians as ploughmen, weavers, tanners, shoemakers, masons, car-penters, blacksmiths, and "various other mechanicks." Even in the 1840s, Marsh continued, the Indians, "when caught young, are most easily domesticated, and manifest a great aptitude to learn what-ever is taught them." They soon learned the language of their mas-ters and performed the labor required of them, showing no dis-position to return to their savage state: "The mind of the wild Indian, of whatever age, appears to be a *tabula rasa,* on which no impressions, except those of mere animal nature, have been made, and ready to receive any impress whatever." Marsh cited several instances in which a white family had settled near an Indian village and "in a short time they would have the whole tribe for willing serfs."[20]

Marsh described the humility and simplicity of the California Indians as "almost inconceivable." Anyone who wished to appro-priate a body of them as laborers could do so with only the slightest effort. "Nothing more is necessary for their complete subjugation but kindness in the beginning, and a little well timed severity when manifestly deserved." He noted that administering such "well timed severity" was not difficult, for the California Indians "submit to flagellation with more humility than the negroes." Marsh concluded his remarks on the "Aborigines of California" with the unambiguous statement "Throughout all California the Indians are the principal laborers; without them the business of the country could hardly be carried on."[21]

Certainly Marsh's own business could not have been carried on without his Indian laborers. From the beginning of his operations at Rancho Los Médanos in 1837, Marsh exploited the local Indians, probably Bay Miwoks and Northern Valley Yokuts. The Indians manufactured the adobe bricks for Marsh's ranch house; they ploughed and cultivated his fields and learned to set traps and collect furs for him. They received no wages for this work, but Marsh fed them beans and beef, gave them a few clothes, and tended to their medi-cal needs. Marsh's biographer, George D. Lyman, has written glow-ingly of this arrangement: "So grateful were they, that in return they became his willing serfs, and he enjoyed a life among them not unlike that of a Southern plantation owner."[22]

Two years after Marsh settled in the San Joaquin Valley, Johann

August Sutter arrived in California. Sutter was an extremely ambitious man, who, having failed in business in Switzerland, had emigrated to the United States in 1834. After a series of false starts in Saint Louis, Santa Fe, and Oregon he arrived in Monterey in July, 1839. Although he was neither an Anglo-American nor an overland pioneer, he became a very significant figure in the history of the American pioneer settlers and their attitudes toward the California Indians. In 1840 he was granted Mexican citizenship and a large tract of land about fifty miles northeast of Marsh's ranch. He grandiloquently named the site New Helvetia and upon it built a barony of sorts complete with a full contingent of Indian serfs. Like Marsh, he took the Spanish mission or Mexican rancho as his model and based his operations on the subjugation and exploitation of the local Indian population. The adobe bricks for "Sutter's Fort" were made by the Indians; the herds and fields and vineyards were tended by the Indians; the workshops inside the fort were staffed by Indian craftsmen who did the weaving, spinning, tanning, and other tasks.[23]

Beginning with the Bidwell-Bartleson party in 1841, the American settlers who arrived overland were welcomed to California by Johann Sutter. After they had made their way through the passes of the Sierra Nevada, Sutter's New Helvetia was a welcome sight. The many Americans who passed through New Helvetia not only received the benefits of Sutter's generous hospitality but also witnessed there a working model of what could be accomplished with the California Indian labor force.[24]

Certainly few travellers who visited Sutter failed to be impressed by the apparent ease with which he had subdued his Indian workers and made them "useful."[25] Edwin Bryant, for example, arrived at Sutter's Fort in August, 1846, as a member of a party of overland immigrants. Bryant's *What I Saw in California* (1848) described Sutter as a man who had "succeeded by degrees in reducing the Indians to obedience, and by means of their labor erected the spacious fortification which now belongs to him." Sutter had only to provide a minimum of sustenance for his primitive workers and their labor was his.[26] John C. Frémont's widely publicized narrative of his exploring expedition to the West Coast in 1843 and 1844 described the Indians around Sutter's Fort as an extremely primitive people who had been easily "domesticated" by Sutter. Frémont explained that at first Sutter had had some difficulties with the Indians, "but by the occasional exercise of well-timed authority, he had succeeded in converting them into peaceable and industrious people." Frémont described how the irrigation system and the adobe bricks for Sutter's buildings were made with Indian labor and all the agricultural operations were performed by Indian workers. The principal compensation they received, Frémont noted, was the clothing on their backs. When the need arose for additional workers, Sutter had assured Frémont, he could easily obtain as many as he wanted.[27]

It is appropriate that we conclude this discussion of the attitudes of the pioneer settlers by taking notice of probably the most active, if misguided, publicist of American settlement in California: Lansford W. Hastings. Hubert Howe Bancroft has labeled Hastings's widely read *Emigrants' Guide to Oregon and California* (1845) as a "worthless book," and indeed it did contain much dangerously misleading information about the routes to California.[28] Hastings first came to California in 1843 after an overland crossing to Oregon the previous year. He was not only an active promoter of California like Bidwell and Marsh but also intent on leading a filibustering action in California. Whatever his faults and ambitions, Hastings produced a classic statement of the great unrealized potential of California under Mexican rule and what it might become as the Anglo-American population began to grow. "We are necessarily driven to this conclusion," wrote Hastings,

> when we consider the vast extent of its plains and valleys, of unequalled fertility and exuberance; the extraordinary variety and abundance, of its productions, its unheard of uniformity, and salubrity of climate; in fine, its unexhausted and inexhaustible resources, as well, as its increasing emigration, which is annually swelling its population, from hundreds to thousands, and which is destined, at no distant day, to revolutionize the whole commercial, political, and moral aspect of all that highly important and delightful country. In a word, I will remark that in my opinion, there is no country . . . now known, which is so eminently calculated, by nature itself, in all respects, to promote the unbounded happiness and prosperity, of civilized and enlightened man.[29]

As for the Indians of California, Hastings reported that they might be "readily employed" for only a trifling payment of coarse clothing or meals or "whatever else you may feel disposed to furnish them." Their manner of living was so primitive, and their expectations so low, that they were easily satisfied with the crudest compensation for their labor. "There are several foreigners, who have from one, to four hundred of them employed on these terms," Hastings mentioned with enthusiasm. What was more, the ranchers had the right to compel their laborers to return to work if they left.[30]

Having described those arrangements, Hastings commented that, although it was generally understood that slavery did not exist in the Mexican Republic, the Indians of California "are in a state of absolute vassalage, even more degrading and more oppressive than that of our slaves in the south." Here Hastings seems to be condemning the California labor system; his remarks echo the comments of La Pérouse and a host of others over the previous half century. Yet he concluded his remarks on a profoundly ambiguous note: "Whether slavery will, eventually, be tolerated in this country, in any form, I do not pretend to say, but it is quite certain, that the labor of Indians will, for many years, be as little expensive to the farmers of that country, as slave labor, being procured for a mere nominal consideration."[31] Hastings's remarks aptly illustrate the change in attitudes toward the California Indians. Lingering in them is a critical posture that demanded some expression of moral outrage at the enslavement of the California Indians, but as an ardent expansionist Hastings was reluctant to pass up an opportunity to attract American settlers to California and therefore he praised the virtually free labor supply.

It is curious indeed how the image of the Indians of California was changing and yet remained the same. Whereas the early European and American visitors had described the Indians as victims of cruel exploitation, the Americans who settled permanently in California began to picture them as a useful class of laborers. In both cases the Indians were acknowledged as primitives and laborers, and in both cases the image of the Indians was part of a larger rationale of expansionism. Put another way, although the American image of the Indians of California was undergoing a fundamental change, the image remained a clear reflection of the needs of the white observers.

4

To Make Them Useful

LANDING at Monterey in early July, 1846, Commodore John Drake Sloat proclaimed, "Henceforth California will be a portion of the United States." A year and a half later at Guadalupe Hidalgo the Republic of Mexico concurred. In a treaty signed on February 2, 1848, Mexico ceded title to California and its other northern provinces to the United States. These events constitute a watershed in California history: the Mexican War and the subsequent transfer of title stand as the great discontinuity in the state's history. California's dominant population and its social, economic, and political institutions were radically different in the decades before and after 1846. The cession also signaled important changes in the nature of Indian and white relations in California. With the inundation of the state by Anglo-Americans in the next few years, hostilities increased between Indians and whites. During the next twenty-five years the Indian population of California would decline at a rate more rapid than at any other time in its history.[1]

While the contrasts between the two periods are both obvious and important, it should not be overlooked that there were also important continuities. To a degree often unrealized, the Hispanic past had a profound impact on the American present. This was particularly true of white attitudes toward California Indians. The evolution of Anglo-American attitudes toward the state's native population did not undergo a great change in 1846. The special interest of the pioneer immigrants—that many of the California Indians were useful laborers—did not end with the Mexican War. In spite of the increase in hostilities, for a quarter century after 1846, California Indians continued to be accepted by many Anglo-Americans as a useful class of laborers, agricultural workers, and domestic servants. Although sometimes reluctant to admit it, the Anglo-Americans who came to California after 1846 perpetuated the system of labor exploitation that had already been established in Hispanic California. Indians

81

continued to be subjected to forced labor; raids on native villages for Indian workers continued uninterrupted by the political changes of the 1840s. In much of northern and southern California, Indians remained in a state of peonage comparable to that which had existed on the Mexican ranchos. This continuity in the status of the Indians in Hispanic and American California will be the subject of this and the following chapter. First we will look at the legal forms devised by the Anglo-Americans to ensure the continued usefulness of the California Indians, and then we will consider the various uses to which the Indians were put.

In the months and years following the landing of Commodore Sloat in 1846, California remained in an unsettled political condition. During the war years California was under American military rule, and the military commanders were obligated under international law to maintain the legal code and practice in California as it had existed under Mexican jurisdiction, making whatever adjustments they deemed necessary. There was considerable ignorance and misunderstanding, however, about what this code and practice had been, and thus the legal system of the old order was not systematically enforced. Following the ratification by Congress of the Treaty of Guadalupe Hidalgo in May, 1848, the situation in California became further muddled. The military government now had no legal basis for further existence, yet Congress failed to authorize an alternative civilian or territorial government. This confusion continued until the impatient Californians began to clarify the situation themselves by forming a Constitutional Convention in 1849 and petitioning Congress for admission as a state in 1850.

During this time of confusion and disorder the status of the California Indians was of considerable concern to the many white Californians who had come to depend upon them for labor. Whites complained that the new American governments were not providing adequate control and regulation of Indian labor, and they argued that steps should be taken to ensure continued access to this valuable resource. Images of idle and dissolute Indians appear frequently in the literature of conquered California. Freed from the restraints of the old order, the labor force was thought to be degenerating. Anglo-Americans who had been in California before the conquest, as well as those who had arrived more recently and had come to appreciate the value of California Indian labor, could all agree: laws or ordinances should be adopted to "reclaim" the Indians, to make them useful. The *California Star*, for example, reported in December, 1847, that ranchers in northern California were unable "to retain their Indian laborers, even by the best and most conciliatory treatment, since it became current that Government did not protect masters from theft and desertion, and *afford* no obstacles to a dissolute mode of life, with apparant indulgence of Indian indolence." The failure of the American government to force the Indians to work, according to these ranchers, "had proved a sad detriment to farming operations throughout the vallies."[2] The *Star* recommended that the new government enact "some stable and *reliable* laws" for the subordination of the Indians because the "domesticated or tame Indians," once so useful, had become idle, dissolute, and destitute: "The vagrants should be schooled to labor—the criminal offenders should be punished."[3] One of the best-considered requests for government action to reclaim the California Indians and to restore their usefulness appeared in a letter to the *Star* in January, 1848, from a correspondent in Sonoma, who was identified only as "Pacific." The letter included a long discussion of the status of the California Indians, offering observations on their past and present condition and on what policies should be adopted for the future. Pacific noted that under the Republic of Mexico the California natives "were *aps de facto*, slaves, and ruled and treated accordingly." Most unwisely, Pacific believed, the United States had put an end to that useful system. "The drunken, roving, vagabond life most have led in California since our flag went up," he commented, ". . . shows the impolicy of having removed all restraints, formerly held over them." If it were possible that all masters were "just, mild and good," he would favor restoration of Indian slavery in California. Recognizing that this was not the case, Pacific suggested an alternative system of reinstating certain restraints over the Indians so that they might continue to be "useful."

The Indians of California, he argued, "are, as we all know, mentally, and morally, an inferior order of our own race; are unfit and incapable of being . . . governed by the same laws; and if retained among us, must necessarily have a code and treatment applicable to their peculiar character and condition." Pacific's proposed "Indian code" included the following features: (1) adoption of a system of written labor contracts that would bind Indians to their employers for a set length of time, under which Indian workers would be compelled to serve out the full term of their obligation; (2) punishment of persons guilty of "enticing" Indians away from their masters by offers of "higher wages or other inducements"; (3) prohibition of Indians' passing through areas inhabited by whites without special passes; and (4) enactment of a system of Indian apprenticeship under which interested whites could legally obtain and control the labor of groups of Indians.[4]

It is indicative of the confusion in California legal and political affairs in the early American period that, apparently unknown to Pacific, several parts of his proposed "Indian code" were already in force. In September, 1846, for example, Commodore John B. Montgomery, naval commander of the American forces in San Francisco, issued a "Proclamation to the Inhabitants of California," in which he announced that he had learned that persons in California had been and were still holding Indians "to service" against their will and without legal contract. He therefore ordered that all Indians so held be released. "The Indian population," he proclaimed, "must not be regarded in the light of slaves." Montgomery then added some important qualifications.

Although Indians were not to be regarded as slaves, they were required to work. Montgomery's proclamation was clear on that point, saying "all Indians must be required to obtain service" and "it is deemed necessary that the Indians within the settlement shall have employment." Any Indians not employed were to be arrested and forced to labor on the public works. Nor were Indians free, except under special circumstances, to leave their employers. Having chosen their employment, Indians must continue to labor unless their employers gave them written permission to leave or a justice of the peace annulled their obligations.[5] Montgomery's proclamation did not exactly fulfill Pacific's request for a system of written labor contracts, but it did establish a basis for compelling Indians to labor.

Similarly, the "enticement" of Indian laborers away from their masters had been prohibited one year before Pacific's letter appeared in the *Star*. On January 11, 1847, Walter Colton, chief magistrate of Monterey, issued an "Ordinance Respecting the Employement of Indians," which declared "no person whatever" would be permitted to hire an Indian without first obtaining a certificate that the Indian's former employer had no claims on him or her. Also Colton ordered, "If it should be proved that any Indian has been enticed away from the service of his master, the person convicted of having so enticed him shall be liable to a fine not exceeding twenty dollars nor less than five dollars."[6]

Pacific's recommended "pass system" to restrict the geographic mobility of Indians had been adopted in August, 1847, when Colonel Richard B. Mason, acting military governor of California, instructed the Indians of southern California not to go any distance from their rancherias except with written permission from government agents.[7] In the following month Lieutenant Henry W. Halleck, acting as California's secretary of state, announced that the governor had issued orders that all persons employing Indians give them a certificate to that effect, "and any Indian found beyond the limits of the town or rancho in which he may be employed, without such certificate or pass, will be liable to arrest as a horse thief, and if, on being brought before a civil magistrate, he fail to give a satisfactory account of himself, he will be subjected to trial and punishment." Indians not employed who wished to visit settlements or towns were also required to obtain a "passport" from a government official.[8]

In these earliest expressions of public policy in American California we see a remarkable continuity with the tradition of Indian relations in preconquest Hispanic California. Montgomery's 1846 proclamation, for instance, which prohibited Indian slavery while requiring all Indians to labor, is reminiscent of the Spanish definition of liberty, worked out in the sixteenth century, that underlay the Hispanic institutions for Indian labor control from encomienda to hacienda: Indians were free, but they were not free to be idle. The force of law was to be applied to compel idle Indians "to obtain service." More specifically, the provision that Indians remain with their employers until given a written discharge was an exact replication of the law of Mexican California that had controlled the mobility of the rancho Indians. The system of fines for employers who enticed Indian laborers away from their previous masters and employed them without gaining the previous masters' written permission also had an exact parallel in Mexican California law. In both cases the minimum fine was set at the same amount: five dollars. Whether the American military leaders were aware of these specific precedents is not known, but it is clear that the policies they adopted had the effect of perpetuating the practices of Indian labor control as they had existed in Mexican California.

In 1849, California's legal and political affairs became more settled with the establishment of constitutional government. Meeting in convention in Monterey, forty-eight delegates from throughout the region devised the fundamental laws for the new state. Of those delegates eight were Californios, and a large majority, including both Hispanos and Anglos, had been in California more than three years. In their deliberations the delegates considered the question of the status of the state's Indian population, and their answer was clear. Indians were to have no political rights and only inferior legal rights. They were to remain essentially what they had been under the previous regime: a subservient class of laborers. Although the delegates voted unanimously to prohibit slavery in California, their attention was on black slavery not on Indian slavery. They debated the question of Indian suffrage and citizenship, especially whether the United States was obligated under the Treaty of Guadalupe Hidalgo to provide such rights. One of the Californio delegates, Pablo de la Guerra, pointed out that, while Indians technically had been citizens under Mexican law, only a few in California had ever been eligible to exercise the franchise, because of strict property requirements. Probably not more than two hundred California Indians, in fact, had possessed the necessary qualifications to make them voters in Mexican California. Delegate de la Guerra argued in favor of granting the franchise to those Indians who had been citizens of Mexico and were subject to taxation, but an amendment introduced to accomplish this was defeated. The Anglo-dominated convention voted finally to limit suffrage along racial (and sexual) lines, providing that only "white male citizens" could vote.[9]

The basic document defining the status of Indians in California was not the state constitution, however, but a law that was adopted by the state's first legislature and entitled "An Act for the Government and Protection of Indians." Passed at the new state capitol in San Jose during April, 1850, the law revealed a continuing concern with subordinating the Indians and facilitating white access to their labor. Thus it suggested further continuity with Indian-white relations in Latin America generally and Hispanic California in particular. It prohibited whites from compelling Indians to work or to perform any service against their will, yet able-bodied Indians were liable to arrest "on the complaint of any resident" if they could not support themselves or were found loitering or "strolling about" or were "leading an immoral or profligate course of life." If it was determined by proper authority that an Indian was a "vagrant," he or she could be hired out within twenty-four hours for the highest price for any term not exceeding four months. In effect, any Indian not employed could be bought from a county or municipal official at public auction.

The law of 1850 further provided that an Indian guilty of any offense for which a fine was imposed could be bailed out by "any white person" willing to pay the fine. The law stated that in such cases "the Indian shall be compelled to work for the person so bailing, until he has discharged or cancelled the fine assessed against him." Thus it was that all Indian convicts were made available to whites who wished to use them as laborers. The law provided that whites taking advantage of the system must treat their Indians humanely and must properly clothe and feed them. One wonders, however, how this provision could have been enforced, for the law also stipulated that "in no case shall a white man be convicted of any offence upon the testimony of an Indian." With this prohibition of Indian testimony it would be virtually impossible for an Indian to win legal redress for mistreatment by his white master or indeed to exercise any legal rights whatever.[10]

A final provision of the 1850 law established a system of Indian apprenticeship, under which any white person wishing to obtain the labor of an Indian child could appear before a justice of the peace with the child's "parents or friends," and, if the justice was convinced that no compulsory means had been used to obtain the child, the justice would issue to the white person a certificate authorizing him to have "the care, custody, control, and earnings of such minor, until he or she obtain the age of majority." Under this law whites could obtain legally the services of any number of Indian males under eighteen years and females under fifteen. The only obligation of the white master was to feed, clothe, and treat humanely his Indian wards. Failure to meet that obligation could result in a ten-dollar fine and the reassignment of the minor to another master.[11] The apprenticeship system that was thus established fulfilled one of the recommendations to the *California Star* of Pacific, who had believed in 1848 that such a system would be well suited to the "peculiar character and condition" of the California Indians.

The 1850 "Act for the Government and Protection of Indians" reminds us of the abiding strength of the image of the California Indians as a useful class, as a resource that should be controlled and properly exploited. The law of 1850 also stands as powerful evidence of the impact of the Hispanic system of Indian relations on American California. In effect, this law and related acts of the legislature were an attempt by the state government to legalize the peonage system that had existed during the Mexican period.[12] The 1850 law contained the familiar provision that Indians were not to be compelled to work; yet the state at the same time assumed responsibility for compelling Indians to labor. The various ways by which whites might obtain Indian laborers under the law are reminiscent of the laws that had evolved during the centuries of Hispanic rule in the New World. Whatever the precise arrangement—whether Indians were sold at the state's public auctions to the highest bidder, bailed out of jail by whites seeking their services, or held as "apprentices"—the relationship established under the law was essentially that of master and serf. As had been true under the various Spanish institutions for the exploitation of Indian labor, the white person who was granted the privilege of exploiting that labor was obligated to care for and treat humanely his Indian charges. In this and other particulars the California apprenticeship system is especially reminiscent of the repartimiento system of the seventeenth century. In both cases a person wishing to obtain the services of a group of Indians had simply to file his request with a government authority, promise to treat them humanely, and a grant would be made.

The California lawmakers in 1850 undoubtedly were not aware of the long history of Spanish Indian policy, but certainly they were aware of conditions in California before the conquest and of conditions as they were in 1850. Certainly they knew that the California Indians long had been held in arrangements whereby whites were able to exploit their labor for little compensation and with little difficulty. They understood that this arrangement long had been beneficial to the Anglo and Hispano settlers of the state and that many Californians now favored the imposition of further controls over the Indians to guarantee their continued usefulness. Indeed, when we look more closely at the legislators involved in the creation of the law of 1850, we are struck by the depth of this understanding.

The author of the 1850 bill, John Bidwell, had been one of the most prominent preconquest Anglo-Californians. As an overland pioneer in 1841, he had observed firsthand the operations of the ranchos of Marsh and Sutter before becoming a naturalized Mexican citizen and obtaining a grant of his own. Bidwell was among those Anglo-Californians who had encouraged further immigration to California by assuring potential immigrants of the ease with which they could obtain cheap Indian labor. From the mid-1840s through at least the mid-1860s, Bidwell was personally dependent upon California Indians for his rancho labor force. On March 14, 1850, Bidwell informed the California Senate that he was interested in introducing a bill for "the protection, punishment, and government of Indians."

Two days later the bill was introduced on Bidwell's behalf (he was absent due to illness) by Senator E. Kirby Chamberlin of San Diego.[13] Meanwhile, in the Assembly a similar bill was introduced by Elam Brown, a pioneer ranchero and former member of the Constitutional Convention. Brown had immigrated overland to California in 1846 and in the following year had acquired the Rancho Acalanes grant in present-day Contra Costa County. Brown, like Bidwell, had readily adopted the Hispanic rancho style as his own and depended upon a staff of vaqueros to tend his herds of cattle.[14] On April 16 the Assembly passed Brown's bill and submitted it to the Senate, where a select committee was appointed to consider and reconcile the Assembly and Senate versions of the proposal.

The final draft of the bill was prepared by a three-member select committee, including John Bidwell, Mariano Guadalupe Vallejo, and David F. Douglas. Vallejo was, of course, the preeminent ranchero of northern California, a nativeborn Californio whose enormous estate was based on the recruitment and control of Indian labor. The Vallejos had been notorious in the 1830s and 1840s for their raids on native villages and the seizure of laborers. The third member of the committee, David Douglas, a Tennessean by birth, had lived in Arkansas, Texas, and Mississippi before his arrival in California in 1848 as a volunteer in the Mexican War.[15] Douglas's contribution to the bill is not known, but his origins in the antebellum South suggest that he would not have been adverse to a system of racial serfdom in California. The final version of the bill was reported from the select committee on April 19 and passed the same day. Following the concurrence of the Assembly, Governor Peter H. Burnett signed the bill into law three days later.[16] With the exception of Douglas, the men most responsible for the creation of the 1850 law (Bidwell, Brown, and Vallejo) were each fully acquainted with the system of Indian labor exploitation in Mexican California. Vallejo and Bidwell, and probably Brown as well, were personally interested in seeing that the advantages of that system were continued in American California. It is thus no mystery that the 1850 law represents a continuity with the Hispanic tradition of Indian labor exploitation; its authors had dedicated their efforts to the achievement of precisely that continuity.

Probably the most generous feature of the law of 1850 was its provision for a system of Indian apprenticeship under which whites could obtain the labor of as many Indian young people as they wanted, promising merely to feed, clothe, and treat them humanely. As liberal as this provision was, it apparently did not go far enough for some Californians. Throughout the 1850s whites called for the enactment of a more comprehensive code dealing with Indian apprenticeship, demanding that Indian apprentices be more easily obtained and that their length of service be lengthened.[17] In 1856 the *Marysville Herald,* expressing concern over the dissipation of the natives around Yuba City, recommended that a new law be passed requiring Indian parents "to bind out their children to farmers and others, for a given period, so as to make them useful, and thus induct them to habits of cleanliness and industry." Such a policy, the *Herald* believed, would render the Indians "useful to the whites" and improve their own condition.[18] In 1860 the *Sacramento Standard* recommended that an enlarged system of apprenticeship would solve much of California's "Indian problem." Under existing conditions, the *Standard* believed, the Indians were deteriorating: "The most humane disposition that could be made of them, is, probably to reduce them to a mild system of servitude. Call them slaves, coolies or apprentices — it is all the same; supply them with christian masters and make them christian servants."[19]

The state government in 1860 authorized a special committee of legislators to investigate Indian affairs in northern California. The committee's minority report, written by state senator J. B. Lamar of Mendocino County, included a discussion of the problems of the "domesticated Indians." These Indians, Lamar argued, would remain useful to themselves and the community only if a proper policy were adopted by the state government for their control, management, and protection. "The State," wrote Lamar in 1860, "should adopt a general system of peonage or apprenticeship, for the proper disposition and distribution of the Indians by families among responsible citizens." Lamar reasoned that "in this manner the whites might be provided with profitable and convenient servants, and the Indians with the best of protection and all the necessaries of life in permanent and comfortable homes."[20]

Although Lamar's proposal was not universally supported, public sentiment was sufficiently favorable to an expansion of the apprenticeship system that in the spring of 1860 the legislature approved an act amending the 1850 law. The legislative history of this act is not as revealing as the history of the 1850 act, though it may be significant that most of the legislators responsible for the amendatory act represented northern California counties, where Indian affairs had become of grave concern by 1860. It was also in the northern counties that the greatest use (or abuse) of the apprenticeship system occurred. Lamar, who had originally proposed an extension of the 1850 law, was from Mendocino, and the author of the 1860 amendment, Lewis M. Burson, was an assemblyman from neighboring Humboldt County.[21] Under the revised statute of 1860 any person wishing to obtain Indian children could appear before a county or district judge to prove that the children had been obtained with the consent of their parents or the consent of "persons having the care or charge of any such child or children." This added phrase was purposely ambiguous: in practice it would allow Indian children to be obtained from third parties and clearly without parental consent. The law further provided that any person could obtain Indians, "whether children or grown persons," who had "no settled habitation or means of livelihood" and were not already "under the protection" of a white person or who were held as prisoners of war. The white person had only to appear before a judge who was empowered under the act to "bind or put out such Indians as apprentices, to trades, husbandry, or other employments." The justice could issue "articles of indenture or apprenticeship" that would authorize the white person to have the "care, custody, control and earnings" of the indentured Indians for a set period of time.

The old law, of course, had provided only for the apprenticeship of minors. The new law considerably lengthened the terms of service and also included adults. Under the 1860 amendment Indian men apprenticed under fourteen could be held until they were twenty-five; those obtained between fourteen and twenty could be held until they were thirty. Indian women could be held until they were twenty-one and twenty-five years old. The terms for adult Indians were limited to ten years at the discretion of the judge. As under the original act, the law of 1860 required the white masters to clothe and provide the necessities of life for their Indian charges. Also, a penalty of $100 to $500 was to be imposed on any person who did "forcibly convey" or compel Indians to work against their will "except as provided in this act."[22]

The number of Indians affected by the law is not known. Robert F. Heizer has estimated that as many as ten thousand Indians were indentured under the laws of 1850 and 1860.[23] The law of 1860 provided that duplicate copies of all indentures were to be filed with the county recorder's office. Before an accurate estimate could be made of the effect of the law, a search would have to be made of the county archives throughout California. Such a search has never been made, but the *Sacramento Daily Union* published a copy of one

91

of the indentures in February, 1861. It included the names of more than forty Indians of Tehama County who were bound to two ranchers "to be used in ranching, farming and housework." To convey some of the human dimensions of the 1860 law the names and terms of service as they appeared in the indenture are given here:

Name	Age	Till When Bound
Simon	17	30 years of age
Big Jack	20	30 do do
Jackass	20	30 do do
Jack White	16	30 do do
Joe	15	30 do do
Elijah	18	30 do do
Judas	18	30 do do
Ben	17	30 do do
Tebalth	19	30 do do
Doc	18	30 do do
Peter	19	30 do do
Big Sam	18	30 do do
Number Two	17	30 do do
Big Abe	19	30 do do
Darly	18	30 do do
Tony	18	30 do do
Ambrose	16	30 do do
Bob	18	30 do do
Bony	15	30 do do
Henry	17	30 do do
Jordan	18	30 do do
Prince	16	30 do do
Yolo Boley	15	30 do do
Little Sam	12	25 do do
Job	12	25 do do
Billy	12	25 do do
Nancy — (she)	15	30 do do
Susan	15	30 do do
Mary	18	30 do do
Laura	10	25 do do
Betsey	15	30 do do
Julliet	17	30 do do
Myra	18	30 do do
Maggie	18	30 do do
Venus	16	30 do do
Sally	17	30 do do

Long Betsey	15	30	do	do
Dido	15	30	do	do
Big Sally	15	30	do	do
Fanny	12	25	do	do
Eliza	15	30	do	do
Van's Billy	17	30	do	do
Trowbridge	12	25	do	do
Cooney	19	30	do	do
George	18	30	do	do[24]

It was popularly understood, when the law of 1860 was passed, that it legalized a system of involuntary servitude in California. The person who sent the above indenture to the *Union* did so, he said, to clear up any misconceptions about the way the law operated in practice. All that a white person had to do, if he or she wanted some Indian apprentices, was to take a list of their names to a judge and have him sign it. In practice the judge made no effort to determine the consent or condition of the Indians or to ensure that the prospective master would clothe, feed, or protect them. In practice the law "made slaves" of the California Indians.[25] A couple of weeks after that indenture was published, the *Humboldt Times*, in an editorial entitled "Apprenticing Indians," wryly remarked: "What a pity the provisions of the law are not extended to greasers, Kanakas, and Asiatics. It would be so convenient to carry on a farm or mine, when all the hard and dirty work is performed by apprentices!"[26] The *Marysville Appeal* meanwhile commented that the apprentice system "smacks of cottondom."[27]

The most perceptive commentary on the new law was provided by the leading newspaper in the state's capital, the *Sacramento Union*. In an editorial published in July, 1860, the *Union* explained in great detail the provisions of the newly enacted law and expressed misgivings about its effect on Indian people. Under the new law, the *Union* believed, many Indians "whose condition differs very little from that of absolute slaves" were being held in domestic servitude. The editorial noted that the new code "with mock earnestness" had forbidden forcible abduction or subjection of Indians "except as provided in this act." With that exception the previous provisions of the act were restored to full force, and Indians could in fact be seized and subjected to labor without their consent. The *Union* editorial concluded, "If this does not fill the measure of the constitutional term, 'involuntary servitude,' we shall be thankful if some one will inform us what is lacking."[28]

The *Union* argued that the 1860 law represented a revival of the "system of Indian slavery" that had existed in the "days of the Spaniards." The paper recalled how at first representatives of the United States had promised to end that system: "One of the first orders issued by the Naval Commanders who hoisted the flag at the ports on this coast in 1846, was aimed at its suppression." The *Union* then printed the text of Montgomery's 1846 proclamation, emphasizing those portions that expressed opposition to Indian slavery. The *Union* predicted that despite this original suppression little effective opposition would be offered to the new law: "The Indians of the country have been so long accustomed, under their Spanish masters, to be treated as menials, that we shall not expect public attention to be called to their case by any determined resistance to the decrees of the Courts."[29]

Set in the context of the national controversy over slavery, the situation in California was certainly ironic. The delegates to the state's constitutional convention had voted unanimously to include a provision in the fundamental law that "neither slavery, nor involuntary servitude, unless for the punishment of crimes, shall ever be tolerated in this State."[30] California's petition for admission into the union as a free state in 1850 had precipitated a national crisis. Yet now the state was approving a form of Indian slavery. The irony of California's position was not lost on contemporary observers. James Delavan, for example, in his *Notes on California and the Placers* (1850), had early remarked that the enslavement of California Indians was being carried out by men supposedly opposed to slavery. "No doubt all these respectable proprietors are *Wilmot proviso* men," Delavan commented, "and eschew slavery, but their mode of recruiting their laborers is something more exceptionable, than if they obtained their supplies from the far-famed slave market at Washington." The condition of the Indian laborers, he believed, was "worse than that of the Peons of Yucatan, and other parts of Mexico, and yet there are no slaves in California!"[31]

During the Civil War the California position became even more of an anomaly. This was brought forcefully to the attention of John Bidwell during his bid for a seat in the House of Representatives in 1864. Bidwell—one of the creators of the original 1850 act and a man who retained a large contingent of Indian workers on his ranch in northern California—ran as a strong Unionist and abolitionist. Thus some of his neighbors charged him with inconsistency. In September, 1864, the *Yreka Semi-Weekly Union* printed a series of questions addressed to "General Bidwell (Abolitionist)," including:

> What compensation do you receive for establishing a (digger) slave pen at Chico, and what is your mode of punishment of your slaves (diggers)?

> If it is not too much trouble, General, I would like you to inform your friends of the manner in which you punished one of your slaves by tying his hands and feet together across a barrel (naked) and in this condition by your authority, beat him with a club so unmercifully that had it been a white man he would have died under the blows?

> Has it ever been recorded that the slaves of the South received such vile treatment as you accord to your Indians?

> As you are such a stickler for freedom of the slaves, why not set the example and comply with the request of your neighbors by giving freedom to your (Indian) slaves?[32]

Yet Bidwell's ranch operations in 1864 were not based on the model of a slave plantation in the South. Although the similarities were there, Bidwell's ranch was a manifestation of a much more local and indigenous model of labor exploitation.

Under cover of the apprenticeship provisions of the laws of 1850 and 1860 the abduction and sale of Indians—especially young women and children—were carried on as a regular business enterprise in California. Whatever the intentions of their framers, the apprenticeship laws had the effect of encouraging the kidnapping and selling of Indians as "apprentices" to white farmers, ranchers, and miners.

In his 1861 report on Indian affairs in California, Superintendent George M. Hanson reported that "a band of desperate men" were kidnapping Indian children in the frontier areas of Humboldt and Mendocino counties and carrying them into the lower counties to sell them virtually as slaves. The superintendent regarded this practice as a crime against humanity and laid the blame for its existence on California's new apprenticeship law. "I beg to call particular attention to the laws of this State providing for 'indenturing Indians,'" Hanson wrote to the United States commissioner of Indian affairs in 1861, "and the sad effects produced by kidnapping under cover of such laws, and I suggest that Congress should in due time provide a remedy."[33] At the end of the following year Hanson informed his superior in Washington that conditions had not changed in California. "The fact is, kidnapping Indians has become quite a business of profit." He described his own efforts to intercept the kidnappers and promised that during the next session of the state legislature he would attempt "to have the law repealed authorizing the indenturing of Indians, under cover of which all this trouble exists."[34]

The Indians of California had long been described as the "slaves" of the priests and rancheros. Yet, although forced recruitment and Indian peonage were part of life at the missions and ranchos, the actual buying and selling of California Indians was an American innovation. The exploitation of Indian labor represented an important continuity between Hispanic and American California. After 1846 the system was simply expanded to include the actual selling of Indians into bondage. As Sherburne F. Cook has noted: "The old Californian and to some extent early American ranchers captured Indian labor for their own use. The American variant which developed in the early 'fifties was to catch or kidnap the natives for sale. In other words, the boundary was at last crossed from technical peonage to actual slavery."[35]

It is impossible to determine the extent of the practice of kidnapping and selling Indian children, since such activities were not often a matter of public record. Although the apprenticeship laws served as a cover for the practice, it is probable that many whites who purchased Indians from kidnappers did not go through the legal formalities of obtaining certificates of indenture. Cook has estimated that from 1852 to 1867 between three and four thousand Indian children were stolen, while a more recent student of the question has suggested that "well over 4,000 Indians" were victims of the practice.[36] Although the exact number of Indians captured and sold as "apprentices" may never be known, contemporary accounts lead one to conclude that the practice was far from unusual.[37]

In 1856, Thomas J. Henley, the superintendent of California Indian affairs, reported that the practice of "kidnapping Indians and selling them into servitude" was being carried on "to an extraordinary extent." "I have undoubted evidence," Henley added, "that hundreds of Indians have been stolen and carried into the settlements and sold; in some instances entire tribes were taken en masse."[38] The *Ukiah Herald* commented in 1862 that the practice of stealing Indians was "extensively carried on" in that section of the state and the operations of Indian slavers were "well known" throughout Mendocino County.[39] In the same year the *Sacramento Union* printed a letter that estimated that "every fourth house" in the northern counties contained Indian children who had been purchased by whites as "apprentices."[40] California pioneer Henry Clay Bailey recalled that there was an almost unlimited demand for them.[41]

That Indians were literally being sold in California cannot be doubted. The prices for Indian women and children depended upon such factors as age, sex, and usefulness and ranged from thirty to two hundred dollars.[42] Henry Bailey remembered that in the 1850s "the standard price for the redskin" was about fifty dollars.[43] In Colusa County in 1861 Indian boys and girls aged three and four years were sold at fifty dollars apiece. Near Yuba City a boy between eight and ten years old was sold for eighty dollars as a hog driver, and a younger boy for fifty-five dollars.[44] Prices for Indians in Mendocino County at the same time were said to range from thirty to a hundred and fifty dollars "according to quality."[45] A Humboldt man estimated in 1862 that Indian children still "fetch a market price of between thirty and two hundred dollars."[46] And an employee of the U.S. Mail Department in northern California testified in 1862: "Indians seven or eight years old are worth $100. It is a d——n poor Indian that's not worth $50. There were some last Winter, sold right here for $50. Parties took them right off the hands of Indian hunters for $50. W.'s boys got $60 apiece. Old W. usually gives a Spanish horse for a good little Digger."[47]

Most of the activity centered in the far northern counties where the Indians were actually seized, but the captives were sold throughout the state.[48] One report indicated that Indians seized north of Chico in Butte County had been sold as far away as southern California.[49] A more typical pattern of distribution was suggested in an 1862 *Alta California* editorial entitled "Selling Indian Children":

> Mr. August Hess, who has returned to this city from a prospecting tour through the lower part of Lake county informs us that he saw a number of men driving Indian children before them to sell in Napa, Solano, Yolo, and other counties of the Sacramento basin. In one instance, he saw two men driving nine children; in another, two men with four children; in another, one man with two girls, one of them about fourteen years of age apparently. The age of these children varies from six to fifteen years. Rumor says that about a hundred children have been taken through Lake county this summer, for sale. They do not follow the main roads, but usually take by-paths. Rumor says further, that the hunters catch them in Mendocino and Humboldt counties after killing their parents.[50]

Apparently, the main markets for Indian children, other than in the northern counties themselves, were in the counties of the Sacramento

"A Digger Boy," photographed at Red Bluff, Tehama County. This young-
ster, about ten years old, was from the Feather River area in northern
California.

Valley and the San Francisco Bay area.[51] In 1858 the *San Francisco
Bulletin* claimed that the practice of enslaving Indian children was
far from over and that there "are not a few of these servants in San
Francisco today."[52] William Henry Brewer recorded in his journal
in the early 1860s that for many years there had existed a "regular
business" of stealing Indian children in the northern counties and
taking them "down to the civilized parts of the state, even to San
Francisco, and selling them."[53]

A common feature of the trade was the seizure of Indian girls and
women who were held by their captors as sexual partners or sold
to other whites. Isaac Cox, in his *Annals of Trinity County* (1858),
described the purchase by "Kentuck" of an Indian girl eight or nine
years old "either for his seraglio, to be educated the queen of his

heart, or the handmaid of its gentle emanations." According to Cox, dealers in Indian women in the early 1850s classified their merchandise as "fair, middling, inferior, refuse" and set their prices accordingly. A teamster in Shasta purchased one young Indian woman, her classification not specified, for forty-five dollars.[54] The *Sacramento Union,* in an 1860 editorial entitled "Apprenticing Indians," remarked: "The most disgusting phase of this species of slavery is the concubinage of creatures calling themselves white men with squaws throughout various portions of the State. The details of this portion of the 'apprenticeship' system are unfit to commit to paper."[55] And in December, 1861, the *Marysville Appeal* commented that, while kidnapped Indian children were seized as servants, the young women were made to serve both the "purposes of labor and of lust." Settlers would pay only sixty dollars for a boy, the *Appeal* noticed, but were willing to pay a hundred dollars for "a likely young girl."[56]

Captured Indian children were considered useful at a variety of tasks. Those who were old enough or strong enough were used as stock herders or general agricultural workers.[57] Younger ones were trained as domestic servants to perform general housekeeping chores. The *Marysville Appeal* pointed out that the majority of customers for Indian children were men who were "unmarried but at housekeeping," who willingly purchased Indian children "to cook and wait upon them"[58] The *Sacramento Union* noted that white men in the sparsely settled valleys of the Coast Range and the northern counties compelled Indians "to perform the most menial drudgery of their cabins."[59] White bachelors, however, were not the only customers for Indian children. One pioneer resident recalled that white married men also bought Indians to lighten the work load for their wives. The young Indian servants were assigned such household chores as carrying water, washing dishes and clothes, and tending the younger white children.[60]

Indian children were often described by whites as apt pupils who readily learned new skills, seemed to enjoy their work, and quickly proved themselves very useful.[61] Franklin Buck, a forty-niner, wrote from Weaverville in March, 1853, that whites there owned "lots of little Diggers" who were "bright little boys."[62] A few years later a northern California newspaper commented that Indian children acquired by local whites were "bright little specimens and no doubt will be of much benefit to those who raise and care for them."[63] A resident of Humboldt County commented in 1862 that Indian children sold as servants were "frequently the brightest and cunningest little chaps you ever saw. They are very cheerful, laugh at jokes, and seem fond of playing practical ones occasionally on their white playfellows." This practicular northern Californian kept an Indian bootblack, named Sam, who was "always jolly, and always whistling."[64]

In contrast to those images of docility and contentment, there is evidence that Indian children sometimes proved to be a "troublesome property" for their white masters. Runaway slaves or "apprentices" were a problem, and occasionally whites were the victims of violent revolts by their young charges. Whites commonly complained that Indian children, no matter how long they lived in white homes, still retained their Indian identity and a desire to be free. "So far as my observation extended," Henry Bailey wrote, "contentment and apparently perfect resignation was the result until manhood or womanhood was reached, when all the Indian instincts seemed to return and no influence, moral, mental or physical, could induce them to remain in the positions they had in many instances esteemed highly during their childhood."[65] A correspondent of the *Sacramento Union* commented that Indian children never seemed to forget their Indian ways entirely. He cited the case of an "intelligent looking girl of fifteen" who had lived for years with her white masters and had nearly forgotten her native language. She had escaped and returned to the woods along the Eel River, and there she was recaptured and sent to Fort Humboldt along with a band of "wild depredators." The correspondent remarked with apparent disgust and incredulity that the girl could then be seen at the fort "in the arms of a half-naked 'buck' with whom she is enamoured."[66]

Actual revolts were probably rare, but a few cases have been recorded. A pioneer in Round Valley, Elijah Potter, recalled that in the summer of 1862 three "pet Indians" belonging to a local rancher revolted, and one attempted to poison his master. The revolt was unsuccessful, and the "pets" were executed for their attempt.[67] One of the most notorious Indian fighters in northern California, Hiram Good, kept for many years an Indian child as a household servant. When the child reached the age of sixteen, he revolted and killed his master. The boy was later apprehended and executed by Good's neighbors.[68]

As those examples suggest, revolts were rare, if only because of the harshness with which they were suppressed. Attempts to escape were also met with deadly repression.[69] The *Alta California* commented that it was general practice among Indian kidnappers to shoot any children who tried to escape and that, after the children were sold, they were held under the threat of death. The *Alta* cited the case of a boy in Berreyesa Valley who left a farmer to whom he had been sold and went to another farmer. The purchaser located his runaway Indian "and swore he would hang him if he should run away again."[70] That such threats were not idle was illustrated by a letter that appeared in the *San Francisco Bulletin* in 1860. It was written by a recent visitor from the northern counties who felt obligated to describe to the people of San Francisco some of the "shameful and horrible crimes" being committed in the north.

> Some time in February last, a man named L——, who has a stock ranch on Van Dusen river, had an Indian boy, whose family lived within half a mile of his place. L——'s boy would occasionally run off to visit his relations. This incensed L—— so much, that he went down one morning and slaughtered the whole family — of about six persons — boy and all. He then made a rude raft of logs, put the victims on it, marked it to W. H. Mills — who was known to be opposed to indiscriminate slaughter of the Indians — and started the bodies down the river.[71]

It should not be imagined that the traffic in Indian children was accepted without protest by the Californians of the 1850s and 1860s. Indeed, it is difficult to find a single expression of public approval of the practices of the Indian kidnappers. The apprentice system itself was widely supported; and its extension in 1860 by a majority vote of the state legislature was in response to considerable public demand. But the practices of the kidnappers — operating under cover of the law — were condemned by most Californians. Whenever an account of their activities appeared in the press, it was usually accompanied by a letter or an editorial condemning the kidnappers. The most nefarious aspect of the business of kidnapping Indian children, in the opinion of many Californians, was the brutal method used by the kidnappers in obtaining their "merchandise." Reports were common that kidnappers killed the parents of the children they seized.[72] An 1862 correspondent to the *Sacramento Union*, for example, castigated the "baby killers" of Humboldt County: "You may hear them talk of the operation of cutting to pieces an Indian squaw in their indiscriminate raids for babies as 'like slicing old cheese.' . . . The baby hunters sneak up to a rancheria, kill the bucks, pick out the best looking squaws, ravish them, and make off with their young ones."[73] Obviously, under those circumstances the question of parental consent for the "apprentices" was moot.

Critics of the trade in Indian children often charged—correctly—that the kidnappers' actions were at the root of other difficulties between whites and Indians. The seizure of their children embittered the Indians, critics maintained, so that they made retaliatory raids on white settlers, many of whom were innocent of any involvement in the trade.[74] In 1862 the *Ukiah Herald* described the extensive traffic in Indian children in Mendocino County and concluded, "This affords a key to the history of border Indian difficulties."[75]

In spite of such expressions of public disapproval it is obvious that the trade in Indian slaves would not have existed had there been no demand. Also it is apparent that in spite of public disapproval few Indian kidnappers were ever brought to trial, and fewer still were convicted of any crime. The prosecutions that did occur were at the insistence of federal Indian agents, not because of pressure from outraged white Californians. Indeed, the federal agents, who were the premier opponents of Indian slavery in California, were convinced that it was futile to expect local authorities in the state to take any action to stop the trade. In 1856 the superintendent of California Indian affairs, Thomas J. Henley, reported that the prosecution of several Indian kidnappers in California had had to be handled by special federal prosecutors: "It would have been utterly useless," he wrote, "to depend for one moment on the district attorney of each county to conduct these prosecutions. Being liable to the midnight assaults of these desperadoes, they shrank from the duty of executing the laws and there was no alternative but to employ counsel or fail entirely in the object of suppressing this crime."[76] Earlier, one of Henley's subagents had suggested that the authority of the United States marshal be extended to cover kidnapping so that kidnappers could more easily be apprehended and brought to trial in federal courts.[77] Henley went beyond that suggestion and requested that he be provided with a special detachment of federal troops to assist in arresting kidnappers. The secretary of war, who in 1855 was Jefferson Davis, showed little enthusiasm for using soldiers to suppress the California slave trade. Secretary Davis turned down Henley's request and advised him that such matters should be handled by the civil officials of the state.[78]

Henley's successor as superintendent, George M. Hanson, shared Henley's view that it was the duty of federal authorities to put a stop to the Indian trade. The state or local governments, he was convinced, were not interested in suppressing it. On the contrary, Hanson maintained, the state government was tacitly encouraging the practice by its apprenticeship laws. The kidnapping of Indian children, Hanson wrote in 1862, was "tolerated by an unconstitutional law" in California and the repeal of that law was essential to the suppression of the kidnappers.[79] In the meantime, having little faith in local officials, Hanson appointed some special agents to the areas of the state where the kidnappers were most active and instructed them to intercept the whites as they brought their Indians to market in the settlements. This, he hoped, would at least temporarily put a check on the commerce.[80]

The record of actual arrests and convictions of Indian kidnappers in California is a meager one. The cover provided by the apprenticeship laws, despite the hostile but ineffectual public opinion, produced toleration of the activities of the kidnappers. The kidnapping and selling of Indians may have been technically illegal, but few who engaged in such activities were brought to justice.[81] In 1861, Lieutenant Edward Dillon reported to his commanding officer at Fort Humboldt that the kidnappers seemed to have no fear of being apprehended or charged with a crime: "The parties, I am told, at least some of them, make no secret of it; but boldly assert that they will continue to do so and that the law cannot reach them."[82] In the following year the *Sacramento Union* reported that in spite of "vigorous efforts" by the Grand Jury of Humboldt County, and even though "everybody" there knew of the kidnappers' activities, the local prosecution of such criminals had failed "for want of evidence."[83]

During the 1862 session of the California legislature a bill was introduced to repeal the state's Indian apprenticeship laws. Proponents of the repeal argued that the law of 1860 had encouraged the practice of kidnapping and forcing Indian children into servitude against their will. This was not only morally reprehensible but also the cause of many of the so-called Indian wars on the California frontier. Opponents of the repeal argued that the apprenticeship system was humanitarian and that abuses were rare. Senator William Holden from Mendocino County opposed repeal of the apprenticeship law because he was thoroughly convinced that "great good had grown out of this law" because under its provisions many Indian children had been reared in white homes. The *Sacramento Union* paraphrased Senator Holden as follows: "If he did not know . . . of his own personal knowledge, that the condition of such children was so much better in white families than in their original condition, he would not say a word upon the subject; but he was convinced the law embodied one of the most important measures for their improvement

103

and civilization that had ever been adopted, and he felt disposed, therefore, to give it a further trial."[84]

The repeal bill passed the state Assembly, but did not secure Senate approval until the following year. In 1863 the California legislature repealed the provisions of the "Act for the Government and Protection of Indians" of 1850 and the amendatory act of 1860. There can be little doubt that California, in spite of its status as a free state, had tolerated within its borders a species of human slavery for thirteen years.[85]

California's "peculiar institution" did not, however, come to an end with the repeal of the state's apprenticeship laws. Even without their cover the kidnapping and selling of Indian children and the holding of adults in a form of involuntary servitude continued. Two years after the repeal of the apprenticeship laws a correspondent to the *Sacramento Union* reported that the repeal had had little effect in Mendocino County: Indians there were still being held "as slaves were held in the South; those owning them use them as they please, beat them with clubs and shoot them down like dogs, and no one to say: 'Why do you do so?'"[86] In August, 1865, the *California Police Gazette* called for an investigation of Indian affairs in the state. "It may to some seem a singular statement," the *Gazette* remarked, "but it is nevertheless true that slavery exists in California in precisely the same condition that it did until lately in the Southern States. There the blacks were slaves; here *in almost every county* Indians are unlawfully held as chattels." The only difference between the two systems, in the estimation of the *Gazette*, was that in the South slaves had been held under the right of purchase, whereas in California they were now being kept by the superior might of their white masters. The *Gazette* could not accept the argument that such enslavement benefited the Indians, for "many of them have fallen into cruel hands and the barbarities inflicted upon them by inhuman masters would put to blush the most unfeeling wretch that ever lorded it over a gang on a Southern plantation."[87]

In the following year, 1866, California was visited by a special investigator from the commissioner of Indian affairs. The investigator found that, three years after the emancipation of black slaves in the former Confederacy and one year after the adoption of the Thirteenth Amendment abolishing slavery throughout the United States, Indian slavery still was "not uncommon" in California. White Californians who were in need of servants could still "*buy*, of a degraded class of mountaineers known as *squaw-men*, children of tender years, who must have been stolen from their parents by these reckless outlaws." The special investigator revealed that in the area around Healdsburg, Cloverdale, and Ukiah there were several of these "domesticated" children, most of whom were under the age of fifteen. He observed, "I believe that these involuntary wards are generally well treated, but they almost invariably die at an early age, or, if they attain maturity, they abscond to their native mountains."[88]

Instances of white enslavement of Indians elsewhere in the United States are rare. It is true that Indians in the eastern part of North America were enslaved by Anglo-Americans in the early colonial period, but for a variety of reasons Indian enslavement did not long survive. For a time Indian slavery was fairly common throughout the southern colonies, especially in South Carolina, and it was not unknown even in New England, where Indians were held as slaves by Puritans and other colonists. By the time of the Revolution, however, Indian slavery had declined throughout the thirteen colonies and continued to exist only as an unimportant practice in the shadow of the much more extensive system of Negro slavery.[89] Almon Wheeler Lauber, author of an early study of Indian slavery in the United States, has identified several causes for the decline of Indian slavery, the most important of which was the introduction of indentured white servants and African slaves. These new sources of labor proved superior to the Indians because both white and black laborers could be obtained peacefully and could be controlled more easily, whereas the holding of Indians to involuntary service frequently resulted in armed attacks on the colonies by Indians still at large.[90] More recently, Winthrop D. Jordan concluded that "Indian slavery never became an important institution in the colonies." The Indian slavery that existed did not last for very long and was always "numerically insignificant and typically incidental in character" in North America.[91] The passing of Indian slavery in the early colonial period did not lead to the rise of alternative institutions for the control of Indian labor comparable to the Hispanic systems of encomienda or repartimiento. The use of Indian labor simply never became as important to the Anglo-American economy as it was in Spanish America, nor did the social hierarchy of Anglo-America ever depend upon a foundation of Indian serfdom.

In the larger context of American history the enslavement of Indians in California stands as something of an anomaly. The explanation of that anomaly lies in the peculiar circumstances of California history: before its conquest by the United States, California had been a part of the Spanish empire, in which the Indians' status was different from that of most North American tribes in Anglo-America. In the Hispanic tradition Indians were essential to the structure of the empire. They were the source of labor for the colonial economy and the broad base of the colonial social structure. On the frontier of Alta California that tradition was continued by the Spanish missions, which were dedicated to the transformation of the Indians into useful members of the empire, and by the Mexican ranchos with their system of Indian peonage. Anglo-Americans who settled in Mexican California soon came to appreciate the advantages of the Hispanic system of Indian labor exploitation, and they came also to adopt it and the traditional Hispanic view of the Indians as a useful class of laborers. This process of appreciation and adoption did not stop in 1846 but continued unbroken into the American period of California history. The early laws that we have looked at reflected that continuity. The important change after 1846 was that Anglo-Americans, rather than simply seizing Indians for their own use as the rancheros had done, came to realize that a profit could be made in securing Indian "apprentices" for other whites and so began a traffic in Indian slaves. This traffic was a grotesque extrapolation of the traditional image of the Indians as a useful class.

To explain why Indian laborers played a major role in the development of the Hispanic New World and only a minor role in Anglo-America, historians have argued that the Indians encountered by the Hispanos and the Anglos were different. The argument is advanced that in the major areas of Spanish settlement in America—central Mexico and the Andean country—the native peoples were sedentary, densely concentrated in villages and towns, cultivators of crops, and accustomed to regular industry. Such a population, once conquered, easily could be parceled out and forced to labor by their European masters—especially where the natives were already accustomed to systems of tribute and compulsory labor in the preconquest period. In British North America, by contrast, the Indian people were neither as numerous nor as densely settled as the Indians of central Mexico and Peru. Native agriculture generally was on a more rudimentary level, and many bands subsisted as nomadic hunters. In spite of efforts by Anglo-Americans to establish Indian slavery, the natives failed to adjust to the demand for constant labor and fled to the frontier, where they maintained their freedom. Thus the Indians in Anglo-America successfully resisted attempts by white settlers to put them to work. They were driven back or exterminated, but they were not converted into a permanent servile population.[92]

California represents a striking exception to that general view because in California the Anglo-Americans found an Indian population that had already been conditioned by the earlier Hispanic colonizers. Substantial numbers of Indians from the various California aboriginal cultures had already been trained to regular industry by the Spanish priests and Mexican rancheros when the first Anglo-Americans arrived. Thus Indian-American relations developed differently because the California Indians were different: they had been made different by generations of contact with the Hispanos.

There is another possible explanation for the appearance of Indian slavery in California. As many contemporary observers commented, relations between whites and Indians in California seemed to parallel closely those of whites and blacks in the American South. Perhaps the continuity we should identify in California is not between the exploitation of Indian labor in both Hispanic and American California but between the enslavement by whites of members of another race in both California and the American South. This explanation seems especially compelling when we recall that slavery in California, unlike the debt peonage typical of the Mexican hacienda or rancho, was an Anglo-American innovation. If American attitudes toward the Indians in California were Hispanicized, it is also true that the Anglos Americanized the Hispanic system of Indian exploitation.

The parallels between California and the South are particularly striking when one considers the Black Codes that were created by the former Confederate states after the Civil War. The California prohibition of the enticement of Indian workers from their masters, for instance, was paralleled by the stern provisions in most southern states against "enticing or persuading a Negro to desert his legal employment before the expiration of his contract." The system of Indian passes and other restrictions on the mobility of Indians in California were also similar to the restrictions placed on blacks in the post-war South.[93] Likewise, Montgomery's proclamation of 1846, which required Indians to contract their labor for a set period, during which time they were not free to leave except with special permission, was similar to restrictions placed on black laborers by many southern state governments. Louisiana, for example, required Negro agricultural laborers to make contracts with landholders that were binding for a year, and thereafter the black workers were not permitted to leave their employment without specific permission.[94] The 1850 California law for the "Government and Protection of the Indians" contained further parallels with the Black Codes. The vagrancy and bail-out provisions, for example, were similar to statutes in several southern states. Mississippi provided that all Negroes not employed were to be arrested as vagrants, and, if convicted and unable to pay a fine, they could be hired out to any white person willing to pay the fine.[95] Also, most southern states prohibited blacks from testifying in cases involving whites, just as the California law prohibited Indian testimony.[96]

These parallels are instructive and serve to remind us that Anglo-Americans in the middle of the nineteenth century did not need to learn from Spaniards or Mexicans how to erect a system of law that was racially discriminatory and that permitted the exploitation of the labor of another race. Yet the parallels and the precedent of black slavery do not explain the appearance of Indian slavery in California. If white exploitation of blacks before and after the Civil War was a model for the exploitation of Indian labor in California, why was that model not adopted elsewhere? Indian slavery had been tried earlier in American history and had been abandoned, why was it revived in California? Again one is forced back to the peculiar circumstances of California history for an explanation.

108

5

The Varieties of Exploitation

IN surveying Indian and white re-
lations in the early American period, one immediately is struck by
the great variety of tasks performed by California Indians for white
settlers. Wherever there was a need for semiskilled or unskilled
labor, Indians were available for the job. Indian labor was especially
prized during the early gold-rush years when all other laborers were
heading for the gold fields. In those flush times it was often impossible
to procure white labor at any price, and the Indians helped fill the
gap between supply and demand.[1] Benjamin D. Wilson reported in
1852 that Indians "are a large majority of the laborers, mechanics,
and servants of San Diego and Los Angeles counties." The "domesticated" Indian workers, he added, "mix with us daily and hourly;
and, with all their faults, appear to be a necessary part of the domestic economy. They are almost the only house or farm servants
we have."[2] At about the same time farther north Indians were working as lumbermen in Monterey, launderers in Mariposa, deckhands
on vessels plying San Francisco Bay and the Sacramento River, and
sheep shearers along the Tule River.[3] Indians were also working at
a variety of odd jobs—gardening, carpentry, yard work, wood gathering, domestic help—providing the state with its first class of casual
laborers.[4]

The most important use of California Indian labor in the early American period was in agriculture. The rancho economy of Mexican California continued after the conquest and indeed reached its heyday
in the early 1850s, when the Argonauts' demand for beef produced
a California cattle boom.[5] As in the Mexican period, the bulk of
labor on the cattle ranches, at least through the early fifties, was
performed by Indian workers. In 1856, Captain E. O. C. Ord reported that Indians were still the main labor force on the southern

ranches. In a letter to his commanding officer in August of that year Ord reported that as laborers the Indians were "the best and cheapest the southern country affords" and that they were generally submissive and appeared contented with their lot. Ord visited several large cattle ranches in Los Angeles and San Bernardino counties and found that each ranch had from fifteen to thirty Indians permanently attached to it who were held in a state of peonage identical to their status in Hispanic California. This was done, Ord pointed out, under state laws that provided for the subordination of Indian labor: "The system thus legalised provides labour in a hot climate where otherwise there would be none, and it being a continuation of the system to which the Indians were accustomed under the Mexican rule, it works well."[6]

Likewise, on the ranches of northern California in the early 1850s the "domesticated" Indians continued to be an important source of cheap labor. As in southern California, the northern Indians often lived permanently on the large ranches and were bound to the landowners in a state of peonage.[7] In 1850 an Argonaut visiting the ranches along the American River was "perfectly astonished" at the fields of grain and herds of cattle being tended by Indian workmen. At one ranch, belonging to a man named Norris, the visitor observed that the entire work force consisted of Indians who were "no better than slaves. Norris is their big chief, and seems to have absolute authority over them."[8] Another early visitor to the northern part of the state reported that many Indians there were "belonging to" local ranchers. "They are called civilized," he noted, "to distinguish them from the naked wild ones, who roam about with bows and arrows; and are occasionally employed to drive in cattle and do the drudgery about the place."[9] George Gibbs, a traveler in northern California in 1851, likewise noted that there were Indians on the ranches around Santa Rosa who seemed willing to work for the barest kind of remuneration. Observing them at work in the fields, Gibbs commented that they were "perfectly under control" of their masters, who "always treated them as *péons,* and inculcated the idea of their obligation to labor."[10]

The cattle ranches of California fell on hard times in the late 1850s and early 1860s. Depression followed flood and drought, and finally the "great drought" of 1862–64 put an end to cattle raising as a distinctive industry in California.[11] In the aftermath of the drought California agriculture went through several changes. First, much of the land, especially in the central and southern parts of the state, that previously had been held in large tracts now began to be divided into smaller parcels. With the decline of the cattle industry many large landowners hastened to dispose of their land by subdividing and selling it in lots suitable for small farms. This process of subdivision may have been inevitable, but clearly the drought hastened the demise of the ranchos. The owners of the smaller ranches and farms that replaced the ranchos began a more intensive cultivation of the soil, the initiation of numerous irrigation projects, and greater development of horticulture and viticulture.[12]

The decline of the cattle ranches also meant the decline of the large-scale demand for adult Indian labor. The smaller farms that appeared in the wake of the drought of the early 1860s simply could not exploit Indian labor as profitably as the large ranchos had. Also, by the late 1850s the California labor market had been glutted with thousands of former miners (both white and Chinese) who were willing now to take the kinds of jobs previously filled only by Indian workers. As a result the demand for Indian labor further diminished.[13]

Nevertheless, throughout the 1860s, Indian laborers continued to be a part of the California agricultural labor force, working whenever possible on the new farms and vineyards.[14] In 1869 an Indian agent from Los Angeles reported that "those Indians who were christianized by the Catholic priests" and "brought into a state of semi-civilization" were still employed as servants on the ranches or in the vineyards throughout Los Angeles, San Diego, and San Bernardino counties.[15] As late as 1872 a visitor to San Diego commented that in southern California "it was thought a great advantage for a man to 'have' Indians." The Mission Indians, he reported, were generally regarded "as tolerably steady, and very useful and indispensable laborers," and he judged that the Spanish missionaries had done a "noble work" because "Southern California is to-day indebted [to them] for a valuable laboring force."[16]

In spite of such reports on their continued usefulness, by the late 1860s the Indians of southern California had entered a period of crisis. The drought, the decline of the cattle industry, the changes in patterns of land ownership, and the reduction in the demand for their labor were all threats to their survival. As the superintendent of California Indian affairs described the situation in 1871:

In former years their villages were fostered and encouraged upon the large stock ranchos, from which the proprietors of the latter obtained their herdsmen and farm hands. Most of these large tracts have passed from the original owners and been subdivided. The necessity for the Indian no longer exists, and the field he occupied is now required by the owner of the soil. The condition of those upon the public lands is scarcely better, as settlers are rapidly absorbing them irrespective of the prior possession of the Indians.[17]

The Indians were being dispossessed of the lands that they had formerly occupied and reduced to the status of homeless vagabonds. In 1874, Charles A. Wetmore, a special United States commissioner for Indian affairs, met with a group of San Diego citizens to consider the declining status of the local Indians. Wetmore reminded the San Diegans that the Mission Indians had long been regarded as peaceable and valuable assistants on the ranches of southern California: "This relationship was preserved in this country until a few years ago, when the new era of farming, and settlement forced the abandonment of the more primitive pastoral life . . . and the Indians are found suddenly changed from their feudal and comparatively prosperous condition as vassals of the ranchero, into a life of vagrancy, crime, complaint and conflict. Their condition now is wretched in the extreme, and is becoming each year worse." Wetmore suggested that the situation could be reversed if the Indians were given clear title to tracts of land around the ranches of whites who were interested in employing them. "This idea has been suggested to a number of landholders in this county especially those engaged in raising stock," Wetmore reported, "and in nearly every case . . . they express a desire to adopt it at once and will be glad to give the Indians a home to secure their services."[18]

The plan that Wetmore proposed was not adopted, and the Mission Indians continued to decline. It was their wretched condition that Helen Hunt Jackson hoped to ameliorate in the 1880s with the publication of her *Ramona*. Throughout the 1870s the Mission Indians remained a homeless people, but even so they continued to provide southern California with a valuable supply of cheap labor. In 1875 the *Alta California* reported on the wide public concern for the problems of the Mission Indians. Lands formerly occupied by them had been seized by white settlers. "No provision has yet been made to secure rights of settlement for these outcasts," the *Alta California* observed. "Notwithstanding they constitute a valuable working force in the country, and are now considered indispensable to its development."[19] At the end of the decade, in 1879, the commissioner of Indian affairs reported that about three thousand

Mission Indians were left in California. For many years these native people had lived on the vast ranches of southern California. The *Sacramento Union* reported: "In many cases the owners of these ranches have availed themselves of the labor of the Indians in cultivating the land, frequently, however, at most unjust and oppressively low rates . . . but now, desiring to dispose of the ranches, or use the whole for their own purposes, the owners have threatened the Indians with summary ejectment." Removed from their traditional homes, the Indians were scattered in small bands over the counties of San Diego, San Bernardino, and Los Angeles, "earning a precarious livelihood by cultivating small patches of land and working for ranchmen and white settlers when opportunity offers."[20]

The decline of cattle ranching also presaged the rise of wheat farming as a major California industry. The drought of the early 1860s was followed by several rainy winters, and vast acreages in the Sacramento and San Joaquin valleys were planted in wheat. For twenty years wheat remained California's largest and most profitable crop; the American wheat farms soon matched and even exceeded the Mexican cattle ranches in size and importance. At first the California wheat growers used primitive methods of cultivation and thus needed a large force of unskilled hand laborers. Throughout the Central Valley and in the northern part of the state California Indians were an important part of that labor force. Machine sowing, multishared plows, and mechanical harvesters were soon introduced, however, and California agriculture became more rapidly and thoroughly mechanized than farming anywhere else in the country. This rapid adoption of highly sophisticated agricultural techniques drastically reduced the growers' demand for manual labor. "The large number of Indians who had been employed on the ranches," Carey McWilliams observed, "became, in fact, superfluous. White labor, single men, migratory workers, began to supply the limited demand for labor on the large scale wheat ranches."[21] Thus the demand for Indian labor on the wheat ranches was short-lived. In the later decades of the nineteenth century, with the growth of further diversified agriculture in California, the demand for cheap, unskilled, agricultural labor once again rose. Fruit growers and other speciality farmers, in order to compete successfully with the wheat growers who had cheapened productivity through mechanization, were forced to reduce production costs by cheapening labor. By the time of this revitalized demand for cheap labor in the 1880s the number of adult

California Indians had become inadequate to fill the need. The Chinese filled this later demand, though they too in time were to be replaced by unemployed whites, Japanese, Mexicans, and a host of others.[22]

Reports from the farms of central and northern California throughout the 1860s indicate that "domesticated" Indians continued to supply at least part of the demand for harvesters.[23] In Mendocino County, California's superintendent of Indian affairs, Thomas J. Henley, reported in 1856 that "many" Indian men were working on farms. Ten years later Superintendent Charles Maltby made a similar report.[24] In 1867 Robert J. Stevens, a special commissioner appointed to investigate California Indian affairs, noted that at Little Lake and Walker's Valley in Mendocino County three to four hundred local Indians were working as harvesters for local farmers.[25] Farther south, in the counties just north of San Francisco Bay, a similar situation prevailed. In 1862 the *San Francisco Bulletin* reported that a "large number" of Clear Lake Indians had come to the Napa Valley to work in the harvest. Many white workers had recently left in pursuit of new gold strikes in the northern mines, and their exodus threatened a scarcity of field hands, "but these Indians are helping to fill the gap."[26] Five years later the California superintendent reported that Indian agricultural workers were in the fields from Petaluma through Healdsburg and into Lake County. "At Clear Lake there were a few Indians, peaceable, docile, and in good condition," he observed. "They had been at work harvesting for the surrounding settlements."[27]

It is impossible to calculate how many Indian agricultural workers were held or employed by whites during those years. It is probably fair to say, however, that Indians made up the bulk of workers on the cattle ranches of the early 1850s and constituted an important part of the labor force on the wheat farms of the early 1860s. Clearly, Indian labor continued to be exploited on large and small farms, ranches, and vineyards throughout California for decades, but it was only in those earlier years that their numbers were significant.

The only demand for Indian labor that remained fairly constant during the 1850s and 1860s was for domestic servants. As we have seen, the kidnapping and "indenturing" of Indian women and children was one manifestation of this continued demand. As in the case of agricultural labor, the Indians' status as domestic servants represented a continuation of their condition in Hispanic California. For at least twenty years after the American conquest whites viewed the

114

California Indians as well suited for domestic servitude.[28] Jessie Benton Frémont, in her accounts of life in California in the early American period, offered an interesting commentary on the use of Indian domestics in California. There was a striking similarity, she thought, between the typical California household and the "life of our Southern people." In California homes it was not unusual to find the lady of the house "surrounded by domesticated Indian girls at their sewing." When Frémont herself needed some work done, she found that Indians were the only domestic help available. Consequently, she had several Mission Indians brought to her to do laundering and other chores. In an account of life in Mariposa County in the late 1850s, Frémont described "playing Missionary" to a group of local Indian women—plaiting their hair, dressing them in clean white undergarments and starched calico, and teaching them to serve her as domestic servants. She was pleased at her success in transforming the native women into "picturesque peasants":

> I had grown up among slaves and could make allowance for untutored people, as I knew them of all grades, from the carefully trained and refined house-servants to the common fieldhands; and knew that with them, as with us, they must have nature's stamp of intelligence and good-humor, without which any teaching and training is not much use. As the early Mission Fathers had taught weaving and cooking to the women, and simple agriculture and the care of flocks and herds to the men, and left in the fine mission buildings proof of their capacity as workmen, so I experimented on these Indian women with advantage to them as well as to ourselves.[29]

The dominant economic activity in California in the early years following the American conquest was not cattle ranching nor wheat growing, but rather the mining of gold. Mining had been unknown in Hispanic California, and no Indians had been employed there as mine workers. Would the perception of the California Indians as a useful laboring class be shared by those whites who engaged in this new California industry? Would the "usefulness" of the California Indians be limited mainly to the traditional roles—as laborers and servants—that they had played in Hispanic California?

To a remarkable extent California Indians did participate in the gold rush as miners. One government report estimated in 1848 that more than half of the gold diggers in the California mines were Indians.[30] At first many Indian miners worked as laborers for white

Argonauts. In effect, the Hispanic system of Indian labor exploitation was transferred from the ranchos to the mines, where the relationship of white miner and Indian mine worker was often the same as that of the Mexican ranchero and his Indian peon. Sometimes Indians were coerced into working for white miners, and in such cases the Indian workers generally received no compensation for their labor other than food and clothing. On other occasions Indians entered a freer relationship with the white miner and agreed to labor in the mines for a modest wage. Other Indians even became independent agents, trading their gold to white merchants for a variety of goods. The distinction, however, between the independent Indian miners and those who were either held or employed by whites was often confused and fluctuating. Whatever the exact nature of the relationship, it is clear that a large number of California Indians were active during the gold rush as mine workers and that as a consequence they were often regarded by white miners as a useful class. As in California agriculture, however, changing economic and social conditions in the mines soon rendered the position of the Indian workers precarious, and very rapidly and very thoroughly their "usefulness" diminished. For two or three years after the gold discovery the image of the "useful" California Indian persisted in the mining country, but, as hostilities increased between Indians and whites, that attitude disappeared.

The immediate background to the gold discovery is well known. In the late 1840s, Johann Sutter decided to supplement his income by establishing a sawmill in the foothills of the Sierra. James Wilson Marshall, one of Sutter's retainers, became a partner in the sawmill venture and was placed in charge of the project. When Marshall set out to select a site for the mill, in May, 1847, he was led by an Indian guide up the American River to a Maidu village site, known as "Kolo-ma." The site had an abundance of timber, the necessary water supply, and offered the possibility of a direct route back to Sutter's Fort. Marshall also may have been prompted to select the Coloma site because of the availability of nearby Indian labor.[31] About half of the laborers at the mill were Indians. During the final stages of its construction, on January 24, 1848, gold was discovered in the race of the mill.

In the flush times immediately following the discovery at Coloma, Indian laborers were a common sight in the California mines. Early reports from California stated that the country was blessed with not only an abundance of gold but also a readily available, easily exploit-

116

able supply of labor. The *New York Journal of Commerce* carried a letter from Monterey, dated August 29, 1848, in which the correspondent reported that the people of California were rushing about here and there literally picking gold out of the earth. The correspondent explained: "They make the most who employ the wild Indians to hunt it for them. There is one man who has sixty Indians in his employ; his profits are a dollar a minute. The wild Indians know nothing of its value, and wonder what the pale faces want to do with it; they will give an ounce of it for the same weight of coined silver, or a thimbleful of glass beads, or a glass of grog."[32] With similar enthusiasm a European guidebook to the gold region, Schmölder's *Emigrant's Guide to California* (1849), advised its readers to hasten to the California mines "to enrich themselves by the gold, which they may gather themselves, or to make the Indians work out for them." The California Indians, Schmölder promised, "being most of them docile, can be made to be of great service, after they are once trained into submission."[33]

The Indians who were "controlled" or "owned" or "employed" by the white miners often received the same compensation that Indian workers had received on the Mexican ranchos: food and clothing.[34] Those Indians who also received a daily wage for their labor in the mines were often singled out for special comment. Henry Simpson's fraudulent *Three Weeks in California* (1848) reported that most of the Indian miners "work by the day for some employer, who furnishes them with food, and pays a regular per diem—sometimes as much as twenty dollars a day, but more generally at the rate of an ounce and a half of gold, the current rate of which is from $10 to $12 per ounce."[35] It is doubtful whether this generous wage scale was widely adopted by employers of Indian labor. Probably more realistic was Bayard Taylor's estimate that in the latter half of 1849 many whites in California were employing Indian miners at the rate of "a dollar daily."[36] In May of the following year Thomas J. Green, major general of the California militia, criticized the white miners who were monopolizing Indian labor by giving them a little calico and food. "This is not only wrong," Green announced, "but highly disgraceful, when they would be content with the pay of one-fourth of the wages of a white man."[37] Indeed, most Indian miners had to be content with a good deal less.

How many Indian miners were there in the early days of the gold rush? The San Francisco *Californian* reported on August 1, 1848: "There are probably 3000 people, including Indians, engaged in

The Indian presence at the gold discovery is suggested by the group of natives in the right foreground of this 1853 lithograph of Sutter's Mill.

collecting gold." Slightly more helpful was one Argonaut's estimate that at the beginning of 1849 "thousands" of Indians were employed by whites in gathering gold.[38] James Clyman claimed that in December, 1848, two thousand whites "and more than double that number of Indians" were at work in the mines.[39] Albert Lyman, a member of the Connecticut Mining and Trading Company, commented that, "within three months after the discovery, it was computed that there were near four thousand persons, including Indians, who were mostly employed by the whites, engaged in washing for gold."[40]

The computation referred to by Lyman was probably that made by Colonel Richard B. Mason in his official report to the United States adjutant general in August, 1848. Mason estimated that of the four thousand men then working in the gold districts more than half were Indians.[41] Mason's report was one of the earliest and most complete accounts of the use of Indian labor in the mines. It was also a prime contemporary source of information about life in gold-rush California. In addition to its appearance as a government document in 1848, it was published in at least half a dozen other forms within a year.[42] The report was based on a tour of the mining regions made by Mason and Lieutenant William Tecumseh Sherman in June, 1848. Throughout the areas that they toured, Mason and Sherman reported an extensive system of Indian labor exploitation.

At one of their first stops, the Mormon Diggings on the South Fork of the American River, Mason's party encountered both whites and Indians at work washing for gold with tin pans and willow baskets.[43] On a tributary to the American River, Weber's Creek, Mason reported that a party of Spanish-speaking miners, known as Suñol and Company, "had about thirty Indians employed, whom they pay in merchandise." Farther up the stream Mason observed "a great many people and Indians" working the bed of the stream and in the small valleys along its edge. In one of those valleys Mason learned that two men, William Daylor and Perry McCoon, had extracted $17,000 worth of gold. "Captain Weber informed me," Mason reported, "that he knew these two men had employed four white men, and about a hundred Indians, and that, at the end of one week's work, they paid off their party and had left $10,000 worth of this gold." Mason's informant, Charles M. Weber, was himself one of the largest and most successful employers of Indian labor in the mines. Profits similar to those of Daylor and McCoon were also being reaped by John Sinclair on the North Fork of the American River. Sinclair employed about fifty Indians to gather gold in their closely

In this panorama of mining activity along the western bank of the Sacramento River, two Indian miners are at work with a large sifting basket while a third points to a likely spot for others to dig. Note also the use of baskets, probably of native manufacture, by miners along the opposite bank.

woven baskets, and Mason estimated his net proceeds at about $16,000. Farther north on the Feather River, Mason reported that a mining company with fifty Indian washers had extracted 273 pounds of gold in about seven weeks.[44]

The individuals named in Mason's report were typical of the Anglo-American pioneers who had immigrated to Hispanic California in the previous decades and who early had realized the advantages of the Mexican system of Indian labor exploitation. Although evidence is incomplete for the operations of many of these early California pioneers, it appears that most had taken their Indian laborers directly from the ranchos to the mining districts. This process was alluded to by one forty-niner who commented, "The Indians on the ranchos in California, are considered as stock, and are sold with it as cattle, and the purchaser has the right to work them on the rancho, or take

120

them into the mines."[45] Naturally those whites who were already in California and able to control a body of Indian laborers had a great advantage in the months following the discovery of gold.

That the Spanish-speaking Californios did not fail to grasp this opportunity is indicated by Mason's mention of the company of Spanish-born Antonio Maria Suñol on the American River. Suñol, a prominent ranchero of the Bay Area, began mining operations in 1848, taking with him more than a score of his Indian workers.[46] Echoing Mason's description of Suñol and Company, Henry Simpson commented, "These gentlemen employ about thirty Indians, and pay them principally in merchandise of various kinds."[47] Another party of Californios, which included members of the Coronel and Sepúlveda families, organized a mining expedition in August, 1848. Information and gold provided by Indians in the mining districts, as well as the labor of Indian workers taken with them, contributed significantly to the success of their operations.[48] Leonard Pitt has estimated that about 1,300 Californios mined gold in 1848, but it is not clear how many of these depended on Indian labor.[49]

One name that figured prominently in Mason's report was that of Charles M. Weber. Weber, an overland immigrant with the Bidwell-Bartleson party of 1841, had worked for Sutter before acquiring a rancho of his own near the site of present-day Stockton. According to E. Gould Buffum, a member of Colonel J. D. Stevenson's regiment of New York Volunteers, Weber began mining early in 1848 on Weber's Creek near Dry Diggings (later known as Placerville). "He carried with him articles of trade," Buffum recalled, "and soon gathered around him a thousand Indians, who worked for him in consideration of the necessaries of life and of little trinkets that so win an Indian's heart. He was soon joined by William Dalor [Daylor], a *ranchero* near Sutter's Fort, and the two together with the labour of the Indians, soon realized at least fifty thousand dollars."[50]

Sometime in the summer of 1848, Weber and several other whites formed the Stockton Mining Company. Fundamental to the company's success was Weber's ability to secure the services of Indian laborers. Consequently, Weber entered into an agreement with a group of Northern Valley Yokuts whose rancheria was not far from his rancho. Weber and the headman of the rancheria, José Jesús, agreed that, in exchange for any gold that the Indians discovered, the company would give them clothing or other merchandise. Some of the Yokuts accompanied Weber to the diggings near Placerville to learn the techniques of mining, while the rest began searching for gold in the Calaveras-Stanislaus region. As it turned out, these Indians were successful in locating some of the richest auriferous areas in California. They discovered gold on Carson's Creek and on Wood's Creek—the first discoveries made in what would be called the Southern Mines.[51] James Carson, one of the earliest whites to benefit from these discoveries, later recalled that the Indians had given "leading information" to Weber's company "so that they were enabled to know the direction in which new discoveries were to be made." Carson himself later was led by Indians to a site on the creek that bears his name, where, according to his own account, he was able to pan out 180 ounces of gold in ten days. The strikes in the Southern Mines proved so rich that by August, 1848, the Stockton Mining Company had moved its entire Indian labor force to the Stanislaus River.[52]

One member of Weber's company soon began his own independent mining operations on the Stanislaus River. John M. Murphy, who had been an overland pioneer with the Stevens party in 1844, was able to acquire a small fortune in 1848 and 1849 at what is now the town of Murphys in Calaveras County.[53] Walter Colton, in his *Three Years in California* (1850), described Murphy's lucrative operations: "His tent is pitched in the midst of a small tribe of wild Indians who gather gold for him, and receive in return provisions and blankets. He knocks down two bullocks a day to furnish them with meat."[54] Another major employer of Indian labor mentioned in Mason's report was John Sinclair. Sinclair had arrived in California in 1839 and, like Weber, had worked for Sutter before becoming a ranchero himself. Sometime around June 1, 1848, Sinclair had removed to the gold fields, taking with him about forty of his "peaceable and useful" Indian workers. He and the Indians had been at work about five weeks when Mason came upon them on the North Fork of the American River. As on the rancho, the workers received food as compensation for their labor as gold diggers.[55]

Weber, Murphy, and Sinclair were not the only California pioneers who successfully transferred their operations from the ranchos to the placers. Although not mentioned in Mason's report, other leading rancheros in this class included John Marsh, John Bidwell, and Pierson B. Reading. Marsh left his Rancho los Médanos in 1848 for a brief visit to the gold fields above Marysville. While there he was able to procure from the Indians a large quantity of gold dust in exchange for sugar, cloth, and beads.[56] After a visit to Sutter's mill in 1848, John Bidwell began mining the bars of the Feather

River with a group of native workers.[57] Bidwell and his Indian miners were still at work in late September and early October when an immigrant from Oregon passed through the Feather River area. The Oregonian later recalled that Bidwell and three other whites "were working Indians in the mines at Bidwell's Bar washing gold in wooden bowls which had been dug out for that purpose."[58] In March, at about the same time as Bidwell's visit to Coloma, Pierson Reading came down to inspect the scene at Sutter's mill. Reading, who had come overland to California in the Chiles-Walker party of 1843, was the grantee of the northernmost rancho in California. After a brief visit to the mill, he returned to his ranch at the north end of the Sacramento Valley and, taking his "domesticated Indians" with him, began mining operations on Clear Creek. In July, Reading crossed over the mountains west of the valley and began working the waters of the Trinity River at a spot subsequently known as Reading's Bar. Reading later recalled that his party included three whites, one Delaware, one Walla Walla, one Chinook, and "about sixty Indians from the Sacramento Valley. With this force I worked the bar bearing my name."[59]

The most successful pioneer ranchero, Johann Sutter, also attempted to transfer his Indian labor force to the mines. Mason apparently was not aware of this, for he described Sutter as among the minority of rancheros who had not abandoned their fields for the mines.[60] It is true that Sutter did not succeed in his mining operations; and it remains one of the great ironies of California history that this man, who was so closely associated with the discovery of gold, was so thoroughly ruined by its consequences. Sutter himself later exclaimed, "What a great misfortune was this sudden gold discovery for me!" In early 1848 most of Sutter's white and Indian laborers left for the mines, and Sutter's operations at New Helvetia came to a standstill. As Indians returned to the fort, displaying the clothing and other items given them for their labor in the gold fields, Sutter's remaining Indian workers expressed a desire to go into the hills and dig for gold. "At last I consented," Sutter recalled in 1857, "got a number of wagons ready, loaded them with provisions and goods of all kinds, employed a clerk, and left with about one hundred Indians and about fifty Sandwich Islanders." Sutter took his Indian and Hawaiian workmen up the South Fork of the American River, near the mouth of Weber Creek, and then in July, 1848, to a spot known later as Sutter Creek. Sutter soon abandoned his mining operations, however, and returned to the fort. "After this,"

Sutter concluded bitterly, "I would have nothing more to do with the gold affairs." He did, however, profit by supplying Indian workers to other whites engaged in mining. He demanded fifty percent of the gold recovered by "his" Indians and received over one thousand dollars from one such contract.[61]

Indian mining activities in the California gold rush were not limited to laboring for white employers, as some Indians became independent miners and bartered as free agents with whites for trade goods.[62] At first the California Indians often were unaware of the true value of the gold that they were trading, and the whites seem to have competed with each other to see who could make (or at least relate) the most lopsided deal with Indians.[63] Later they developed a finer appreciation of the white man's high regard for gold and became increasingly able traders. "When the gold was first discovered," E. Gould Buffum explained, "they had very little conception of its value, and would readily exchange handfuls of it for any article of food they might desire, or any old garment gaudy enough to tickle their fancy. Latterly, however, they have become more careful, and exhibit a profounder appreciation of the worth of the precious metal."[64]

That the profits of the Indian trade were high is well illustrated by the career of James D. Savage. Savage has often been viewed as something of a mysterious figure in California history, but, when he is placed in the context of his fellow white traders, he does not appear quite so unusual. Savage came overland to California in 1846, worked for a time at Sutter's fort, and in the fall of 1847 moved up the Merced River, where he began life as an Indian trader. He apparently married several Yokuts women and gained a position of some power over the Chowchillas. Thus, when gold was discovered a few months later, Savage was able to command a considerable body of Indian labor. In addition to his original store on the Merced, Savage also set up trading posts on the Mariposa and Fresno rivers. In 1849, in partnership with other whites, he had claims on the Tuolumne River near Jamestown and in the Big Oak Flat mining district. In all his operations he depended upon the labor of Indian miners.[65] Probably he was no more nor less scrupulous in his dealings with his Indian customers than the average trader in the mines. More than one forty-niner witnessed Savage trading to Indians equal weights of goods for gold.[66] Estimates of his profits from this trade were extremely high. Benjamin Butler Harris, a forty-niner from Texas, pointed out that Savage's Indian miners "numbering thousands, were earliest in prospecting and finding the shiny metal." His

"An Indian Woman Panning Out Gold," an engraving probably by Charles Nahl. First published in *Hutchings' Illustrated California Magazine* (April, 1859).

practice of trading food and blankets for Indian gold led Harris to estimate that Savage's profits per day often amounted to ten or twenty thousand dollars.[67] Another contemporary observer, Indian agent Oliver M. Wozencraft, estimated that Indian miners gave Savage gold that was worth between four and five hundred thousand dollars.[68]

This profitable trade with independent Indian miners had virtually disappeared by the early 1850s. Indeed, after the midcentury mark descriptions of any Indian miners, "independent" or "employed," are rare.[69] One of the reasons for the decline in their numbers may have been the change in the kind of mining being done in California. In the flush times the bulk of the gold taken from California was from the shallow placer deposits. During this early period only the most primitive technology was necessary, and whites and Indians alike were able to gather great quantities of gold with little difficulty. As the placers became exhausted, mining became more difficult. Placer mining gave way to tertiary mining, hydraulic mining, and quartz mining, all of which required equipment, capital, and skills that were unavailable to the Indians.[70] As in agriculture, the changing technology of mining reduced the opportunities for Indian labor.

The fundamental reason for the disappearance of the Indian miners, however, was that after 1849 the gold fields of California came to be dominated by men who had had no contact with the Hispanic system of Indian labor exploitation. From experiences on other American frontiers or in crossing the plains to California, many of these newcomers had come to regard Indians as threats to their physical safety or as obstacles in the path of their economic success. The newcomers also manifested a jealous opposition to the whites already in California who were able to control or otherwise exploit the labor of Indian miners. Such exploitation was viewed by the newly arrived Californians as an unfair advantage in the pursuit of California gold. Similar hostility was expressed toward white southerners who attempted to bring black slaves to work their claims. It is a familiar aspect of gold-rush history.[71]

In seeking the causes of the breakdown of the old order of Indian-white relations and the growth of the fatal spirit of enmity between the forty-niners and Indians, it is useful to examine the experiences of the first miners who came into the state after the gold discovery. One of the first areas outside of California to respond to the news of the discovery was the Oregon Territory.[72] In the summer of 1848 pioneer settlers in the Willamette Valley and elsewhere began making preparations to leave for the gold regions, and by August, 1848, the first Oregon Argonauts had arrived in California. Passing through the northern part of the state, the Oregonians encountered parties of California pioneers at work with their Indian miners. One of the first such encounters occurred in early August at Reading's Bar on the Trinity River, where Pierson B. Reading and his sixty Indians had been at work for over a month. In a scene that was to be repeated many times during the next few months, the newcomers expressed opposition to the Californians' labor system. Reading later recalled his encounter with the Oregonians: "After about six week's work, parties came in from Oregon, who at once protested against my Indian labor. I then left the stream and returned to my home."[73]

The following spring an incident occurred which, like the protest over Reading's Indian laborers, darkly foreshadowed the shape of things to come. In about March, 1849, a party of seven Oregon miners prospecting on the American River came upon a rancheria of Southern Maidus. Although reports of what happened next are contradictory, probably the Oregon men raped some of the Maidu women. When several Indian men attempted to interfere, they were summarily shot by the miners. A short while later five of the Oregonians were attacked and killed by a party of Indians at a spot on the Middle Fork of the American River, later known as Murderer's Bar. About twenty Oregon men then banded together and retaliated by attacking a village of Indians near Coloma, killing a dozen or more and taking many prisoners. Apparently, several of those captured were Indians who had been employed by James Marshall and other California miners. About seven of the captured Indians were subsequently executed by the band of whites.[74]

The various versions of this incident and the reactions to it are a case study in contrasting attitudes toward the California Indians. The incident also throws into sharp relief the origins of the mutual hostilities that were to prove very subversive to the white Californians' system of Indian labor exploitation.

James Marshall gave his version of the action both in a first-person account, which was published in Edward Dunbar's *The Romance of the Age: Or, the Discovery of Gold* (1867), and in a biography published by him but written by George Frederic Parsons, *The Life and Adventures of James W. Marshall: The Discoverer of Gold in California* (1870). Marshall pictured himself and his Indian workmen peacefully and harmoniously at work at the mill before the arrival of the Oregonians. According to Parson's biography, "These Indians had been peaceable and industrious, and [Marshall] had obtained considerable ascendancy over the tribe by fair dealing with them on all occasions."[75] After the arrival of the outsiders and the subsequent rapes and murders of the Indians and the deaths of the five whites, the surviving

"The Attack," an 1850 engraving by Charles Nahl depicting the hostilities between whites and Indians on the California gold-rush frontier.

Oregonians started out to hunt the Indians involved. In his own abbreviated style Marshall reported that the avenging whites "found our friendly Indians; induced a part to come, telling them I wanted to talk to them; brought them to Coloma; picked out eight which were most friendly to me, and dismissed the others; drank plenty of whiskey; took out the eight Indians; placed them in the direction of our work-hands, whites and Indians; bid them run, commenced shooting, killed seven of the eight prisoners and one of my workhands, an Indian."[76] Parsons commented that "there was not the shadow of justification for the atrocious deed, for the whole of the slaughtered men were constantly employed as mill-hands by

128

Marshall and his partners, and therefore could not have had anything to do with the killing of the white men at Murderer's Bar; besides which, they belonged to a different tribe from that of the hostile Indians."[77]

This attack may have been a typical case of indiscriminate frontier revenge, but it is also possible that the victims were carefully chosen. The attack may have been motivated by the same hostility toward white control of Indian labor exhibited by the Oregonians at Reading's Bar. If it was in fact the intention of the Oregonians to put an end to the Californians' labor system by intimidating their Indian workers, then their execution of the Coloma Indians was a success. An article in the *Placer Times and Transcript* reported in May, 1849, that Indians who had been employed as miners were abandoning the gold fields and withdrawing to their villages. They were fleeing, it was reported, out of fear of further white attacks.[78]

The hostile attitude of the Oregonians was an obvious threat to the exploitive practices that the Californians had so carefully nurtured. Consequently, Marshall and others attempted to prevent the breakdown of their friendly relations with the Indians. John E. Ross, a butcher, was one of the Oregonians present at the Coloma execution. He later recalled that, when Marshall "started in to advocate the cause of the Indians," a man named Everman raised his gun to shoot Marshall. "Marshall was given five minutes to leave the place," Ross remembered, "in which he gladly availed himself of."[79] Marshall was not the only Californian to attempt to protect the Indians from the Oregon men. According to Ross's recollections, one of the Indian captives to be executed was secreted in the house of Mrs. Peter Wimmer, the wife of Marshall's assistant at the mill.[80] Later William Daylor, an English sailor who had come to California around 1835 and employed a hundred Indian miners, gave shelter to several Indians who fled to his rancho on the Cosumnes to escape the Oregonians' wrath.[81]

To the Oregon men their actions in California were justifiable and even reasonable. Indian-white relations in the Oregon Territory immediately before 1848 had been marked by bloody encounters, such as the attack on the Whitman Mission at Walla Walla and the Cayuse War.[82] These recent experiences, coupled with the Oregon men's opposition to the Californians' economically advantageous relations with the Indian miners, explain much of their actions in California. The Oregonians apparently had come to the conclusion that safety lay only in vigorous retaliatory attacks on the aborigines. John Ross,

129

one of the few Oregon miners who left a record of his experiences, had been a volunteer in December, 1847, in the party of Oregon settlers organized to avenge the Whitman deaths. Eight months later he left for California. On the way south, according to Ross's recollections, his party encountered hostile Indians "at every point" until they reached the Shasta Valley in northern California. As for the hostilities around Coloma, Ross made no mention of the raping of Indian women. Rather, he described the Oregonians as having suffered an unprovoked attack by Indians that resulted in the death of five miners. Following this attack the Oregon men made a conscientious effort to locate the murderers, took many Indian prisoners, and from these selected five whom they believed were guilty. These five they intended to try for their crimes, but, when they attempted to escape, four of them were shot. Ross was puzzled that these actions should have raised the antagonism of Marshall and the other Californians. "There seemed to be a jealousy," Ross remarked, "manifested by the California miners against the Oregonians."[83]

The significance of the actions of the Oregonians and the subsequent growth of hostilities between the two races was not lost on contemporary observers.[84] Before hostilities had commenced, Indians in the mining region were viewed predominately as a cheap labor force or an easy source of gold. Now, because of the mutual fear and outrage, many Indians began to flee the mining camps. Their exodus meant an end — at least in the mines — to the system of labor exploitation that the Californians had transferred so successfully from the ranchos to the placers. In the popular mind the termination of the system was attributed specifically to the presence of the newcomers from Oregon or generally to the hostilities brought on by the increase in the mining population. J. E. Gould Buffum's narrative, for example, contains frequent comments on the usefulness of the California Indians on the ranchos, at Sutter's fort and mill, and in the mining regions. He reported that, in the summer of 1848, Weber and Daylor had a thousand Indians working for them in the area of Weber's Creek, but that after the following spring the Indian miners had virtually disappeared. He identified the tragic events at Coloma as the essential cause of the change. In reference to the execution of the Indians at Sutter's mill, he wrote, "Soon after this several expeditions were fitted out, who scoured the country in quest of Indians, until now a redskin is scarcely ever seen in the inhabited portion of the northern mining region."[85]

"A Road Scene in California." The Indian group in the left foreground, in cast-off clothing, is presumably leaving the diggings. The Chinese miners, on the right, are heading for the hills. From a letter sheet drawing by Charles Nahl.

James Delavan also identified the events at Weber's Creek and Coloma as the beginning of the end of Indian commerce in the mines. After describing the long-standing system of Indian labor exploitation in California, Delavan commented that the coming of the Oregonians and the "bloody contest" between them and the California Indians had brought about a fundamental change. "In consequence of this outbreak with the natives," Delavan observed, "the trade with them, hitherto so profitable, was at an end, and many who had brought out lots of trinkets and rings of *simular* gold, in the hope of getting *bags* of the real stuff in exchange for it, found their merchandise unsalable, and they were forced to go to the mines and dig for themselves, in order to replenish their exchequers."[86]

The affair at Coloma was emblematic of changing conditions throughout the California gold country. Everywhere the pattern was the same: violent hostilities between the evergrowing white majority and the Indians put an end to the "usefulness" of the latter as miners. The most perceptive discussion of this change in the nature of Indian-white relations in California appeared in the narrative of Theodore Johnson. Johnson admired the Indian policies of men such as Sutter and John Sinclair and was impressed with the obvious advantages of a system in which native labor could be exploited with such apparent ease and profit.[87] In the mines, he observed, the Indians had continued to be useful as laborers and traders of gold dust. "Now all was changed," he reported with bitterness and regret. "The late emigrants across the mountains, and especially from Oregon, had commenced a war of extermination upon them, shooting them down like wolves, men, women and children, wherever they could find them":

> Some of the Indians were undoubtedly bad and needed punishment, but generally the whites were the aggressors; and as a matter of course the Indians retaliated whenever opportunities occurred; and in this way several unarmed or careless Oregonians had become, in turn, their victims. Thus has been renewed in California the war of extermination against the aborigines, commenced in effect at the landing of Columbus, and continued to this day, gradually and surely tending to the final and utter extinction of the race. And never has this policy proved so injurious to the interests of the whites, as in California.
> The profitable trade with them in exchange for their gold dust is

132

entirely at an end. *Their labor once very useful, and, in fact, indispensable in a country where no other species of laborers were to be obtained at any price, and which might now be rendered of immense value by pursuing a judicious policy, has been utterly sacrificed by this extensive system of indiscriminate revenge* [Italics added].[88]

For many white Californians the sacrifice meant the loss of a labor system. For the California Indians it was a sacrifice of blood.

PART III

Obstacles

THE company had been prospecting for several days, when an obstacle that I had not met before presented itself. The word reached camp that unfriendly Indians were on the warpath. — Richard L. Hale, *The Log of a Forty-Niner: Journal of a Voyage from Newbury-port to San Francisco*

THE Indian, if he becomes an obstacle, is classed with wild animals, and is hunted to the death; this antagonism becomes mutual and is perhaps as natural as the antipathies of cats and dogs. — Edward E. Cheever, "The Indians of California," *American Naturalist*

6

Removal and Reservation

IN his second Annual Message, delivered in December, 1830, Andrew Jackson expressed sentiments widely shared by his countrymen: "Humanity has often wept over the fate of the aborigines of this country, and Philanthropy has been long busily employed in devising means to avert it, but its progress has never for a moment been arrested, and one by one have many powerful tribes disappeared from the earth." While the extinction of the Indian nations may "excite melancholy reflections," Jackson told his fellow Americans that true philanthropy reconciles the mind to this inevitable process. "What good man," he asked, "would prefer a country covered with forests and ranged by a few thousand savages to our extensive Republic, studded with cities, towns, and prosperous farms, embellished with all the improvements which art can devise or industry execute, occupied by more than 12,000,000 happy people, and filled with all the blessings of liberty, civilization, and religion?"[1]

In 1830 the fate of the North American Indians was generally accepted as a melancholy fact of American life. Indeed, there were few "good men" who entertained the notion that the continent ought to be restored to its aboriginal occupants. Most of Jackson's twelve million constituents agreed that the progress of American civilization was justification in itself for the "extinction" of the Indian people. They had come to view the presence of the Indians as an impediment, a block, an obstacle in the path of American progress and to accept as a sad necessity their elimination through disease, homicide, or relocation farther west.[2]

When Andrew Jackson delivered his Annual Message in 1830, the official Indian policy of the United States prescribed the removal of all Indians east of the Mississippi onto "unsettled" western lands. Jackson is often identified as the initiator of this policy, but its roots lay deep in colonial history. Since the earliest days of English settlement, Anglo-American attitudes toward the Indians had been marked by a sense of incompatibility and inevitable conflict. Whites had concluded that the Indian presence was a block to development of the land and that the elimination of Indians was a necessary stage in the progress of white civilization. It is true that at times Anglo-Americans had regarded Indians as useful consumers of European trade goods, trappers of furs, and military allies. These functions, however, were always best performed beyond the pale of white settlement and became considerably less important as American settlement advanced.[3]

The Anglo-American colonial system did not produce a body of imperial law for the protection or acculturation of Indians on the scale of Spanish legislation on the subject. Unlike the Spanish, the British did not develop a colonial policy giving the Indians a place or a future within the structure of empire. This is not to say, of course, that Anglo-American efforts at conversion and assimilation were nonexistent. Indeed, the charters and patents of most of the early English colonies contained injunctions similar to those found in the edicts of the Spanish monarchs, instructing the colonists to convert and "civilize" the Indians. English missionary efforts established some churches and schools for Indians and achieved some notable successes among groups such as the Praying Indians of New England. In the end, however, the English missionary program must be judged a failure. The missionaries worked with great dedication and energy in Anglo-America, but their enterprise was never as extensive nor as well supported by the government as was that of their Catholic brethren on the south.[4] A loss of faith in conversion and assimilation soon became apparent in each of the English colonies. Following the devastating Indian assault on the Virginia colony in 1622, for example, efforts at "civilizing" the Indians were abandoned there. As Roy Harvey Pearce has concluded, "the Indian became for seventeenth century Virginians a symbol not of a man in a grip of devilish ignorance, but of a man standing fiercely and grimly in the path of civilization."[5] A similar loss of faith and abandonment of assimilationist goals marked Indian and white relations in New England. The early settlers there had anticipated that the Indians could somehow be "rescued from their savagery." By the late seventeenth century, however, "this optimism had subsided into the grimmer realization that Indians—all Indians—were somehow irredeemably different from the whites. Hopes of assimilation gave way to policies of segregation and discriminatory legislation."[6]

Once the English colonists had lost faith in assimilation, the Indians came to be viewed as undesirable creatures standing in the path of the advance of white civilization. The Indians became obstacles, objects that somehow must be removed. Interest in Indian education, conversion, and assimilation continued to be a part of Anglo-American Indian policy, but by the end of the colonial period the main effect of that policy was Indian removal and separation. The Proclamation of 1763, which established a line along the Appalachian Mountains separating Indian lands from non-Indian lands, reflected the realization by the English crown that the only hope for peace between the English colonists and the Indians lay in the separation of the two groups.[7]

After 1776 the Continental Congress made repeated efforts to restrict white settlement from western Indian lands, but these efforts were insufficient to restrain the advance of settlers and speculators. The Constitution delegated to the federal government the exclusive right to manage Indian affairs, and beginning in the 1790s a series of congressional acts were adopted to regulate trade and intercourse with the Indians and to restrict white encroachment on Indian lands. With the final elimination of the British after the War of 1812 the white pressure on Indian lands increased, and the federal government's ability or willingness to protect those lands remained inadequate. Francis Paul Prucha has concluded:

> The federal government was sincerely interested in preventing settlement on Indian lands only up to a point, and it readily acquiesced in illegal settlements when they had gone so far as to be irremediable. The basic policy of the United States intended that white settlement should advance and the Indians withdraw. Its interest was primarily that this process should be as free of disorder and injustice as possible. The government meant to restrain and govern the advance of the whites, not to prevent it forever.[8]

Thus the main thrust of federal Indian policy in the first half of the nineteenth century was to remove Indians from the settled areas east of the Mississippi River to new territories farther west. In the early years efforts to remove and segregate Indians beyond the Mississippi River rested on the voluntary cooperation of eastern tribes who agreed through treaties to an exchange of territory. The policy of removal had originated during the administration of Thomas Jefferson, for it was then that the vast western territories beyond the Mississippi were first acquired by the United States. The removal

139

policy was regarded by most whites, on the frontier and elsewhere, as a logical means of eliminating the Indians—that is, of removing obstacles—from the path of American settlement. Other supporters of removal believed that "only if the Indians were removed beyond contact with whites could the slow process of education, civilization, and Christianization take place."[9] In other words, the removal policy was viewed not just as a means of opening more lands for white settlement, but also as a philanthropic policy that would remove the Indians from harm's way until at their own pace they became integrated by education and religious persuasion into American society. Meanwhile, the opponents of removal regarded the latter view as so much cant and claimed that removal represented an inhumane abandonment of assimilationist goals and the triumph of the view that Indians were obstacles to be cast aside from the path of white civilization.

Whatever the motives that lay behind the removal policy, its effect was to relocate thousands of Indian people beyond the pale of white settlement. Jefferson's successors—Presidents Madison, Monroe, and Adams—continued the policy of encouraging voluntary migration of eastern Indians, and under their direction the United States entered into a great number of treaties with eastern tribes in which the Indians ceded their tribal lands in exchange for lands farther west. Under the administration of Andrew Jackson the removal policy accelerated and took on a more coercive character. "Jackson's solution," Wilcomb Washburn has concluded, "involved a cold-blooded removal of the problem from the concern and consciousness of white Americans."[10] By midcentury only a few Indian tribes were left east of what was then called the "permanent Indian frontier," a line extending from Texas to the Great Lakes.

The discovery of gold in California sealed the fate of the removal policy. Just as Anglo-Americans believed that they finally had solved their "Indian problem," it became again a matter of pressing national concern. The rush to California greatly accelerated the process that had already been begun by the settlement of Oregon, the Mormon migration to Utah, the annexation of Texas, and the war with Mexico. In 1848 the boundaries of the United States were extended to the Pacific Ocean, and the notion of a permanent Indian frontier was suddenly and forever rendered obsolete. The settlement of the territories on the Pacific slope forced a readjustment in American Indian policy. No longer was it possible to remove Indians farther west ahead of Anglo-American settlement, because beyond California

140

there was no more West. California, because it was the most rapidly developing region of the new far western territories, became the crucible in which the United States was compelled to design an alternative method of handling its Indian population.

During the quarter century after the American conquest, federal Indian policy in California, as elsewhere, was a manifestation of basic attitudes or assumptions generally held by whites about Indians. In California the evolution of federal policy was also shaped by local circumstances and by the particular attitudes of whites within the state. There is evidence of the lingering influence of the Hispanic tradition governing Indian relations in California as well as the ascendancy of traditional Anglo-American attitudes.

Shortly after its admission to the union, California was visited by three federal Indian commissioners. These men, Dr. Oliver M. Wozencraft, George W. Barbour and Redick McKee, urged the Californians to accept the implications of their own geography: "As there is *no further west*, to which they *can* be removed, the General Government and the people of California appear to have left but one alternative in relation to these remnants of once numerous and powerful tribes, viz: *extermination or domestication*."[11] Beginning in February, 1851, and continuing for more than a year, the three commissioners negotiated eighteen treaties involving about twenty-five thousand California Indians. In each of the treaties the natives acknowledged the jurisdiction of the United States, agreed to refrain from hostilities, and relinquished all claims to the territory that they had held. In return the commissioners promised the Indians provisions, cattle, and large tracts of land to be set apart for reservations. William Henry Ellison, an early student of these treaties, has estimated that the proposed reservations would have contained about 7,488,000 acres or 7.5 percent of the land area of the state[12] (see map 3). After the conclusion of one treaty in May, 1851, George Barbour wrote to the commissioner of Indian affairs, "You will probably think that the amount agreed to be given to those tribes with whom we have treated too great; but when you take into consideration their poverty, the country they surrender, and particularly the expense of a war with them that would necessarily last for years, to say nothing of the gold mines they give up, I do not think you will conceive that we have given them too much."[13]

The objections that Barbour foresaw did not come from the commissioner, however, but from the people of California. The treaties and proposed reservations became the subject of a vigorous debate. A substantial minority of Californians supported the work of the commissioners and argued that considerations of geography, humanity, and economic self-interest dictated that provision be made for the Indians within the state's borders. The majority sentiment, however, was hostile to the commissioners' proposals and demanded the extension of the traditional removal policy to California. Advocates of removal argued that it was intolerable that vast tracts of rich agricultural and mineral lands within the state should be made the exclusive domain of Indians. Basing their arguments on the precedents in American history, they demanded that California's Indians be treated the same as those in the eastern states — that is, expelled to some distant territory. If there was no further West for them, then they should be removed eastward. There were still vast tracts of unsettled land east of Sierra Nevada. Why not place them there?

One of the most consistent supporters of Wozencraft, Barbour, and McKee was the *San Francisco Alta California.* The paper heralded their arrival in January, 1851, and called upon the governor and legislature not to impede the commissioners' work. The *Alta* agreed with the commissioners that removal was not a feasible policy for the California Indians: "It was fortunate that the eastern states had a kind of Van Dieman's land on the western side of the great river where they could transport these poor red children of the forrest [*sic*]. It is not so, however, with California." The state had either to accept the right of the Indians to live within its boundaries or else annihilate them. Regarding the latter possibility, the *Alta* commented optimistically: "No one of human feelings can advocate such a course. . . . The Indians have a right to a portion of the soil, a better right than we have to the whole of it. And if we deprive them of that we must afford them the means of sustenance in some other way."[14] Likewise, a correspondent to the *Alta*, identified only as "Shasta," argued that for every acre set aside for the reservations there were a hundred or a thousand still inviting white settlement. Shasta argued that those who called for removal of the Indians to the arid plains east of California were unrealistic, because California Indians could not survive such a drastic change of environment. He concluded, "You have but one choice — KILL, MURDER, EXTERMINATE OR DOMESTICATE AND IMPROVE THEM."[15]

In spite of this vocal support for the commissioners' plan, Cali-

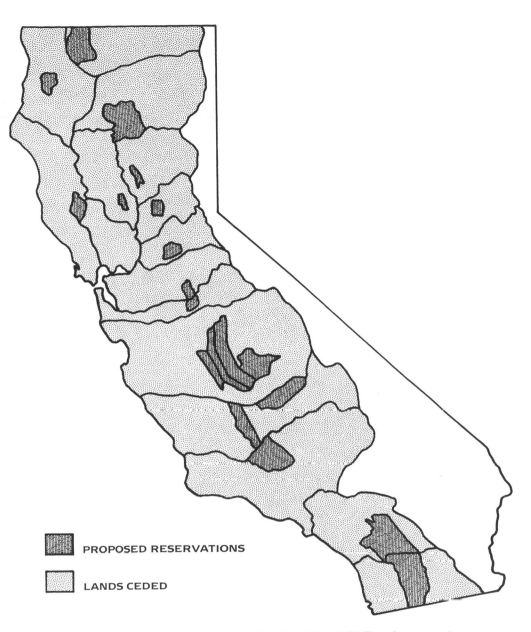

PROPOSED RESERVATIONS

LANDS CEDED

MAP 3. Unratified Treaty Lands in California, 1851–1852. Based on maps in George H. Phillips, *The Enduring Struggle: Indians in California History*, and Robert F. Heizer, *The Eighteen Unratified Treaties of 1851–1852 between the California Indians and the United States Government.*

143

fornia sentiment was clearly hostile to the proposed reservations. On January 5, 1852, Democratic Governor John McDougal, a native of Ohio and a veteran of the Black Hawk War, delivered his Annual Message to the legislature and declared that the Indians were a "source of much annoyance" in California and would continue to be so as long as they resided in close proximity to whites. The governor reminded the legislators of the traditional solution offered by the federal government to this problem: "The last effort which was made by our Government was the policy strongly recommended by President Jackson, of removing them to some isolated position distant from all contact with the whites." Governor McDougal suggested that the best plan for California would be a continuation of the policy of Jackson. A few days after McDougal's address his successor, John Bigler, was inaugurated, and the new governor expressed views identical to those of his predecessor. In a special message delivered on January 30, Governor Bigler urged the rejection of the Indian treaties and the prohibition of the proposed reservations.[16]

One of the first orders of business of the new legislative session in 1852 was the creation of special committees to draft resolutions instructing the California congressional delegation. The committees were charged with investigating the eighteen recent treaties with California tribes which "reserve to them extensive tracts of valuable mineral and agricultural lands, embracing populous mining towns, large portions of which are already in possession of, and improved by, American citizens." With these somewhat stacked charges it was no surprise that the majority reports of the committees urged rejection of the treaties, on the grounds that they would guarantee Indian occupation of lands rich in mineral and agricultural wealth, and recommended instead that the Indians be removed from the state.[17]

This recommendation was tempered, however, by the realization that some of the state's Indians were useful laborers. The senate committee was careful to distinguish between the state's "useful" and "wild" Indians. The former were those who had been influenced by the missions and now were an important source of labor for whites engaged in farming and ranching. The senators recommended that these Indians be left alone: "If thus treated, they will resume their former occupation, and supply, to a great extent, what is so much needed, that labor, without which, it will be long before California can feed herself." Concerning the "wild" Indians the committee reported, "To take any portion of the country west of the

144

Sierra Nevada, for the home of the wild, and generally hostile Indians, would be so manifestly unwise and impolitic, that your committee cannot think that anything more is necessary, than thus to present it to public consideration."[18]

Despite that careful distinction between "wild" and "useful" Indians, a minority on the senate committee objected altogether to the majority recommendations. A minority report, prepared by Jonathan Trumbull Warner, argued that removal was not only impractical and inhumane but also economically unwise. Warner, a senator from San Diego, had immigrated to California in 1831, had become a naturalized Mexican citizen and taken the name Juan José. On his Agua Caliente rancho in southern California, Warner had long been dependent on the labor of the local Cupeños.[19] In his minority report Warner recommended that, instead of removal of the Indians, sufficient land should be provided for them within the state, so that they might continue to be useful to the white population: "Here philanthropy and charity, hand in hand, might find a field in which to labor. From them, the farmer, grazier, and owners of vineyards, might derive their accustomed and needed laborers."[20] Warner had had difficulties with the Indians, but he also appreciated their value as workers. Obviously he was reluctant to see any of them banished from the state.

Again in the majority and minority reports of the Senate we see the influence of the two traditions of Indian relations in California. The majority report's recommendation that the "wild" Indians be removed from the state is a manifestation of the traditional Anglo-American view of Indians as obstacles that must be eliminated. The Hispanic view of Indians as a valuable resource is represented in the majority report's recognition that because of the peculiar circumstances of California history some Indians had been rendered "useful" and were now a valuable source of labor. The senators believed that the latter group should be left as it was—a dependent class of laborers on California's farms and ranches. Warner's minority report is a very clear illustration of the continuity of the Hispanic tradition. Warner was personally familiar with the advantages of the California Indian labor system, and he recommended that that system be preserved. Removal, like the rise of violent hostilities across the state, represented a threat to the old order of Indian relations and therefore should be opposed. Unfortunately, the important point for us is that a majority of the legislature had defined a substantial portion of the California Indians as obstacles and demanded that the

145

A remarkable illustration of the split image of the California Indians. This lithograph, published in *The Annals of San Francisco* (1855), was captioned "1. *Wahla*, chief of the Yuba tribe—civilized and employed by Mr. S. Brannan. 2. A Partly civilized Indian. 3. A Wild Indian."

federal government remove them from the state. Undeniably, the tradition of Jackson had arrived in California.

In June, 1852, the United States Senate, meeting in secret session, rejected the California treaties. Thus the vast reservations proposed by Wozencraft, Barbour, and McKee were never created. The most important reason for the rejection of the treaties was the vigorous opposition to them by the California congressional delegation.[21] These men had faithfully transmitted to Congress the sentiments of the governor, the state legislature, and the majority of the people

146

of California. The proposed reservations contained lands of great potential value, and Californians were simply unwilling to set them aside for the exclusive use of Indians.[22] The actions and proposals of the commissioners prompted one California representative to remark, "The absurdity and ridiculousness of their official action almost forbids one from characterizing and denouncing it in terms it deserves."[23]

Subsequent judgments on the work of Wozencraft, Barbour, and McKee have often reflected the views of the commissioners' contemporary critics. William Henry Ellison concluded in 1919 that, if the treaties had been approved, "some of what are now the most populous and prosperous regions of California would have been today peopled by a few undeveloped natives. . . . The judgement of history must be that the Commissioners badly blundered, and that it was fortunate that their work was rejected."[24] In a more recent study, *The Other Californians* (1971), Robert F. Heizer and Alan J. Almquist also censured the commissioners: "One can only conclude that the treaty-making of 1851–1852 was something other than an honest and sincere attempt on the part of the federal government, through its three commissioners, to help the Indians whose lands had been overrun."[25] In the light of the subsequent history of Indian-white hostilities in California—which included the deaths of thousands of Indians and hundreds of whites—perhaps the commissioners' proposals should not be condemned out of hand.[26] If sufficiently large tracts of land had been set aside for the exclusive use of the California Indians, as proposed by the commissioners, the chances for survival of the native peoples and their cultures would have been greatly increased and the occasions for conflicts with whites proportionately reduced.[27] In 1852 the majority of Californians were not concerned with Indian survival on the land, however. Their concern was precisely the opposite: ejection of the Indians from the land so that it might be occupied by whites.

Although Congress acted in accord with the wishes of the Californians and rejected the eighteen treaties, it did not approve their request for the removal of the state's Indians. Nor did the Californians exert further pressure to have the Indians removed from the state. It is tempting to interpret the diminished demand for removal as a triumph for indigenous Hispanic attitudes toward the Indians—to believe that their usefulness as laborers outweighed the impediment that they represented to white progress—but such was not the case. We know that the rise of Indian-white hostilities, the changing economic conditions, and the decline in the numbers of available Indian laborers meant that the image of Indians as a useful class was declining, not increasing. It is most likely that support for removal diminished because Californians accepted that the state's geography had rendered removal impossible.[28] As a joint committee of the state legislature concluded in 1860, "there is no longer a wilderness west of us that can be assigned them, and our interest, as well as our duty and the promptings of humanity, dictate to us the necessity of making some disposition of the Indian tribes within our borders."[29]

In March, 1852, before taking action on the eighteen California treaties, Congress created an independent Indian superintendency for California.[30] Appointed as superintendent was Edward Fitzgerald Beale. He was to have an important impact on federal Indian policy in California and throughout the Far West. The scion of a distinguished military family, Beale had participated as a naval lieutenant in the American conquest of California. Beale was commissioned as the first superintendent of Indian affairs in California just a month after his thirtieth birthday.[31] Almost immediately after arriving in the state in September, 1852, he forwarded to Washington a set of specific proposals for dealing with the California Indians:

> In the first place, I propose a system of "military posts" to be established on reservations, for the convenience and protection of the Indians; these reservations to be regarded as military reservations, or government reservations. The Indians to be invited to assemble within these reserves.
>
> A system of discipline and instruction to be adopted by the agent who is to live at the post.
>
> Each reservation to contain a military establishment, the number of troops being in proportion to the population of the tribes there assembled.
>
> The expenses of the troops to be borne by the surplus produce of Indian labor.[32]

Unlike Wozencraft, Barbour, and McKee, who had proposed reserving several millions of acres of land for the Indians through formal treaties, Beale proposed a handful of modest reservations occupying about 75,000 acres each. No treaties were to be negotiated with the Indians, they were simply to be "invited to assemble" on government lands.

148

Beale's proposal is significant because it included the essential features of the reservation system that was to be adopted in California and eventually extended across the West. Although reservations had been created by English colonists as early as the mid-1600s, and elements of the reservation system can be traced back to the earliest formulations of United States Indian policy in the eighteenth century, Superintendent Beale's proposal was innovative. Robert A. Trennert has demonstrated that since 1846 officials of the Office of Indian Affairs had been experimenting with the idea of a reservation system for the Plains Indians similar to the one proposed by Beale in 1852. Trennert acknowledges, however, that it was in California that the first modern reservation was actually established. Under the removal policy Indians had been assigned "reservations" in the unorganized lands of the trans-Mississippi west. This vast "Indian Country" was an area supposedly beyond the borders of white settlement that required little supervision or regulation by white agents. Beale's reservation system, on the other hand, called for the concentration of Indians on relatively small parcels of land, the borders of which were to be precisely defined. The reservations were to be created within a state and were surrounded by areas of white settlement. The new reservations would be located on government land, whereas the earlier reserves had occupied land recognized by treaty as belonging to the Indians. Also, unlike the "reservations" in Indian Country, the California reservations were to be places where Indian people were subject to "a system of discipline and instruction" administered by government agents.[33]

Superintendent Beale's proposed reservation system was a distinctly California product in several respects. In the first place, it was necessitated by the rapid migration of whites to California, a demographic fact that put an end to the "permanent Indian frontier" and Indian removal. Secondly, Beale had found the inspiration for his system in the California missions. He expected the reservations to be self-supporting: the Indians would be trained in mechanical and agricultural skills, and the surplus of their labor would support the troops and agents assigned to the reservation. As proof that this was possible, Beale cited the accomplishments of the Spanish colonizers of the state. In a letter to the commissioner of Indian affairs in November, 1852, Beale wrote: "Indian labor, directed by white intelligence, may be made as effective as that of any other purely laboring class. Let us take, as an exemplification of this assertion,

149

the stately missions reared by Indian labor, which at one time flourished in every part of California, the ruins of which to this day astonish those who have visited them." Under the mission system the Indians had been taught to labor, and it seemed to Beale that they had been taught to labor well: "It is this system, modified and adopted to the present time, which I propose for your consideration; nor can I conceive of any other which would preserve this unfortunate people from total extinction, and our government from everlasting disgrace."[34]

Beale's enthusiasm for the mission system may have been influenced by the views of the subagent for Indian affairs in southern California, Benjamin D. Wilson, a pioneer settler who had immigrated to California in 1841. Beale requested in 1852 that Wilson prepare a report on the condition of the Indians in the southern part of the state and give his views on what policy ought to be adopted. Wilson recommended essentially the same policy that Beale was already formulating. Like Beale, Wilson argued that the concentration and instruction of the Indians would succeed in California because the missions had demonstrated that such a policy would produce results. He wrote to Beale that the missions had been "one of the grandest experiments ever made for the elevation of this unfortunate race" and that it was now "the province of our own Government to check the downward career of these children of the Missions, and put them anew in the broad road they followed to happiness and convey to their brethren who never yet have felt them a taste of the comforts and blessings of civilization." Americans were to establish missionlike reservations and bring to fruition the work of civilization and uplift that the Franciscans had begun.[35] Wilson prepared his report, as George H. Phillips has pointed out, in the aftermath of an abortive uprising of the Indians of southern California. Thus the report was tinged with a note of urgency, imploring Beale to take prompt action to implement the new policy.[36]

There is a third sense in which the reservation system was a California product. An important distinction between the Beale reservations and previous federal policy was that the Indians were to be placed on reserved *government* lands (or lands leased by the government) rather than on land whose title was recognized as belonging to the Indians. It was often argued that Spain and Mexico had not recognized Indian title and that the United States should not alter that precedent.[37] T. Butler King had reported in 1850 that the California Indians "never pretended to hold any interest

150

in the soil, nor have they been treated by the Spanish or American immigrants as possessing any. The Mexican government never treated with them for the purchase of land, or the relinquishment of any claim to it whatever."[38] The majority report of the state senate committee that investigated the eighteen treaties had argued that it would be unprecedented and unwise for the federal government to recognize Indian title in California: "It is well known to all those who are acquainted with the history of the Indian policy of Spain and Mexico, that the right of the Indian in the soil was never admitted nor recognized."[39] After the defeat of the treaties the federal government made no further effort to extinguish Indian title in California. Thus the new government reservations reflected the unwillingness of the white Californians to reverse what they regarded as a local precedent and to recognize the title of the California natives to any of the land within the state.[40]

Under the Indian appropriation act of 1852 Congress provided $100,000 for California Indian affairs. Superintendent Beale regarded that sum as inadequate for the system of reservations that he envisioned and decided to concentrate the entire amount in the development of a single reserve. Yet before even this prototype could be created, Beale believed it necessary to return to Washington to lobby for his proposal and to win a larger appropriation. His trip was a success. In March, 1853, Congress provided for the establishment of five reservations in California (or surrounding territories) and an appropriation of $250,000.[41] By August the superintendent was back in California, ready to inaugurate the new system. For several reasons Beale chose the Tejon Pass area at the southern end of the San Joaquin Valley for the state's first reservation.[42] As the surrounding Indians were gathered there in the fall and winter, he expressed satisfaction at what was being accomplished, and in February, 1854, he reported that over 2,500 acres had been cultivated by the Indians at Tejon:

> It is impossible to do justice to the docility and energy which these poor people possess. They work not only without murmur or complaint, but with the most cheerful alacrity, and as the fruits of their labor begin to show itself [sic] in the immense field now covered with its verdant promise of future plenty, they look at it in amazement, and with delight.[43]

Then, in July, Beale was surprised to learn that he had been removed from his office as California superintendent. He had been accused by political opponents, apparently unjustly, of financial malfeasance.[44]

Beale's removal did not, however, mean a change in federal policy. His successor, Thomas J. Henley, attempted to duplicate Beale's Tejon success at other sites in the state. In September, 1854, Superintendent Henley established a second reservation on the western side of the Sacramento Valley in present-day Tehama County at a site known as Nome Lackee.[45] During Henley's administration three additional reserves and two "Indian farms" were established. In 1854 the Fresno reservation in the San Joaquin Valley was established. The following year Henley founded the Klamath reservation at the mouth of the Klamath River and the Mendocino reservation along the coast about fifty miles south of Cape Mendocino. The Kings River "farm" in the southern San Joaquin Valley was established in 1854. Henley created the Nome Cult Indian "farm" in Mendocino County in 1856. Nome Cult later became the Round Valley reservation. In 1857 the superintendent summarized his accomplishments as follows:

Name	Indian Population
Tejon Reservation	700
Nome Lackee Reservation	2,000
Attached is Nome Cult Farm	3,000
Mendocino Reservation	500
Fresno Reservation	900
Attached is King's River Farm	400
Klamath Reservation	2,500[46]

Henley reported that at all the reservations and "farms" the agents were dutifully instructing Indians in agricultural skills and that they were supervising their charges in cultivating hundreds of acres of land. His report probably exaggerated the numbers of the Indians on the reserves, but even so in 1857, when the reservation system was at its peak, as many as 10,000 of the estimated 50,000 California Indians may have been affected by the system.

In the early 1860s the system began to contract. The Fresno reservation was closed in 1861 and the following year both the Kings River "farm" and the Klamath reservation were abandoned. A few Klamath Indians were relocated to the new Smith River reserve, which was founded in 1862 above Crescent City in the northwestern corner of the state, but Smith River too was abandoned in 1869. By 1862 most of the Indians had left the Nome Lackee

"Tejon Indians" at the site of California's first reservation. Based on a drawing probably by Charles Koppel, first published in 1853.

reservation, and it was abandoned. The remaining Nome Lackee Indians were transferred to the Round Valley reserve. The Tejon reservation was closed in 1864. Most of its Indians had moved to a "farm" established in 1858 on the Tule River that was designated a reservation in 1863. The Mendocino reservation was abandoned in 1864, and its Indians were moved to Round Valley. The only important new reservation founded in the 1860s was the Hoopa Valley reserve, which was founded in 1864 on the Trinity River near its junction with the Klamath River. In southern California two small reservations were established in 1870 at San Pasqual and Pala in San Diego County, but they were closed in 1871.[47]

During the early 1850s support for the accomplishments of Beale and Henley was widespread in the press of San Francisco, Sacramento, Stockton, and Los Angeles.[48] The reservations were regarded by many whites as humanitarian institutions that would benefit both

153

whites and Indians. During those years Californians demonstrated considerable faith in the capacity of the California Indians for "civilization." Nowhere was this early faith in the "civilizing" mission of the reservations more evident than in the columns of the *San Francisco Alta California*. For example, after Beale's return to California from Washington in August, 1853, the *Alta* expressed enthusiasm and optimism for his reservations:

> Five years after the first settlement is made and put into successful operation, the Indian affairs of California will cease to be an item of expense to the General or State Government; all hostilities will be over; the whites will be entirely free from annoyance by the Indians; the Indians will be transformed from a state of semibarbarism, indolence, mental imbecility and moral debasement to a condition of civilization, Christianity, industry, virtue, frugality, social and domestic happiness and public usefulness.[49]

The *Alta* followed carefully Beale's progress as he established his prototype at Tejon, and by June, 1854, it judged his efforts to be a success: "We had scarcely supposed it possible that in so short a time so much could have been done with the raw material upon which Mr. Beale was called to operate." When the news came that Beale had been removed from office, the *Alta* expressed confidence in his integrity and the hope that his departure would not mean an abandonment of the policies that he had inaugurated. The results of that policy, the *Alta* pointed out, had been "beyond the fondest anticipations of the most sanguine."[50]

Beale's successor, Thomas J. Henley, also received widespread support for his extension of the reservation system.[51] The *San Francisco Placer Times and Transcript* in September, 1854, expressed faith that under his superintendency the success of Tejon would be reproduced at the new Nome Lackee reserve and that the new reservation would provide "protection and domestication" for more California Indians and thereby contribute to the peace and prosperity of the state.[52] Early visitors to Nome Lackee confirmed the optimism of the *Placer Times*. In December, 1854, one traveler reported that the Indians there were "doing better than the most sanguine friends of the system could have anticipated," and in the spring of 1858 the *Alta* published a glowing account of the California reservations written by the paper's "travelling correspondent." The correspondent was especially enthusiastic about the progress made at Nome Lackee, where he had observed the Indians harvesting a crop of wild oats:

154

Some fifty or more field hands have been mowing and raking, and cocking this grain for the last fortnight and are now gathering a hundred bushels a day for home consumption. As I write, the Diggers, clad in the most fantastic dress imaginable, from the Georgia costume to military suits and plug hats, may be seen swinging the scythe, and handling the rake in as artistic style as the Dutch farmers on the banks of the Hudson. They enjoy the work and labor cheerfully from early morn to dewey eve.[53]

Such positive images of reservation operations were almost exclusively products of the 1850s. At the end of the decade and in the 1860s and 1870s descriptions of the reservations became more critical. Increasingly the state's leading newspapers began to reflect a different reality: the Indians were victims of corrupt or negligent agents, and the reservations themselves were dreary and unproductive places. The early promise that the reservations would become self-supporting went unfulfilled. Perhaps of greatest importance, the inchoate faith in the "civilizing" mission of the reservations was lost. After more than a decade of operations many Californians concluded that the reservation system had been unable to accomplish its objectives.

In January, 1855, the *San Francisco Sun* and the *Sacramento Union* published a challenge to the prevailing sentiment regarding the reservations:

It has been too much the custom of the press in this country to represent the Indian Reservations as flourishing, merely on the representations of parties making temporary visits, or of persons interested in publishing such statements; we have, however, good reason to believe that those glowing accounts are far too highly colored, and that all is not *coleur de rose* at these Reservations as they would have us believe.

The article charged that reservation agents were neglecting their duties and that many of the white employees on the reserves were brutal and immoral men who mistreated the Indians and subjected them to "cruel outrages."[54] In September, 1856, the *San Francisco Bulletin* expressed faith in the reservation system generally but called into question its administrators. The *Bulletin* recommended a special investigation of the California reserves: "We feel convinced that the appointment of a competent secret agent by the Indian Department to visit the reservations and the Indian frontier and report upon the state of things really existing, would develop a set of facts which would open the eyes of those at home."[55]

Eventually the recommendation of the *Bulletin* bore fruit. In May, 1857, a special agent of the U.S. Treasury Department, J. Ross Browne, was appointed to investigate the condition of Indian affairs on the Pacific Coast. Browne toured California the following year, and during the course of his investigation he uncovered evidence of fraud and malfeasance in the superintendency of Thomas J. Henley. Money and supplies allocated for the reservations had been used for private purposes; the labor of Indians from the reserves had been used to benefit the pecuniary interests of agents. As a consequence, Browne wrote from the Mendocino reservation in April, 1858, that the Indians were suffering very keenly from the lack of proper care: "I regret to say that my anticipations in regard to the progress of this reservation have not been realized."[56] In October, 1859, Browne reported that Nome Lackee presented an appearance of "utter neglect and ruin." He estimated that not more than fifty Indians were left on the reservation: "No evidence of the results of attention, labor, or the expenditure of public money is anywhere manifest. When it is considered that forty-five or fifty thousand dollars have been expended on this Reservation during the last year, it must be conceded that the result is very discouraging."[57]

Browne later amplified his views on the California reservations in an article for *Harpers' Magazine.* The Spanish missions, Browne recalled, had demonstrated the capacity of the California Indians "for the acquisition of civilized habits." Therefore, when the Tejon reservation had been founded in 1853, "there had been every reason to hope that the experiment would prove successful." Then through the patronage system, incompetent and venal men had been appointed as Indian agents, and fraud became commonplace. Although the tone of Browne's *Harpers* article is one of bemused detachment, it is clear that his sympathies lay with the Indians who had been victimized by the corrupt system. His discussion of the blankets distributed to the reservation Indians is typical:

> The blankets, to be sure, were very thin, and cost a great deal of money in proportion to their value; but, then, peculiar advantages were to be derived from the transparency of the fabric. In some respects the worst material might be considered the most economical. By holding his blanket to the light an Indian could enjoy the contemplation of both sides of it at the same time; and it would require a little instruction in architecture to enable him to use it occasionally as a window to his wigwam.

156

"Distribution of Rations to the Indians," an unsigned drawing from 1858. The setting is the Mendocino reservation, which was established along the northwest coast of California in 1855 and abandoned in 1864.

Browne charged that the agents grossly exaggerated the numbers of Indians whom they had placed on the reservations and that they had defrauded the government on a grand scale. The reservations certainly had not been made self-supporting, and, while the condition of the Indians had deteriorated, the prosperity of the white employees had increased. Browne concluded, "So the end of it is, that the reservations are practically abandoned—the remainder of the Indians are being exterminated every day, and the Spanish Mission System has signally failed."[58] As a result of Browne's investigation, Superintendent Henley was removed from office by the commissioner of Indian affairs.

After Browne's report in 1858 it is difficult to find much evidence of the optimism and enthusiasm that had characterized the early images of life on the California reservations.[59] Under the headline

157

"EXPOSÉ OF THE INDIAN DEPARTMENT IN CALIFORNIA: Gross Frauds and Mismanagement," the *Sacramento Union* in July, 1860, published the original correspondence between Browne and the commissioner of Indian affairs. In an accompanying editorial the *Union* acknowledged that the whole reservation system in California had proved to be a failure. Not only had the reservations not become self-supporting but also their administrators had not delivered on the promise that the reservation Indians would gradually become "civilized."[60] The *San Francisco Alta California*, earlier the most enthusiastic supporter of the reservation system, became in the 1860s one of the system's most strident critics. In 1867 the *Alta* proclaimed: "The Indian Department in California has been a disastrous failure from the first. Under no administration, in no part of the State, has it given satisfaction."[61] The *Alta* charged, in June, 1868, that after seventeen years and the expenditure of $2 million the reservation system, "so far as we can learn, has not taught a solitary red man to live in the fashion of civilization."[62]

Discontent with the management of Indian affairs, of course, was not limited to California. The charges of fraud and corruption in California were part of a national protest against the federal Indian service.[63] When Ulysses S. Grant became president in 1869, he attempted to reform federal management of Indian affairs by appointing military officers as Indian superintendents and agents. He also placed several agencies under the direction of the Society of Friends. In 1870, Congress forbade military personnel from holding civil offices, and Grant turned to what was known popularly as the "Quaker policy," appointing individuals nominated by various religious denominations to offices in the Indian service.[64]

By 1869, when Grant assumed office, the reservation system in California had been virtually abandoned. All but three of the state's reservations and Indian farms had been closed. Those that remained were the Hoopa Valley reservation in Humboldt County, with 700 Indians; the Round Valley reservation in Mendocino, with 700 Indians; and the Tule River reservation in Tulare County, with about 300 Indians.[65] Under Grant's Quaker policy the staff positions on these remaining reservations were assigned to individuals nominated by the Methodist Episcopal Church.[66] In 1870, Methodist ministers and laymen were selected to man the California agencies, and under their direction a program of religious and secular education was begun on the reservations.[67] Although it was recognized that the number of California Indians who would benefit from this last change of administration was small, the Methodists were generally credited with making a positive contribution. Under their administration one can detect the glimmering of a revival in Indian affairs, and for a while at least the positive images that had characterized the early days of the reservation system began to reappear.[68]

The *New York Tribune,* for example, in 1871 reported on the "Good Effects of Kindness, Education, and Christian Influences" on the California Indians. In particular, the *Tribune* described the successful harvesting of 500 acres of grain by contented and willing Indians at the Hoopa reservation and noted that "numbers of Indian children who had no idea of the alphabet are now rapidly learning to write, and can readily read words of five or six letters."[69] Similar progress was reported at the other reserves. Schools were established, and the instructors (usually wives of the agents or of other white employees) described enthusiastically their progress in teaching Indian children to read and write. Flora Saxbe, for example, said her students at Tule River were "obedient and attentive, and I think they have done as well as the same number of white children placed in the same circumstances."

At Round Valley the Reverend Hugh Gibson rated the success of his wife's school as beyond expectations, saying the Indian children "evince both ability and disposition to learn, although their education has been generally conceded to be an impossibility." Mary Gibson said that, although the "prevailing impression was that the Indians were incapable of learning," she had found the opposite to be true.[70]

In spite of the initial enthusiasm with which the Methodists were greeted, it soon became apparent that the change in personnel had not brought the millenium to California Indian affairs. In the fall of 1871 the *San Francisco Bulletin* special correspondent visited the reservation at Round Valley. He carefully examined the operations there and interviewed the Reverend Hugh Gibson, who was still the resident agent. The correspondent's report, published in the *Bulletin* on November 10, called into question the improvements claimed for the reservation. He judged that the reservation was still not self-supporting and probably never would be. The Indians could be made to work only with the greatest difficulty; their houses were still constructed "in the primitive manner"; and their sanitation and health were far from satisfactory. "Such a weeping, blinking, moping, red-eyed company of human beings as these Round Valley Indians are I never saw before," he reported. Mrs. Gibson demonstrated the ability of her students to read simple sentences, but the correspondent showed no enthusiasm for their accomplishments. When the Reverend Gibson was asked whether he thought there was "a single Indian of the eight hundred that had any genuine religion," the minister answered "rather evasively, but the substance of his reply was that he hoped there were a few who knew and loved their saviour." From his observations the *Bulletin* correspondent concluded that it was "absolutely hopeless" to attempt to convert to Christianity any of the Indians at Round Valley. "What then is this Reservation?" he asked. "With all due respect to the worthy Agent, it is simply a farce, like all others."[71]

In October, 1873, three years after the introduction of Methodist agents the *Alta California* could find no great improvement in California Indian affairs. The agents were still of poor calibre, often dishonest; the Indians had not materially benefited. The *Alta* called for the replacement of all civilian agents once again with military personnel, preferably graduates of West Point, and favored transferring the Bureau of Indian Affairs from the Interior Department back to the War Department: "Until they shall become civilized—which they never will, according to our ideas of civilization—it is absurd to entrust their government to any other Department."[72] In an 1874 editorial, entitled "The Horrors of the Indian Reservations," the *Alta* condemned the reserves as "nurseries of idleness and prostitution, and discreditable to the Government in every respect." The paper ridiculed reports that conditions had improved at the reserves and that under the new order hundreds of Indians had been Christianized and "civilized."[73]

One of the strongest indictments of the "reformed" reservation system came from Stephen Powers, who was later the author of a richly detailed survey of the *Tribes of California* (1877). Powers was convinced that the Methodists were hopelessly naive and ineffectual and the Indians had not benefited under their supervision. In spite of all the missionaries' talk of teaching theology and other ethereal subjects the Indians in their care remained in truly pitiful condition. In an article published in the *Overland Monthly* in April, 1872, Powers derided the Christian agents and their much vaunted reservations: "I have seen [the reservations]—and they are so raw, so bald, so primitive in their uses, and so crude in their outcome, that they were scarce worth the visiting, except for the opportunity they afforded of noting the workings of the natural and unregenerate Indian mind." Powers branded as useless the efforts of the reservation agents to "civilize" the Indians. As for the likelihood of their success, he said "the chasm between them and the wretched, unhappy Indian is world-wide."[74]

These reports from the California reservations reveal a loss of faith in conversion and acculturation that is reminiscent of the attitudes of the English colonists two hundred years earlier. At first the effort to "civilize" the California Indians had been greeted with considerable optimism, but soon the effort was judged a failure, and confident expectations of success turned to disappointment. When Powers concluded in 1872 that the "chasm" between whites and Indians was "unbridgeable," he employed a metaphor that was by then commonplace. For a century or more Anglo-Americans had come to see the differences between themselves and Indians in terms of an unbridgeable or impassable gulf. Indians were seen as inextricably bound to their primitiveness, and it appeared that no amount of effort by whites could break the bond. Anglo-Americans in California believed for a time that the new reservation policy might bridge the gap between red and white. Soon, however, that faith was abandoned.

As one considers popular attitudes toward the reservation system on the California frontier, one soon realizes that a different set of assumptions and expectations were in operation there than in settled and secure places, such as San Francisco or Sacramento. Because the whites on the frontier viewed the Indians as obstacles to the development of the areas in which they had settled, they looked for ways to eliminate the Indians. The reservations represented one possibility. Generally unconcerned with the "civilizing" or ameliorative purposes of the reserves, many frontier whites regarded them as a system of Indian prisons or concentration camps, to which Indians should be taken by force if necessary. If the Indians escaped, the whites believed that they should be punished by death. On the frontier ineffective protests against the concentration of Indians were occasionally made, especially by whites who feared that the reserves would interfere with their access to Indian labor, but such objections were usually disregarded by an outraged white majority.

On the frontier attitudes toward the Indians and the reservations were marked by a greater sense of urgency than in the cities. Often whites on the frontier viewed the Indians as an immediate danger to life and property, and they demanded their removal to reservations as an urgent necessity. Such demands often came amid or

161

immediately following outbreaks of violent hostilities between the two races, and in this atmosphere the call for removal was expressed in extreme terms. Settlers in a particular county or district would demand that their area be rid of all its Indians. All of them, friendly and hostile alike, must be expelled and concentrated under guard on the reservations. It seemed to matter little whether the Indians were killed in the process of relocation or reached their destination on distant reservations. Once they were on the reserves, it was of little concern what happened to the Indians so long as they were prevented from leaving. The paramount concern on the frontier was that these dangerous hindrances to local safety and development be eliminated. Soon it became apparent that the reservations would not eliminate the problem. Only a fraction of the California Indians ever saw a reservation, and those who were placed on a reserve easily escaped. Then opposition to them grew. Discontent was especially strong among whites in the areas immediately surrounding the reserves. They denounced them as a blight or a curse and demanded that the reservations be terminated. In some cases this opposition led to violent attacks and acts of sabotage by white settlers against the reserves.

Wherever Indian hostilities posed a threat to development of a community, whites on the California frontier looked to the reservations to reduce the threat. Northwestern California, for example, was the scene of devastating "Indian wars" during the 1850s and early 1860s, and the reservations there were accepted as possible solutions to the region's difficulties.[75] In 1858 the *Humboldt Times* reported that the nearly constant Indian hostilities, the attendant loss of life and property, and the general "stagnation of business" had deterred the community from "experimenting" any longer with Indians within the county's borders. The only hope for a return to peace and prosperity appeared to lie in the removal of all local Indians to reservations. The *Times* argued that removal must be total because the so-called "friendly" Indians often harbored those who were hostile. The paper stated the terms under which removal or expulsion should be carried out: "A force of armed men must be sent among them sufficiently strong to hold a rod over them. They must be informed that they will be provided for and protected on the Reservations, and that a war of extermination will be waged against all who are caught off of it."[76]

Similarly, in the foothills of the Sierra Nevada and the northern Sacramento Valley, Indian-white hostilities led to demands for the removal of the Indians to the reservations. The murder of two white children in Butte County in 1863 (probably in retaliation against the hanging of five Indians by whites) prompted a mass meeting in Chico. The assembly of about 300 whites called upon Superintendent Hanson to remove every Indian in Butte County to the reservations within thirty days. Any left at liberty after that time would be killed.[77] The *Butte County Appeal,* in an editorial entitled "Indians! Indians!!," called upon the citizens of the county to aid in the "removal of these festering devils from our midst." Committees were to be formed to round up the county's native people, and a fund established to defray the expenses of removal. The *Appeal* called for the gathering in of "the last remaining son of the forest" to the reservations where each Indian should be put to work "with the positive assurance that when again seen meandering upon our valleys and mountains his life will pay for his audacity."[78] As in the northwest, the local press concluded that it was impossible any longer to separate the "friendly" and "hostile" Indians and that security for the county lay in total removal.[79]

A common complaint on the frontier was that government agents were not resolute enough in recruiting and holding Indians to the reservations. As a result volunteer militia and vigilante groups conducted their own recruitment campaigns. Reservation agents sometimes found themselves responsible for a hundred or more Indians delivered to them under guard by armed whites, who warned the agents that the Indians would be killed if the agents allowed them to escape from the reservation. These campaigns dramatically illustrate the expectation on the frontier that concentrating Indians on the reserves would permanently eliminate these serious obstacles to local development.[80]

In the fall of 1858 a group of white residents in Fresno and Tulare counties gathered about two hundred Southern Valley Yokuts from Kings River and Tulare Lake and escorted them to the Fresno reservation. As they collected the Indians, the whites burned the vacated villages.[81] In a letter to the subagent in charge of the Fresno reserve the citizens group explained that they had taken this action because of "depredations" by these Indians on the cattle and hogs of local ranchers: "The presence of these Indians in a region so densely populated by whites whose exclusive business is stock raising is prejudicial to their interest in many ways. These Indians and a community of stock growing people cannot inhabit the same country." The citizens warned that, if any of the Yokuts attempted to return, they would be dealt with harshly, *"as abide with us they shall not."*[82]

At about the same time in Shasta, Trinity, and Humboldt counties a militia company, known as the Kibbe Guards (after its leader, state Adjutant General William C. Kibbe), forcibly collected several hundred Indians for the Mendocino reservation. One member of the guards, Elisha Renshaw Potter, later recalled that their collection methods consisted mainly of locating Indian camps, surrounding them at night, and attacking them at dawn. Indians who survived the attacks were taken to the reservations.[83] Meanwhile, in Mendocino County, Captain Jarboe's Rangers killed twenty-five "bucks" in the course of capturing fifty-five others for the Mendocino reservation. In a letter to the *Sonoma Journal* in October, 1859, one resident of the Eel River valley praised Jarboe's work and expressed the hope that he would continue to have success. With these Indians eliminated, the correspondent explained, a tract of range land seventy miles square had been opened up: "To persons seeking good stock ranches, I would say, so soon as the Indian difficulties are disposed of, you cannot fail to find satisfactory locations in this region."[84] Jarboe himself claimed that in four months he and his men had killed 283 "warriors" and delivered 292 others to the reservation.[85]

The forced removal of Indians to the reserves was criticized by some whites as a cruel injustice. Others objected to it for a more practical reason: they feared the reservations would deprive them of their Indian laborers.[86] To counter that objection, federal agents in California permitted local whites to hire reservation Indians to work off the reserve. It is not clear, however, how common such permits were in practice. In 1856 the agent on the Mendocino reservation reported that "most" of the able-bodied men on the reserve had permits to work for local farmers.[87] In the same year the agent at the Fresno reserve estimated that, with the exception of harvest time, about one-fifth of the Indians under his supervision worked for whites.[88]

Despite the permit system some Californians continued to oppose the reservations because they removed a part of the local labor force.[89] For example, the agent at Nome Lackee reported to the California superintendent of Indian affairs in 1856 that many of the Indians who were brought to the reservation were "followed and demanded by persons claiming them as private property." The agent explained that many of the Indians had previously worked on ranches and farms in the vicinity and that their employers seemed "to have adopted the principle that they belong to them as much as an African slave does to his master."[90] In the early 1870s residents of

164

"Protecting the Settlers," an ironic comment by reservation critic
J. Ross Browne in 1864.

Inyo County opposed the removal of "their Indians" to the Tule River reservation because removal would hurt farming operations and impoverish the Indians. The *Inyo Independent* predicted, "The consequence will be that large numbers of working Indians, now peaceably and profitably employed on farms, will be transmogrified into vagabonds, forced to steal or starve, if compelled to go on this worthless piece of ground." The *Independent* reported that white farmers would be willing to take extreme measures to prevent the removal of the Indians.[91] Meanwhile a similar protest was being mounted by farmers in Sonoma County who were concerned that the removal of about 300 local Indians to the Round Valley Reservation would reduce the available supply of farm labor.[92]

Although these objections to the reserves may be evidence of the continuity of the Hispanic tradition in California, they also illustrate the decline of that tradition. By the late 1850s the major objection to the reservations on the California frontier was not that they had removed too many Indians, but rather that they had failed to ensure total and permanent Indian relocation. As prisoner-of-war or concentration camps the California reservations proved to be hopelessly ineffective. Although hundreds of Indians were forcibly removed to the reserves by the volunteer militia groups, many of them remained there only temporarily. Food and other supplies were often inadequate to support the reservation population, and the Indians were faced with the choice of starvation or leaving the reserves and raiding neighboring farms and ranches.[93] To the extent that the reservations were unable to guarantee the permanent concentrations of Indians, they were opposed by whites on the California frontier. The reservations themselves came to be regarded by many whites as "obstacles," and demands were made that they be closed or moved to more distant sites. The attitudes of frontier whites toward the reservations were thus an extension of their attitudes toward the Indians: whatever blocked local development should be eliminated.

Opposition to the reservations, as one might expect, became especially strong in those areas immediately surrounding the reserves.[94] For example, in 1859 a group of Tehama residents presented a petition to the secretary of the interior demanding that the Nome Lackee reservation be "removed beyond the pale of our thickly settled districts." Although only eleven men had drawn up the document, they assured the secretary that "every respectable citizen of Tehama County . . . as well as a large portion of those in Colusa County" would have been willing to sign if asked. The petitioners claimed that they were "aggrieved" by the presence of the reservation in their immediate neighborhood. The reservation Indians committed "depredations" on local hogs and calves, and the lands that they occupied "are among the best in our State and capable of subsisting a valuable community of settlers." If the land were turned over to white settlers, they would be able to afford themselves "a much purer and better protection" against depredations than that provided by the reservation.[95]

The reservation was not immediately closed, and three years later the residents of Tehama again lodged complaints against Nome Lackee. In 1862 they gathered in a public meeting and passed resolutions calling for the removal of all the Indians from the reservation. The Indians there, one local editor noted, were "without constraint of any kind, and must therefore depredate upon the property of citizens." He asked: "Where is Hanson, Indian Agent for this District? He seems to have entirely neglected his duties. Is the government paying him a salary of $3,000 per annum, and perquisites, for doing nothing?"[96] Superintendent Hanson, in fact, was well aware of the problems at Nome Lackee and also favored its abandonment. In September, 1862, he recommended that the Nome Lackee and Mendocino reservations be sold and that the Indians on those reservations be transferred to Round Valley in northeastern Mendocino County.[97] Hanson's analysis of the difficulties with the Nome Lackee site, however, differed markedly from those of the residents of Tehama. The superintendent complained that local ranchers had allowed their stock to overrun the reservation. The abandonment of Nome Lackee, Hanson informed the commissioner of Indian affairs, would remove the Indians from contact with "a population of whites who are more degraded than the Indians themselves."[98]

In closing the Mendocino and Nome Lackee reservations, Hanson hoped to introduce greater security and economy into the California reservation system by concentrating the northern Indians at Round Valley. This turned out to be a vain hope. As at the other sites, the whites in the Round Valley area became bitterly opposed to the presence of the nearby reservation. They complained that Indians frequently escaped from the reservation and stole or killed valuable stock.[99] In 1862 whites in Round Valley began a campaign of direct action against the reservation. In August a group of whites attacked and killed several reservation Indians. The local subagent wrote to Superintendent Hanson that "their only excuse for killing the Indians was, *they were afraid they would leave the reservation some night*

167

and run off with some of their stock, &c. [italics in the original]."[100]
Whites also took the rather contradictory course of destroying the
reservation's food supply, apparently in the hope that the Indians
would be forced to leave not only the reservation but Round Valley
as well.[101] At a mass meeting in November, 1862, local whites adopted
resolutions declaring the presence of the Indians "quartered on this
reservation in our midst" to be intolerable. They said that the reservation was the source of "serious difficulties," that it had "signally
failed" to provide for the maintenance of its Indian population, and
as a consequence the Indians, "prompted by that necessity which
knows no law, have taken our stock, thereby causing a serious loss
to many." If the government was unwilling to remove the reservation, the settlers demanded that they be given "just compensation"
for their property and improvements. They believed that the valley
must be all Indian, or all white.[102] In spite of these protests, the
reservation at Round Valley survived and remained one of the few
reservations still functioning in northern California at the turn of
the century.

Frontier discontent with the reservation system led to a curious
and short-lived revival of interest in the removal policy. If security
could not be ensured by concentrating Indians on reserves within the
state—from which they could easily escape and continue to commit
"depredations" on white lives and property—then the whites believed that they should be removed still farther away. White settlement of the intermontane West had convinced most Californians
that it was no longer practical to remove the state's Indians east of
the Sierra. Yet, as incredible as it might seem, in the early 1860s
some white Californians clung to the hope that the Indians might
yet be removed farther west—even if this meant placing them on
islands in the Pacific. California geography might be defied after all,
and a permanent Indian frontier erected at the ocean's shore!

James Beith, a forty-niner who had settled south of Arcata in
Humboldt County, was one Californian who entertained that hope.
In a series of letters written in the early 1860s, Beith complained
that Indian depredations were ruining the prospects of the county's
development. The reservation policy, he believed, was not a sufficient solution to the problem.[103]

I can never tolerate the idea of moving [the Indians] to some reserve
close at hand, for such a course is fatal and most dissastrous [*sic*] to
our interests. A combination of such has served to render this County

168

the poorest in the State, and will only prolong our misery by entailing a fresh curse upon us. Could we give security to the Indian and an asylum, & at the same time prevent his return—we would—from our eligible position become one of the first counties, in this best of all States.[104]

Beith and his neighbors concluded in 1862 that one sure means by which Humboldt County could reach its destined preeminence was "the entire removal of the Indians to some Island on the Pacific." If the Indians were removed beyond the Pacific shore, it would at last "give to the peaceful settler a full security and possession of the soil. This would induce an influx of settlers, and assist in the development of the County amazingly, for it is unquestionably one of the best grazing counties in the State."[105]

One of the leading public figures in northern California was Austin Wiley, editor of the *Humboldt Times* and state assemblyman. Wiley shared the sentiments of Beith and his neighbors. He believed that the presence of Indians, whether on or off the reservations, was responsible for the suspension of Humboldt's development. In an editorial for the *Times* on December 19, 1863, Wiley wrote:

The issue is about to be fairly and squarely presented to the citizens and the military authorities whether this district which is second to none in California for grazing, agricultural and lumbering resources, but which is now depleted in population, and its property ruinously depreciated by this curse fastened upon it by former neglect, mismanagement and untoward sympathy, shall be abandoned altogether by the white man and be given over to the remorseless red skin or whether they shall be at once subdued by a force adequate to that purpose and the last one removed to parts so far remote as to render their return impossible.

Four months later Wiley was appointed superintendent of Indian affairs for California (a post that he held for less than a year).[106] As superintendent he officially recommended in June, 1864, that the hostile Indians of the northern counties be removed to San Pedro or Santa Catalina Island off the southern California coast.[107] He presumed that these "parts" were sufficiently remote to render impossible the Indians' return to Humboldt County.

Wiley's recommendation was rejected by the commissioner of Indian affairs as impractical, but it received wide public support in the northern counties of the state.[108] The *San Francisco Bulletin* reported that all efforts at pacification on the state's northern frontier had failed: "All attempts to domesticate these free sons of the hills, to coop them within the limits of reservations removed but a short distance from their native haunts have hitherto failed." As a consequence, the *Bulletin* reported, Superintendent Wiley's suggestion regarding Santa Catalina Island had been greeted with enthusiasm: "The proposition is approved by the citizens of the northern counties who have suffered the ruinous results of Indian hostilities and who express the opinion that deportation or extermination must be the fate of their savage neighbors." Then, apparently in sympathy with the Catalina proposal, the *Bulletin* concluded, "The Government has frequently removed Indian tribes of the Atlantic side a much greater distance from their native wilds than it is proposed to take the mountain Indians of Northern California." The only possible objection that the editors of the San Francisco newspaper could foresee might come from whites who recently had begun development of the mineral resources on the Channel Islands.[109]

Of course, the California Indians were never exiled to an island reserve, and probably most Californians who thought about it at all considered it unlikely that they ever would be. That the notion was even considered indicates the intense dissatisfaction with which Californians had come to regard the reservation system. They had simply lost faith in its ability to solve the problems posed by the Indians' presence in the state. It was but a small step from this loss of faith in the system to the demand for Indian removal beyond the Pacific shoreline—or to the demand for Indian extermination. Today there seems to be a quantum difference in the last step, but to many whites on the California frontier in the 1850s and 1860s there was little difference between concentration of the Indians on distant reservations and their extermination. In either event Indians would be eliminated, expelled, or removed from lands desired by whites. The method used to accomplish that elimination was not so important as the certainty that it would be done.

7

Extermination

DURING the first quarter century following the American occupation of California in 1846, the state's Indian population declined from an estimated 150,000 in 1845 to less than 30,000 in 1870. Many Anglo-Americans, witnessing this rapid and dramatic depopulation, concluded that the California Indians were destined to extinction. Evidence was all about them: throughout the state, in areas where once thousands of Indians had lived, only a remnant remained.

Generally, whites regarded this process as inevitable. The extinction of the Indian population by disease and violent conflict was seen as an unavoidable consequence of contact between the two races. Furthermore, there were whites on the California frontier who had dedicated themselves to making extinction a certainty. They advocated and carried out a program of genocide that was popularly called "extermination," and in the process thousands of California Indians were killed.[1] Miners and ranchers temporarily banded together for the purpose of killing Indians. More permanently organized groups—the volunteer militia—ranged the hills and valleys of California killing hundreds of Indians. As late as 1870 frontier communities were raising subscriptions to support the volunteers and paid bounties for Indian scalps and Indian heads. How are we to account for this horrible business? Why did white Californians demand and attempt the extermination of the state's Indian people?

Behind the demands for extermination lay the abiding conviction, nurtured on countless other American frontiers, that Indians were obstacles to progress that somehow had to be removed. Anglo-Americans arriving in California were convinced that conflict between themselves and the Indians was inevitable and that, as long as Indians remained in an area, its development would be retarded or blocked. With the elimination of the native population mines could be worked in security, and acres of new land opened for cultivation and grazing.

The same conviction had led whites to demand the removal of Indians from the state or the concentration of Indians on reservations. The difference between the demands for removal and concentration and extermination was the degree of desperation of the whites. Extermination was clearly the last resort or "final solution." Advocates argued that extermination was necessitated by the failure of all other courses of policy. It was believed that Indian "depredations" on white property and lives could not be eliminated through such relatively pacific means as treaties, removal, or reservations. Only with the total extermination of the Indians could white security and prosperity be ensured.

As early as 1849 it seemed to many Americans that the fate of the California Indians was sealed.[2] In the aftermath of hostilities at Coloma in the spring of that year, E. Gould Buffum observed that the number of Indians in the mining regions had begun to decline: "Their *rancherias* are deserted, the graves of their ancesters are left to be desecrated by the white man's foot-print, and they have gone, —some of them to seek a home beyond the rugged crest of the Sierra Nevada, while others have emigrated to the valley of the Tulares, and the whole race is fast becoming extinct."[3] Thirty years later Horace Bell reported that the process was complete, that the Indians' destiny had been fulfilled. He recalled that, when the Americans had first arrived in California, the state had been "densely populated with Indians. You couldn't go amiss for them. Mountain and valley, forest and plain, were covered with Indians." Yet, after little more than a quarter century of American contact, the Indians were extinct: "At the present time, passing over the Tulare plains not a vestige is to be seen of its former thousands of Indian population. They are gone! all gone! It is sad to contemplate. . . . But what is the use of useless lamentation? The Indians are all gone and that is the end of it, and we can only hope that they have all gone to happy hunting grounds."[4]

It is a strange irony that the death and extinction of the California Indians were often described with poetic imagery. The "Diggers" had been denied any status as noble savages as long as they were numerous, but in their passing Anglo-Americans managed to see something picturesque.[5] "Men of the desert, forest and prairie! O how short is they destiny!" exclaimed an 1857 article in *Hutchings' Magazine:*

172

A solitary Indian horseman in the San Joaquin Valley in 1853.

Wherever thou plantest thy foot, the sure onward march of the white man treads on thy heel, crowding thee out. . . . Alas! what has civilization done for thee? The pathless waste, the stunted glade, the barren rock, the lonely shores, await the remnants of thy tribes; their solitudes groan for the last of thy race, and soon shall the hollow winds howl their last dirge over thee.[6]

The process of extinction was often cast in a metaphor in which "advancing white civilization" was likened to the sun and the "dying Indians" to evaporating moisture.[7] The image implied a natural and inevitable process; certainly the sun was relieved of any moral responsibility for the effects of its rays. For example, in 1850 the *San Francisco Alta California* described the destruction inflicted on the Indians as "unavoidable"; they must fade away "like a dissipating mist before the morning sun from the presence of the Saxon."[8] In the following year the *Alta* returned to that image in a discussion of the "certain

173

In 1857, *Hutchings' Illustrated California Magazine* published a series of illustrations of various national and racial types in California. Shown here is "The Indian." Note the cast-off white clothing draping the figures.

doom" of the Indians who were then engaged in hostilities in Mariposa County: "They must fade away before the Saxon race as the cloud in the west before the light and heat of a greater power."[9] And twenty years later California pioneer Harry Clark looked back on the settlement of the state by Americans and commented that in the process the Indians had "melted away before the scorching heat of immigration, as frost-work dissolves in the morning sun."[10]

When Californians asked themselves why the Indians were "dissipating," "fading," or "melting" away, they could suggest several reasons. It was commonly understood in California, as on other American frontiers, that contact between the two races often led to the "degradation" of the Indians. Rather than being elevated by exposure to white civilization, the Indians adopted its vices and contracted its ills—alcoholism, venereal disease, and other afflictions.[11] As Governor John B. Weller explained in 1859, the California Indians "are fast fading away, particularly those who are located in the vicinity of our towns and settlements. The vices of the white men, which they readily adopt, will soon remove them from amongst us."[12] Alcoholism was early recognized as a special and often fatal malady of Indians who remained in close contact with whites.[13] A coroner's jury in Los Angeles, possessed of a grim sense of humor, ruled in the case of an Indian found dead on the city's streets: "death from intoxication, or the visitation of God."[14] Likewise, venereal disease was regarded by whites as a special agent in the decline of the Indian population. Sandford Seymour, in his *Emigrant's Guide to the Gold Mines of Upper California* (1849), noted that the California Indians were "rapidly decreasing under the influence of malignant disease, among which is an hereditary syphlis [*sic*] which preys alike upon old and young."[15]

Sherburne F. Cook has estimated that 60 percent of the population decline in the years 1848 to 1870 was due to disease. Of this 60 percent he attributed about 15 percent to the effects of syphilis and the remaining 45 percent to various acute and epidemic diseases, including cholera, measles, smallpox, pneumonia, malaria, tuberculosis, and typhoid.[16] The effects of all those diseases were duly noted by contemporary Anglo-American observers.[17] Charles Pancoast, a Quaker forty-niner from Pennsylvania, described the decimation by cholera of the Indians along the Trinity River. A surviving member of the Hupa tribe showed Pancoast a large grove and explained that beneath each tree lay the bones of several Indians who had died from the disease.[18] Meanwhile, a visitor to southern California, Albert S.

175

Evans, confirmed that smallpox had devastated many of the villages of the Cahuillas in San Bernardino County. Passing through an afflicted village, Evans reported overhearing the cry of one desperate survivor of the disease: "'Lo, the curse of the white man is upon us!'"[19]

While disease was the primary cause of Indian depopulation, it was not the most dramatic. More striking were the violent deaths of Indians who fell victim to the campaigns of extermination being waged on the California frontier. A considerable part of the heat and light of the Saxon sun that caused Indians so inexorably to "melt" or "fade" away was generated by whites actively engaged in the process of killing Indians. Sherburne F. Cook has estimated that during the years 1848 to 1880 at least 4,500 California Indians were killed by whites.[20]

As the metaphor of the rising sun suggests, violent conflict between Indians and whites was generally regarded by the latter as inevitable.[21] "Whenever the white man has come in contact with the red," the *Alta California* observed in 1850, "discord has been engendered and blood has poured out like water." Such discord was "impossible to prevent," according to the *Alta*.[22] Newspapers on the frontier readily agreed. "Time and sad experience has fully established the impossibility of Indians and whites living peaceably together," the *Humboldt Times* concluded in 1858. In 1860 the same newspaper pronounced, "It is as impossible for the white man and the wild Indian to live together as it is to unite oil and water."[23] In 1862 the *Mendocino Herald* restated what by then must have been a very settled fact indeed: "It is a settled fact that the two races cannot live . . . in harmony together."[24]

To a surprising degree Anglo-Americans recognized that their own presence in the state posed a threat to the survival of the Indians and that, in order to survive, the natives had been forced to take actions threatening to whites.[25] It was apparent, for example, that placer mining had interrupted the salmon runs in the interior waterways; that deer and other game had been killed or frightened away by white settlers. While a substantial number of California Indians adapted to the changed conditions by becoming, sometimes under duress, a part of the new economy, others adapted quite differently. As their access to traditional food sources was interrupted, many natives appropriated the more readily available livestock and supplies brought in by whites.[26] Such dietary substitutions may have been necessary for the Indians' survival, but they were, of course, opposed by whites. Retaliatory raids were launched against Indian settlements—raids that often resulted in the death of Indians not involved in the initial "depredations." Motivated by revenge and a desire to eliminate the whites who threatened their survival, Indians responded by attacking isolated outposts of white settlement. In this cycle of hostilities each side viewed the other as the aggressor; each represented a threat to the other's continued prosperity or survival on the land.

An especially clear account of the process appeared in the *Alta California* in 1851. In the opinion of the *Alta,* the violent conflict between Indians and whites was a consequence of the futile attempts of the two races to occupy the same soil: "The settlement of the whites in the plains and vallies has necessarily driven the game from the grounds whence the Indians derived their supplies." Faced with "threatened starvation," they were forced to raid white settlements and storehouses for food. And "reasoning as they have ever reasoned since our ancestors came into their country, they very naturally have come to the conclusion that if they could exterminate the whites the old condition of things would return." Their attempts to act on this conclusion infuriated the whites: "The Saxon blood is up, and when it is so, like the rolling Mississippi, no slight levee will stay it within its channels."[27]

Everywhere the pattern seems to have been the same. As friendly relations devolved into hostilities, the Indians became obstacles blocking white access to areas desired for mineral or agricultural development. Extermination was embraced as one sure way of eliminating those obstacles. First the miners saw their success in the diggings endangered by Indian hostilities.[28] As early as April, 1849, following the Oregonians' attack at Coloma, the *Alta California* reported that the white miners were "becoming impressed with the belief that it will be absolutely necessary to exterminate the savages before they can labor much longer in the mines with security."[29] The events at Coloma foreshadowed hostilities throughout the mining regions. Whenever the miners advanced into new districts, the problem presented itself in similar terms.[30] A miner in the Auburn area in 1852 reported that mining activity there had been suspended by Indian hostilities. Indians had stolen or killed some mules and oxen and had attacked several miners: "We are kept in constant fear, especially nights, lest the red man should pierce us with arrows." To put an

177

end to the depredations, the miners organized themselves into several armed parties "determined to exterminate these merciless foes, or drive them far from us." After an attack on a nearby Southern Maidu village—in which thirty natives were killed outright and those wounded were knifed to death—the miners resumed their search for gold.[31] Meanwhile, in the southern mines the recorder of the Coso mining district in Owens Valley reported in 1862 that mining activities there had been abandoned on account of the Indians. Millions of dollars were at stake, and yet the miners were "compelled to abandon their mills and claims and fly for their lives. They can not proceed until a sufficient force is sent to chastise and drive out the hostile and thieving Indians."[32] In the spring of 1863 whites in the area commenced a war "to exterminate the whole race" so that they might resume their mining in security.[33] One miner explained that, even if they were compelled to leave their claims temporarily, they would soon be able to labor in peace "after the Indians are exterminated."[34]

Indian hostilities became even more burdensome as permanent settlements—farms, ranches, towns—began to replace the mining industry in the frontier areas. Wide expanses of land were needed for crops, grazing, timber harvesting. As in the mining districts, California Indians were perceived and described as obstacles to white development and settlement. One resident of Humboldt County complained in 1862 that Indian hostilities were responsible for the depopulation of towns and farms throughout the north: "The savages are paralizing [sic] our best interests, already they have destroyed all our grazing ground; and have driven the settlers from their homes; they have killed their stock, and daily commit outrages of the most terrible character."[35] Rather than progressing, the area was retrograding. Farming and commerce were decreasing, and the county was becoming deserted. "A savage & withering Indian War has blighted all the fair prospects. Driving out all the pastoral population. Burning and destroying fine homes and beautiful farms. . . . All kinds of business is pretty near at a standstill, on account of the terrible nature of the strugle [sic] going on around us."[36] Another settler claimed in 1863 that Indian hostilities had become so serious that a large stretch of valuable land in the northern counties might have to be entirely abandoned to the Indians. Farms, grazing lands, forests of valuable timber were all threatened by the Indians' presence.[37] Meanwhile, the *Humboldt Times* complained that for years hostile Indians had "been a serious drawback to all kinds of business, prevented the development of our agricultural resources and retarded the progress of our county generally."[38]

It was the task of the volunteer militia to eliminate that "serious drawback." As we have seen, the volunteers often aided in the work of concentrating the Indians on reservations while at the same time they waged a "war of extermination." It was not uncommon for their operations to produce an equal number of Indian homicides and candidates for the reservations.[39] The *Humboldt Times* was an enthusiastic supporter of the work of the militia companies and expressed the hope that they "will succeed in totally breaking up or exterminating the skulking bands of savages." Following the destruction of one inland tribelet by a volunteer unit called the Kibbe Guards, the *Times* reported that the land they had occupied contained excellent grazing lands and "will afford pasturage for from twenty to thirty thousand head of cattle."[40] William Kibbe claimed that his men had killed over two hundred California Indians in the process of opening up new lands for white settlement. His own view of the significance of this action was similar to that of the *Times:* "Some twenty-five families of this year's immigration have already taken up claims in these valleys. And this is the country which has been hitherto almost exclusively occupied by Indians."[41] In the spring of 1859 the *Times* praised the work of another group of volunteer Indian fighters who had succeeded in "clearing out" some Indians (probably Whilkuts) from the eastern section of the county: "The importance of this successful termination of the expedition to this section can scarcely be estimated. . . . The fine body of grazing and agricultural lands on upper Mad River can now be occupied without danger to life or stock; trade and travel can be resumed in safety, our Weaverville mail will arrive with regularity, and hunters can enjoy their sport without the fear of being waylaid by the skulking savage."[42]

During the 1850s the agricultural prospects of neighboring Siskiyou County were also clouded by Indian hostilities. Relations between the two races deteriorated in a series of bitter conflicts. Whites found their cattle and horses slaughtered, and several ranchers were killed. One early resident wrote in 1853 that the county offered some of the richest agricultural land in the state, "but few Emigrants have come into this country this year, on account of the trouble with the Indians."[43] In August it was reported that Indian hostilities had produced a general stagnation in the county's business. The two Siskiyou newspapers, the *Shasta Courier* and the *Yreka Herald,* both demanded "a war of extermination, death to all opposition, white men or Indians."[44] The *Yreka Herald* made its position unequivocally clear:

> Now that general hostilities against the Indians have commenced we hope that the Government will render such aid as will enable the citizens of the north to carry on a war of extermination until the last Redskin of these tribes has been killed. Extermination is no longer a question of time—the time has arrived, the work has commenced, and let the first man that says treaty or peace be regarded as a traitor.[45]

Farther south, in Mendocino County, hostile Indians posed a similar threat to white settlement, and a similar conclusion was reached. "The only remedy," a rancher near Ukiah announced in February, 1861, "is a war of extermination."[46]

Evidently, white advocacy of Indian extermination was based on the perception that Indians were obstacles to the white settlement and development of California. While that is an accurate statement of the white views, it fails to convey the desperation of the whites or the fevered intensity with which extermination was carried out. Extermination was not only the product of coldly rational calculations of the numbers of mines or acres of grazing land that would be opened up by the deaths of certain Indians. It was that, obviously, but it was also more. When we look closely at the immediate circumstances surrounding white assaults on Indians, we see premeditation dissolving into hysteria. Indians inspired a special terror: they were not just obstacles, like stones in a field, they were savages capable of committing the most atrocious and horrible acts.[47] Gripped by hysterical fears and the most powerful feelings of revenge, whites responded with their own horrible atrocities. This sequence of events was hardly unique to the California frontier. Similar situations have obtained elsewhere on Anglo-American frontiers and, for that matter, throughout human history. Fearing the savage without, if not within themselves, "civilized" men have destroyed "savages" with a special fury.

Illustrations of such fury are not hard to find in California.[48] William Jackson Barry, in his memoirs of California in the early 1850s, described the discovery of the remains of an emigrant train in northeastern California: "In the morning we soon arrived at the place, and a horrible sight was presented, the naked bodies of murdered men, women, and children lying about in all directions among the charred waggons [*sic*] and household goods. The Indians had stripped all the dead bodies before leaving. The sight was indescribably horrible, and made every man clench his hands and set his teeth hard with a half-muttered vow of vengeance." To carry out their vow, Barry and his companions launched a surprise attack on a nearby village of (according to Barry) over six hundred natives: "We immediately charged them, shooting down men, squaws, and papooses indiscriminately. The slaughter—for it could hardly be called a fight—was over in half an hour, and we reckoned that scarcely fifty out of the mob escaped; the rest were dispatched to the 'happy hunting grounds' without the slightest show of mercy, and the poor emigrants were fearfully avenged." Later Barry recounted the discovery of a farm in the Shasta area that had been attacked by the Pit River Indians (Achumawis). Once again, "a horrible sight was presented, dead and mutilated bodies lying in all directions among the wreck of their household goods." The whites quickly organized themselves "to go and exterminate the Indians" and "showed no quarter, but slaughtered all they fell in with, men, women, and children. It certainly seemed a savage retaliation, but there was no other course open, and it was long ere Shasta was again troubled with Indians."[49]

A similar cycle of "savage retaliation" occurred in Butte and Tehama counties in the following decade. One of the area's most active Indian fighters, Sim Moak, described a sequence of hostilities in the 1860s involving the Mill Creeks (Yahis). His story forms the background to Theodora Kroeber's powerful biography of the last of the Yahis, *Ishi in Two Worlds* (1961). In the summer of 1862 three white children were kidnapped, and two were killed by the Mill Creek Indians. The body of one of the slain children was discovered "scalped with his throat cut. Seventeen arrows had been shot in him and seven had gone partly through so that they had to be pulled out the opposite side."[50] The *Oroville Union,* after recounting in detail the kidnapping of the children and other "Indian outrages," expressed the conviction that now everyone would agree on the necessity of extermination: "What will those say to this catalogue of outrages, who are opposed to killing off these 'devils of the forest'?" The *Union* reported that a party of whites bent on destroying the Yahis "have already sent several to the 'big hunting ground.' May unbounded success attend them, and they never take one male prisoner."[51] The *Red Bluff Independent* agreed: "It is becoming evident that extermination of the red devils will have to be resorted to before the people . . . will be safe."[52]

Three years later a farm house in Butte County's Concow Valley was attacked, and its occupants—a young woman and an older man—were killed by Indians. According to Sim Moak's recollections: "They cut Miss Smith's throat, scalped her and mutilated her body in such a shocking manner it is unprintable. They then cut the old man's throat and scalped him." A party of fifteen whites, including Moak and led by Hiram Good and Robert Anderson, was organized to pursue the murderers. It was assumed that the same Indians from Mill Creek who had attacked the children in 1862 had also committed this more recent act. The party made their attack on a village of Yahis—an attack aimed at the total annihilation of the tribe. "It came like a thunderbolt out of a clear sky," Moak recalled. "The plan had been carried out with such discretion that they did not dream of a white man being within miles of them."[53]

Anderson later remembered that on that day the men from the Concow Valley "were intensely wrought up over the horrible atrocities practiced by the Indians on the white woman whom they killed, and I told them that they were at liberty to deal with the Indians as they saw fit."[54] Moak rendered in detail the actions taken by these men thus "intensely wrought up": "The Concow men who had seen how horribly Miss Smith had been mutilated could not get enough revenge, it seemed. I saw one of them, after an Indian was killed and scalped, cut his throat and twist his head half off and said, 'You will not kill any more women and children.'"[55]

As these grisly scenes indicate, the rhetoric (and the reality) of extermination was shot through with a sense of extreme desperation. Extermination was the only sure way to white security; nothing else would suffice. We should not conclude from this that in every case whites had actually tried other means of ending Indian hostilities and that they resorted to extermination only after careful consideration of the alternatives. As a matter of fact, demands for extermination antedated the negotiation of the first treaty or the establishment of the first reservation in California. Yet we may conclude that extermination was the result of a complete lack of faith in alternative methods. Whites on the California frontier came to believe that diplomatic and humane methods of eliminating hostile Indians simply would not work.[56] For example, a resident of Humboldt County in the 1850s argued that extermination at the hands of the volunteer militia "in regular old-fashioned, backwoods, bushwhacking style is the only way that Indian disturbances will ever be brought to a close in this section. Dilly-dallying, establishing Reservations and making treaties with such a set of murdering, house-burning, women-and-children butchering fiendish devils, will not answer the purpose. To be tolerant with them—treat them anything like human beings—will no longer suffice."[57] In 1866 the *Chico Courant* objected to further "temporizing" with the Indians. Any policy short of extermination would be inadequate: "It is a mercy to the red devils to exterminate them, and a saving of many white lives. Treaties are played out—there is only one kind of treaty that is effective—cold lead."[58] Seven years later, during the conflict known as the Modoc War, the *Yreka Journal* expressed the view that it was futile to attempt to negotiate with the Indians or place them on reservations. "Those who were at first favorable to peace . . . ," the *Journal* reported, "are becoming more eager to have the fight go on towards extermination, as there is no safety in trusting such treacherous devils anywhere, a fact we have always believed from the very commencement of hostilities."[59]

The destruction of the Indians still did not progress without protests from whites. The actions of the volunteer militia were denounced; the Indian fighters were vilified and censured. Criticism was strongest in urban areas, such as San Francisco and Sacramento, but occurred throughout the state. One of the best-known protests to the slaughter of California Indians came from the pen of young Bret Harte. In 1860, while Harte was serving briefly as substitute editor of the *Northern Californian Union* in Arcata, local whites launched a brutal attack on a settlement of Indians on Humboldt Bay. Harte denounced the action in the *Californian* as an "indiscriminate massacre" and condemned the perpetrators. His courageous protest stirred considerable resentment against him, and within a month he departed Humboldt County.[60]

While Harte's objection was based on humanitarian principles, others argued that the rise of hostilities between whites and Indians threatened to end white access to Indian labor.[61] In the hysteria of revenge killings "tame" as well as "wild" Indians often fell victim to extermination.[62] Here again we see the familiar conflict in Californian attitudes toward the Indians. Whites who perceived the Indians as a useful class of laborers objected to the actions of whites who regarded the Indians only as obstacles to be eliminated. We have seen, for example, that in the aftermath of the hostilities at Coloma in 1849, Theodore T. Johnson and others objected that "wars of extermination" and "indiscriminate revenge" had sacrificed the system of Indian labor exploitation in the mines. Later, in March, 1850, several employers of Indian labor in the Napa Valley organized to restrain a group of whites bent on exterminating the local Indians in retaliation for the death of two settlers. The employers eventually prevailed, but only after several Indians had been slain.[63] During the hostilities in Butte County in the early 1860s John Bidwell objected to the demand for extermination. Bidwell, who still employed large numbers of Indian workers, pled successfully that his own Indians should be spared from death.[64]

Perhaps the most important aspect of the protest to extermination was what it condoned: objections were more often raised to the method of extermination than to extermination itself. Critics were careful not to question the inevitability of conflict between the two races, nor even the proposed extinction of the Indians. All that was asked was that the process be carried out in a "civilized" fashion. The *Alta California,* for example, in 1860 denounced a particularly ruthless campaign by a northern California militia company, but carefully couched its protest so that it did not question the inevitability, or even the basic necessity, of the larger process:

> We are not among those who entertain so warm a degree of sympathy for the Indians as to hold that they should be suffered to occupy the country at the expense of sacrificing its settlement. It is a too well established fact that as civilization advances the aboriginal races must go down before its tread, the contact of the two races always resulting in the gradual extermination of the red man. But holding this to be a necessary sequence following in the train of the progress of civilization, we at the same time . . . fail to recognize any existing right on the part of our race, to become savages in turn, and perform acts of barbarity precisely similar to those for which it is found necessary to wage war against the red man.
>
> This horrible massacre must not be justified by the incontrovertible rule by which the Indians are made to succumb before the advance of civilized races. The fact that in the contact of the two races, the one must eventually fade away before the other and become extinct, is no plea in justification of the slaughter of women and children in the cold-blooded and heartless manner which characterized [this] massacre.[65]

The *Alta* recognized that, if new lands were to be developed, "a war of extermination seems to be the only course of policy that can be pursued": "As a matter of course, civilization must advance and the savage must give way before it. The only question to be considered is, what is the most expeditious, economical and humane method of disposing of the difficulty?"[66] At the heart of the *Alta*'s protest lay an unresolved dilemma. In effect, the newspaper's editors were calling for a war of extermination that was free of "acts of barbarity" and could be conducted with "humane methods."

The *Alta*'s dilemma was shared by other Californians who spoke out against the extermination policy.[67] State Senator Robert Kirkpatrick, in a debate over a proposal that the state assume the expenses of the volunteer militia, contended that the government should have nothing to do with these men and their "diabolical" actions: "I would rather my right arm should fall from its socket than vote one dollar to the payment of men who had disgraced the banners of a Christian state—who had sunk themselves to a level with the tigers that prowl in the jungles of Africa." And yet Senator Kirkpatrick tempered his objections by concluding: "I am not one of those who entertain a morbid sympathy as to the fate of the Indian tribes, or with respect to the inevitable destiny which awaits them. They are destined to extermination, no doubt; but sir, if war is necessary to be waged against them, it should be conducted on our part as befits a civilized people."[68] Senator Kirkpatrick, like the *Alta*, expected a war of extermination to be waged in a "civilized" way.

It is also important to realize that the work of extermination, though denounced as cruel and barbarous, was supported by public policy. On the local level municipal governments offered bounties for Indian heads or scalps. Shasta City, for example, in 1855 offered five dollars for every Indian head presented at city headquarters. Subsequently, one resident reported that he saw men bringing to town several mules laden with eight to twelve Indian heads. A community near Marysville in 1859 paid bounties that were collected by public subscription "for every scalp or some other satisfactory evidence" that an Indian had been killed. Plans were made in Tehama County in 1861 to raise a fund "to be disbursed in payment of Indian scalps," and two years later the citizens of Honey Lake paid twenty-five cents apiece for Indian scalps.[69]

In addition to such local remuneration, men engaged in Indian extermination as members of the various volunteer militia were permitted to submit claims on the state treasury for their expenses. The claims became the subject of extended public debate, but eventually the state legislature honored most of them. In 1851 and 1852 the legislature authorized payment of claims totaling over $1 million, and in 1857 it issued bonds for more than $400,000 to pay the expenses of volunteers engaged in "the suppression of Indian hostilities." Eventually the federal government, while disallowing the most

185

obviously exaggerated claims, reimbursed the state for these expenditures. Thus the murder of Indians on the California frontier was legalized and publicly subsidized.[70] Although the work of extermination was condemned by some California whites, the process went forward with the financial support of local, state, and federal governments.

The American image of the California Indians, fully rounded and complete, was one of men and women immensely different from their white observers, different in ways that whites invariably interpreted as evidence of extreme inferiority or primitiveness. In order to understand the attempt to exterminate the California Indians, we must understand this sense of difference and, more especially, the utter contempt with which Anglo-Americans often regarded the native people. The California Indians, when perceived as obstacles, could be eliminated by savage means because whites regarded them as creatures of little worth. The Indians' inferiority seemed so marked that whites questioned their very humanity. Their physical appearance and conduct seemed so revolting that many whites found it impossible to regret their passing. In California extermination meant the elimination of peoples whose appearance and ways of life evoked a range of emotion bounded by contempt and repulsion. To the white Californians the removing of the "obstacles" indeed meant removing objects, not people.

As many before them had done, Anglo-Americans in California after 1846 frequently compared the local Indians to others that they had encountered elsewhere on the continent. In such comparisons the California natives were nearly always ranked at the bottom.[71] Some observers extended the comparison to include aboriginal people around the world, and here too the California Indians were ranked among the most primitive of societies.[72] One 1849 guide to California, for example, noted that the state's natives "are classed by all who have had an opportunity of studying their character and dispositions, amongst the Hottentots, Patagonians, and the savages of Australia, as the lowest races of mankind."[73] There was even speculation that the California natives should be considered more primitive than any other people. Titus Cronise, in his *Natural Wealth of California* (1868), reported that the California Indians were generally ranked "at the very foot in the scale of humanity": they "were in-

186

ferior in intelligence to the Bosjesmen of Africa, and worse in their habits than the disgusting aborigines of Australia."[74]

Evidence of the inferiority of the California Indians was often assumed to be self-evident. When whites did describe what it was about these people that led them to conclude that they were very primitive, they focused on such things as the quality of Indian art, clothing, housing, religion, and diet. It was frequently remarked, for example, that the California Indians lacked any tradition of artistic or ornamental achievement, though the California tribes, in fact, did manufacture textiles in which design and ornamentation were important aspects of the manufacturing process.[75] Charles Brace explained in 1869 that one of the reasons he classified the "Root Diggers of California" among "the most wretched tribes of man on earth" was their complete "want of inventiveness." He claimed that they created neither monuments nor mounds; nor art, architecture, or painting; nor even pottery, images, or ornaments "except the very rudest." He was, of course, in error. California tribes did produce a variety of plastic and pictorial art.[76] One is struck by the extraordinary ignorance of these early observers, as well as the over-riding tone of their contempt.

As something of an exception in their supposedly impoverished cultures, the California Indians' basketry was singled out for special consideration.[77] One visitor from New Jersey, who regarded the Maidus whom she encountered along the Feather River as "miserably brutish and degraded," remarked that their baskets were "woven with a neatness which is absolutely marvelous, when one considers that they are the handiwork of such degraded wretches." Anthropologist Albert B. Elsasser has observed, "Among the textile arts of native California, basketry is beyond any question the most highly developed, and compared with that of other regions of North America, the basketry of California Indians must be judged to be of the highest quality."[78]

During the mild dry season clothing was often unnecessary for the California tribes, but when appropriate many garments—robes, capes, aprons, hats, and footgear—were manufactured and used. Nevertheless, both the costumes and the nudity of the California tribes seemed to many white observers to be further evidence of their primitiveness.[79] The *San Francisco Bulletin*, for example, argued in 1857 that the near nudity of the California Indians clearly demonstrated that they had "less intellect than the Indians generally inhabiting the country east of the Rocky Mountains."[80] When the Indians began to clothe themselves in the fashion of their white critics, they became the subject of ridicule. Instead of being regarded as a positive accomplishment, the change of costume was seen as further evidence of the Indians' inferiority. Images of Indian men and women in cast-off white garments frequently appear as a kind of comic relief in many California narratives.[81]

Observers also commented on the primitive nature of the California Indians' shelters. Like their clothing, housing was invariably described as minimal or nonexistent.[82] "I have passed through many of their villages," reported one early observer. "They make an appearance precisely like a number of common coal-pits for manufacturing charcoal, having a small vent or opening on one side for a door. . . . their construction displays less mechanical genius than the habitations of the beaver, or even the muskrat."[83] Other observers described native dwellings as mere "heaps of earth" and reported that many California Indians simply lived in "holes in the earth, or crevices in the rocks."[84] Reflecting a tradition of belief that can be traced back at least to the reports of John C. Frémont, Anglo-Americans during the gold rush professed to believe that the "Diggers" not only lived in holes in the ground but also hibernated there during the winter months.[85] Samuel Upham, following a tour among the California tribes in 1849, reported that during the winter the "Digger . . . burrows in the earth like a prairie dog, and emerges from his den in the spring as fat as a grizzly."[86]

When whites had the opportunity to observe the nonmaterial aspects of the Indians' way of life, they described them with the same contempt that marked their descriptions of the more obvious material culture. For example, the possibility of religious belief on the part of the Indians was denied altogether, or else their beliefs were described as barbarous. The *Annals of San Francisco* (1855) reported that the California Indians "appear to have had little or no notion of religion, although they seem to have had a kind of sorcerers among them, who amused or terrified themselves and their patients with sundry superstitious observances." The authors of the *Annals* believed that the Indians had no conception of the supernatural; but then, the whites asked, how could they when their chief characteristics were "stupidity and insensibility, want of knowledge and reflection, inconstancy, impetuosity, and blindness of appetite"?[87] The mortuary customs of the California Indians seemed an equally distasteful part of native life.[88] Alfred T. Jackson, a forty-niner from

A sketch by H. B. Brown in 1852 of houses and acorn granaries in the Sacramento Valley. The location is probably in Patwin territory.

Connecticut, attended the funeral of a Maidu "buck" in Nevada County in 1850 and recorded in his diary a detailed account of the body being placed on a pyre and engulfed in flames. "What heathens they are," he exclaimed, "to dispose of their dead in such a barbarous way instead of burying them decently in the ground!"[89] The mourning practices of the Indians struck whites as not only "heathenish" and "barbarous" but also filthy.[90] An immigrant in Plumas County recorded in his diary in 1853 an encounter with an old woman in mourning who, in traditional Maidu fashion, had blackened part of her face and covered her short-cropped hair with pitch. "Washing & cleanliness," the Argonaut concluded, "is about unknown to them."[91]

In assessing the quality of Indian life in California, the standard most often applied by Anglo-Americans was that of diet: societies that cultivated the soil were superior to hunting societies. By this standard the California native ranked as the most primitive of people, for the "Diggers" often were seen, incorrectly, as neither farmers nor hunters.[92] They were believed to subsist on the crudest and simplest of diets—roots, acorns, berries, nuts, insects. Whites recognized that the Indians did hunt small game and fish, but most descriptions of their diet focused on these other, more "primitive" foods.[93] T. Butler King, for example, in his official report on conditions in California in 1850, described the state's Indians as "the lowest grade of human beings. They live chiefly on acorns, roots, insects, and the kernel of the pine burr; occasionally they catch fish and game. They use the bow and arrow, but are said to be too lazy and effeminate to make successful hunters. They do not appear to have the slightest inclination to cultivate the soil, nor do they attempt it."[94]

It was no great surprise that the California Indians were not farmers—Anglo-Americans were surprised when they encountered native societies that were agricultural—but it was considered extraordinary that they were not hunters. As the statement by King suggests, whites usually explained this unusual circumstance as the result of a lack of spirit or energy or enterprise on the part of the Indians.[95] Thus the Indians' "failure" to become hunters not only demonstrated their primitiveness, but also was supposed to reveal a flaw in character. The *San Francisco Bulletin*, for example, remarked that the California Indians were "less ingenious in catching and killing game" than other natives on the continent: "Instead of being brave and expert in the use of weapons and cunning in trapping

"An Indian Binding the Corpse for Burning or Burial." From *Hutchings'
Illustrated California Magazine* in 1859.

game, they are timid and idiotic, feeding on roots, snakes and insects, and on the grasses of the fields like beasts."[96] Besides being
excessively judgmental, these early observers of Indian diet were
again in error. Hunting was a common practice among California
Indians, and many tribes had great skill in the use of snares, traps,
decoys, and bows. Agriculture, although rare in California, was practiced by the Chemehuevis, Mohaves, and Cahuillas.

The diet of California tribes provoked expressions not only of
contempt but also of revulsion. Whites considered the Indians' foods
at best indiscriminate and unpalatable and at worst filthy and nause-
ating. For example, the staple in the diet of many California tribes
was the acorn, and the whites who had an opportunity to sample
acorn bread or cereal usually described it as unappetizing.[97] After
an attack on a Central Miwok village in 1850 a group of whites

"Indians Burning their Dead," a scene from an 1862 letter sheet published by James Mason Hutchings, drawn by Charles Nahl.

discovered a quantity of bread that they believed had been made from acorns and pine nuts. "This bread we tried to eat," one of the raiders reported, "but found it exceedingly disgusting to the palate; bitter, and with a flavor that was nauseous in the extreme."[98] Another observer, Austin Clark, described in detail the hulling, grinding, and cooking of the acorns. He imagined that the final product might not be unpalatable, but said that in its preparation much "filth and dirt" had accumulated. "I never tasted this food," he confessed.[99]

Clark's objection to "filth and dirt" in the Indians' food is revealing because the Indians, in fact, took great care to prevent the accumulation of sand or other foreign matter in acorn meal. Both the Indian methods of food preparation and the very substance of their diets often seemed to whites to be unclean. As one observer put it, the California Indians ate "dirty-looking victuals."[100] They ate foods that whites considered unfit for human consumption.[101] "Everything that lives, everything that breathes," wrote an observer in 1849, "is good to the Indians' stomach: toads, frogs, grasshoppers, moles, mice, rattlesnakes or other kinds of snakes; they find nothing in nature unworthy of their stomachs."[102] Even when Indians ate beef or venison, whites emphasized the grotesque in describing their diets.[103] Indians were credited with a predilection for raw, uncooked meat and for the "unclean" internal organs. "The Indians lived like Swine," one forty-niner commented, "they ate raw tripe and their filth and gluttony were beyond description."[104] John Perry's account of his *Thrilling Adventures* (1858) included a description of a group of natives along the Sacramento River butchering a deer: "These Indians scraped up the clotted blood in their hands and swallowed it as fast as a Dutchman would sour milk and while some were engaged with the blood, others were engaged in tearing the innards to pieces, each endeavoring to get the most, at the same time drawing them through their fingers and devouring them like dogs."[105]

California Indians who survived at the fringe of white settlements were often forced to subsist on whatever refuse they found in the streets.[106] The diet of these impoverished and truly pitiable people was, of course, filthy and repulsive to whites.[107] Hinton Rowan Helper included the diet of the "filthy and abominable" California Indians among the more unpleasant realities in his version of *The Land of Gold: Reality Versus Fiction* (1855). "A worse set of vagabonds cannot be found bearing the human form," he wrote: "Their chief characteristics are indolence and gluttony. Partially wrapped

"Gathering Acorns," another scene from the Hutchings' 1862 letter sheet drawn by Charles Nahl. The women in the background are digging for roots and handling what appears to be a frog.

in filthy rags, with their persons unwashed, hair uncombed and swarming with vermin, they may be seen loitering about the kitchens and slaughter-houses waiting to seize upon and devour like hungry wolves such offal or garbage as may be thrown to them."[108] Readers familiar with the story of Ishi will recall that his emergence in 1911 from the long concealment came at the corral of a slaughterhouse near Oroville. If this emaciated last survivor of the Yahis was looking there for food, he was acting in a well-established tradition of obtaining sustenance.

Much of the white Californian's aversion to the Indians can be attributed to two closely related assumptions: one, that the California Indians were especially dirty people and, two, that they were unusually ugly and dark-skinned. The identification of dirt with despised people of dark complexion is, of course, not unique to California. The association can be traced to the earliest contacts between whites and members of other races. It may have its origins deep in the recesses of the unconscious.[109] According to longstanding Anglo-American tradition, cleanliness as a virtue was practically co-equal with godliness; by definition things clean were superior to things unclean. And everything about the California "Diggers" seemed dirty. They not only ate "dirty victuals," they lived in "heaps of earth" and mourned their dead by covering themselves with black pitch. The name "Digger" itself—whether it derived from the Indians' alleged burrowing under the ground or from their digging and eating roots—expressed this identification with dirt. The Indians of California were thus ranked not only among the most primitive of people but also among the dirtiest.[110] "Of all the aborigines that are known to travellers within the limits of the western continent," one American began in his discussion of the California natives, "the Digger Indians are certainly the most filthy and abominable."[111] It mattered little which California tribes were being described; wherever travellers encountered the natives they seemed obsessed with their uncleanliness.[112] In the southern mines, for example, Charles Loring Brace considered the Miwoks to be "all disgustingly dirty," while a miner in the northern diggings condemned a village of Maidus as "the dirtiest lot of human beings on earth."[113]

In physical appearance California Indians were the reverse image of the Anglo-American ideal of beauty. In physique, physiognomy, hair, and complexion they were judged exceedingly ugly by white observers.[114] Ida Pfeiffer, for example, described the Maidus around Marysville as "actually uglier" than the Malays of Southeast Asia:

"Their growth is short and stunted; they have short, thick necks and clumsy heads; the forehead is low, the nose flat with broad nostrils, the eyes very narrow and showing no intelligence, the cheek bones prominent, and the mouth large."[115] George Payson, in his *Golden Dreams and Leaden Realities* (1853), considered the California Indians to be so ugly that they appeared deformed: "Their monstrous heads, covered with a thick thatch of long black hair, and mounted on dwarfish bodies and distorted limbs, gave them a peculiarly inhuman and impish aspect."[116]

Although whites might have admiration for the physical appearance of other North American Indians, they found little to admire in California. John Woodhouse Audubon, son of the famous naturalist, seemed genuinely disappointed that the Indians of California were such uninspiring subjects for portraiture. The Miwoks along the Stanislaus River, he noted in his journal, were "not as handsome as the Indians of the east, or even the Yumas, Pimos [*sic*], or the Maricopas on the Gila."[117] In contrast, James Borthwick was so struck by the ugliness of a Southern Maidu woman who visited his cabin near Placerville that he was inspired to attempt a portrait of her: "She was such a particularly ugly specimen of human nature, that I made her sit down, and proceeded to take a sketch of her."[118]

Perhaps the most conspicuous feature in the appearance of the California tribes was the color of their skin. Rather than the tawny red color usually associated with North American Indians, the Californians were described as dark brown or black.[119] Their color was such a salient feature that it bound together the other associations of primitiveness, dirtiness, and ugliness in the whites' minds. One forty-niner, for example, in the midst of his account of the inferior intelligence and animal-like nature of the Californian Indians, commented that the term "redskin" was most inappropriate for them, saying, "Their true color is close to a chocolate-brown."[120] Inevitably their skin color inspired comparisons of the California tribes with Negroes. "Their complexion is a dark mahogany," Theodore Johnson noted in 1850, "or often nearly black, their faces round or square, with features approximating nearer to the African than the Indian."[121] William Redmond Ryan, upon landing in Monterey in 1848, likewise was struck by the unusual complexion of the California natives. These Indians, Ryan reported, "are the most hideous-looking creatures that it is possible to imagine. They are very dark, indeed I may almost say black, with a slight tinge of copper colour;

the features are, in all other respects, as purely African in their cast, the nose being large and flat, the cheek-bones salient, the lips thick and wide, and the forehead as low as is consistent with a fair supposition of a brain, to which their pretentions are miserably small." One of Ryan's companions went so far as to address an Indian whom he was preparing to shoot as "you ugly-looking naygur."[122]

Little elaboration is necessary to suggest the significance of skin color in the attitudes of Anglo-Americans. The dark complexion of the California Indians was their badge of inferiority. It marked them as inferior not only to whites but also to other "redskins." In the minds of Anglo-American observers it identified them with dirt and made their appearance revolting and hideous. It also prevented them from being included among the "noble savages." Since the eighteenth century, European and, less commonly, Anglo-American writers had been describing American Indians as a race of native nobility, and by 1848 the noble savage had become a stock figure in literature. Anglo-Americans explicitly and consistently denied, however, that the California Indians were in any sense noble.[123]

The denial of nobility to these dark-skinned tribes is an interesting confirmation of Winthrop Jordan's argument that the appearance of blacks, not just their enslavement, barred them from acceptance by whites as noble savages. Outside of California, Indian skin color and physiognomy were not matters of primary concern; traditionally, among Anglo-Americans such characteristics were peculiarly the Negroes' burden. As Jordan has pointed out, white observers generally belittled the importance of Indians' complexions and described them as lighter than they were in fact.[124] In California, however, complexion was a major concern, and the distinction between black men and red was blurred.

The line between red and black, however, was not the only distinction that was blurred in California. As on other American frontiers, whites commonly described the California Indians as "beastly" or "brutish" while recognizing that they really were human beings. In California, however, the Indians were considered so primitive (or "degraded" or "wretched") that some whites regarded them very nearly as beasts.[125] California whites used animal metaphors to suggest the status of the Indians and to register their own sense of extreme distance or difference from the people that they described. Many elements of the native cultures seemed to them to reveal a close affinity between the Indians and the animals of the forests or fields. Native housing, we recall, struck Franklin Langworthy as inferior to that of the beaver or muskrat. Indian dancing seemed to him "a most senseless and stupid entertainment, less intellectual in its character than the gambols of quadrupeds."[126] Samuel Upham compared the Indians' subterranean houses to the burrows of prairie dogs and their imagined hibernation to that of a grizzly bear.[127] Another observer, discussing the "nearly nude women" of aboriginal California, speculated, "They may even have a periodical mating season, like most animals."[128] The *San Francisco Chronicle* commented that the Indians' diet consisted of eating "roots, snakes and insects, and the grasses of the fields like beasts."[129] More than one white Californian described Indians "grazing" in fields like cattle.[130] They also were described as eating "like pigs" when they ate acorn meal and as eating "like dogs" or "like hungry wolves" when they ate meat.[131]

Predictably, whites often compared California Indians to creatures that they regarded as especially repulsive. Pigs were a favorite subject of comparison.[132] The California Indians were said to spend their nights "piled one on top of another to keep each other warm like the animals in a pigsty." Another observer stated that they lived "like swine" and looked "like hogs."[133] Perhaps the least flattering comparisons were those made to reptiles. "There were three or four Indians lying in the hut," one forty-niner recalled of his visit to a California village, "coiled up together like a parcel of snakes. They were a naked, filthy, degraded set, and we turned away disgusted."[134] One of the most revealing reptilian metaphors was offered by Ernest de Massey in his discussion of California Indian women. He was struck by these women, who wore "scarcely more than the proverbial fig-leaf," and yet he considered their nudity neither beautiful nor appealing: "Every time I touched their rough, cold, oily skin I had a feeling of repulsion just as if I had put my hand on a toad, tortoise, or huge lizard."[135]

Most commonly, whites likened the California Indians to the beasts that most resemble man, the simians.[136] A traveler along the Mariposa River in 1851 described a group of Southern Miwoks as the most "wretched set" of human beings that he had ever seen. "Two of them," he added, "look as if they had exchanged their humanity with baboons; they are scarcely a shade removed therefrom."[137] Theodore Johnson, while describing the Southern Maidus around Coloma, commented, "Many of them were quite naked, and the men and boys especially, looked more like orang-outangs than human beings."[138] The simian metaphor suggested more than just

198

"The Diggers at Home," an engraving published in 1864 as an illustration for an article by J. Ross Browne.

outward appearance. John Woodhouse Audubon, for instance, extended the comparison to include intellectual qualities. In the spring of 1850, while on the North Fork of the Stanislaus River, Audubon recorded in his journal a description of a Miwok child: "I saw a papoose, too small to walk, with a stone in his hand half as big as his head, shelling out the nuts of the pinecone, cracking and eating them with the judgment of a monkey, and looking very much like one."[139] Samuel Upham believed that the diet of the "Digger Indians" placed them among the beasts: "The Digger eats very little animal food. Like his brother, the gorilla, he is a vegeterian."[140]

Some white observers suggested that, because the California Indians were so different from themselves and so nearly like beasts, they were perhaps an intermediary race or species between man and the lower orders of creation.[141] A correspondent to a San Francisco newspaper in 1848 described the Indians as a "degraded and brutish class . . . the nearest link, of the sort, to the quadrupeds of any on the continent of North America."[142] Later recollections of life in California, written after 1859, when Darwin published the theories of natural selection and the descent of man, continued to describe the California Indians as a "link" to the lower orders. Austin Clark, for example, concluded his recollections of the California Indians by observing: "Taken together, they were the most worthless and miserable set of beings I ever saw, and on the principle of evolution, could not have been far from the 'connecting link' our scientists talk so much about."[143] Meanwhile, Charles Loring Brace found it particularly suggestive that the skulls of the California Indians had an enlarged cerebellum "making the animal organs prominent." Furthermore he said, "It is remarkable that this—one of the lowest tribes on earth—has a widespread tradition of its derivation from animals."[144]

It is hard to overestimate the importance of these images. Some may say that those metaphors of pigs and snakes and apes were nothing more than casual references intended as passing remarks. Although sometimes that may have been the case, the evidence indicates a widely held view that the California Indians—in a variety of specific ways—were like beasts. With those images in mind, the full, horrible significance of the demand for the extermination of the California Indians can be understood. We can appreciate the literal meaning of the statement in a Humboldt County newspaper in 1851 that it was impossible to treat the California Indians "anything like human beings"; or the conviction of one northern California resident in 1853 that "we can never rest in security until the red skins are treated like the other wild beasts of the forest"; or the demand by a Yreka newspaper in 1873 that "every Modoc be treated the same as wild animals."[145] When we read a forty-niner's comment that the whites in California hunted the Indians "as they would wild beasts" and shot them "with as much nonchalance as though they were squirrels," we must hesitate before dismissing his words as hyperbole.[146]

As we have seen, from the moment of first contact the California tribes were regarded by white observers as exceedingly primitive. Their primitiveness was the subject of remarks and speculation among the earliest observers along the coast in the late eighteenth and early nineteenth centuries. Those who came to regard the Indians as victims of Hispanic mistreatment also readily acknowledged that the Indians were utterly primitive. Later, as the Indians came to be seen by the Americans as a useful class of laborers, the quality of extreme primitiveness was hardly less emphasized. The whites believed that, because they were "primitive" and "docile," they could more easily be subjugated and put to useful labor. Finally, the Indians' primitiveness fueled the demands for their extermination as damnable obstacles to white progress. Who could regret the passing of such supposedly beastly and revolting creatures?

The reduction of the Indians of California to the level of beasts was a necessary precondition to their extermination. In the eyes of their Anglo-American beholders the California tribes were the most primitive aborigines in North America if not the entire world. Whites could rarely find a single aspect of their material or nonmaterial cultures to admire. Their housing and clothing were insignificant; their diet and physical appearance abominable. Rather than admiration, the California Indians evoked expressions of contempt and repulsion. They seemed so primitive and degraded that they were more like animals than men. This radical loss of humanity made the prospect of Indian extermination and extinction palatable and even highly desirable, as if with their extermination California would be purified and cleansed of a set of degraded and repulsive creatures. It is by understanding how Anglo-Americans perceived the California Indians' lives that we most clearly, unmistakably, see the Indians' deaths.

Epilogue

IN the very beginning all was water. The sky, as far as one could see, was clear. It did not have any stars, or clouds, or anything in it. Then one day a cloud formed in it, grew lumpy, and turned into Coyote. Next a fog arose, grew lumpy, and became Silver Fox. They became persons.

They both looked down at the world, which was entirely of water, and thought how nice it would be to have a canoe, and a canoe appeared on the water.

"Let's stay here. Let's make it our home," they said to one another.

They floated about for many years and the canoe became old and mossy. They grew very weary of this.

"Do go and lie down," said Silver Fox to Coyote one day.

While Coyote slept Silver Fox combed his hair and saved the combings. When there were many of these combings Silver Fox rolled them in his hands, stretched them out, and flattened them between his hands. Then he laid them upon the water and spread them out until they covered all the surface of the water. This became the earth. Silver Fox looked at it and thought of trees, of shrubs, and rocks, and they were there.

Then he cried to Coyote: "Wake up! We are going to sink."

Coyote woke and looked up. He saw the trees and heard crickets. "Where are we," he asked; "What place is this we have come to?"

"I don't know," Silver Fox replied. "We are just here. We floated up to the shore." But Silver Fox was not telling the truth, for he knew, since he it was who had made the world. He did not want Coyote to know that the world was his creation.

"What shall we do?" Silver Fox asked. "Here is solid ground. I am going ashore, and am going to live here."

So they landed and built a house and lived in it.

After a time they thought about making people. They made little sticks of serviceberry, and thrust them all about in the ceiling of the house. By and by all became people of different sorts, with the names of birds, animals, and fishes.—Achumawi Creation Myth in *California Indian Nights Entertainments: Stories of the Creation of the World, of Man, of the Sun, of Thunder, etc.*, compiled by Edward Winslow Gifford and Gwendolyn Harris Block

Epilogue

THE early 1870s were a watershed in the history of American attitudes toward the California Indians. After 1873 the Indians were no longer perceived by whites as serious threats to the prosperity and development of the state. They presented some minor irritations later, but for the most part their days as "obstacles" were over. The tribal remnants still alive became fit subjects for study by scientists and for the charity of philanthropists.

In the early 1870s California's first true ethnologist, Stephen Powers, published an important series of articles in the *Overland Monthly* on the California tribes. The series marked the beginning of scientific study of the state's Indians, for, although the articles were marred by crude generalizations and many inaccuracies, their systematic descriptions and sympathetic tone distinguished them from previous works. "It has been the melancholy fate of the California Indians," observed Powers in 1872, "to be at once the most foully vilified and least understood":

"Men damn what they do not understand." To have once been the possessors of the most fair and sunny empire ever conquered by the Anglo-Saxon, and to have had it wrenched out of their grip with the most shameless violence; to have been once probably the happiest, and afterward reduced to the most miserable and piteous ruin, of all our American aborigines! Pity for the California Indian that his purple-tinted mountains were filled with dust of gold, and that his green and shining valleys, lying rich and mellow to the sun, were pregnant with so large possibilities of wheat! Pity for the blotched and sweaty toad, "ugly and venomous," that he "wears yet a precious jewel on his head!" Fatal for him was the unconscious guardianship of these apples of Hesperides; and in what proportion the gold of his placers was beautiful in the eyes of the White Man, in that proportion was he the dragon, odious to look upon, and worthy of death.[1]

205

Here Powers gave eloquent, almost poetic expression to the thesis that the American image of the California tribes was more a reflection of the observers than the observed. The expanded version of his articles, Powers's *Tribes of California* (1877), remained the most important volume on the subject until Alfred L. Kroeber's *Handbook of the Indians of California* was published by the Smithsonian Institution in 1925.[2]

Coincident with the publication of Powers's articles, there occurred in northern California the last outbreak of violent hostilities between whites and the California Indians, the so-called Modoc War. In the early 1860s the Modocs had been removed to a reservation in southern Oregon, but conditions there had forced many to move back to their ancestral territory in California. During the winter of 1872–73 about 150 Modocs, who had refused to return to the reservation, battled nearly 1,000 soldiers in the desolate lava beds of eastern Siskiyou County. The *Yreka Journal* testified that local whites were "eager to have the fight go on towards extermination, as there is no safety in trusting such treacherous devils anywhere."[3] Although the Modocs put up a heroic fight against overwhelming odds, ultimately they were dislodged, and many were transported to Oklahoma as prisoners of war. After their defeat several of the Modoc leaders were executed, and, symbolic of the new age, their heads were sent to the Smithsonian for "scientific" investigation.[4]

During the late 1870s and early 1880s humanitarians sympathetic to the plight of the American Indians began to take notice of the California tribes. Their interest was stimulated in large part by the work of Helen Hunt Jackson, who, after the publication of *A Century of Dishonor* in 1881, devoted her attention to the Indians of southern California. In 1883, Jackson was the coauthor of an important but neglected report for the United States Department of the Interior on the condition of California's Mission Indians. She reached a far wider audience the following year with her romantic novel *Ramona*, a book she intended to be the *Uncle Tom's Cabin* of Indian reform. By contrasting the supposed loving-kindness of the old Spanish missionaries with the rapacity of the Anglo-American interlopers, Jackson hoped to arouse sympathy for the dispossessed and mistreated descendants of the mission neophytes.

This newfound interest in the California Indians was also manifest in several organizations of "friends of the Indian." The founding of the national Indian Rights Association in 1882 was paralleled by the organization of the Sequoya League in 1901 by Los Angeles journalist

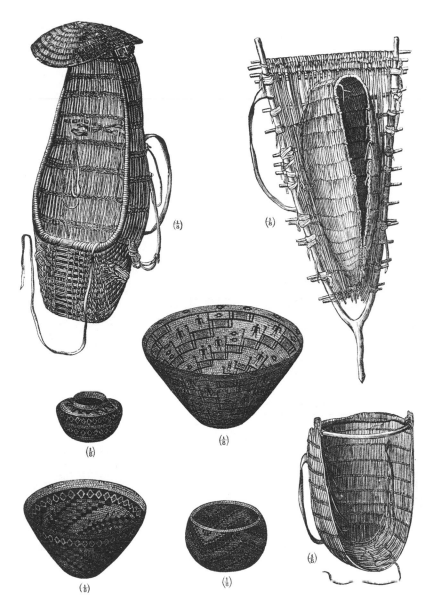

"Baby Baskets and Fancy Baskets," an illustration from Stephen Powers's *Tribes of California* (1877). Note the wealth of ethnographic detail included in the drawings.

"A Modoc Brave on the War Path," one of a series of stereoscopic photographs taken by Eadweard Muybridge during the so-called Modoc War of 1872 and 1873. An engraving made from this photograph was first published in *Harper's Weekly* in 1873.

Charles F. Lummis and other prominent Californians. Lummis was moved to action by the dispossession of the Cupeños, a small group of southern California natives who for years had resided on land around Warner's Hot Springs. When the Supreme Court ordered their removal in 1901, Lummis and his colleagues in the league—Stanford University president David Starr Jordan, anthropologist C. Hart Merriam, and philanthropist Phoebe Apperson Hearst—successfully petitioned the federal government to provide the Cupeños with a new home. Over the next ten years the league obtained food and medical supplies for destitute Indians in the San Diego and Riverside areas, and the league served as a broker for the sale of Indian crafts. In the early 1920s the Sequoya League was succeeded by the Mission Indian Federation, an organization of whites and Indians similarly dedicated to improving the condition of the Indians of southern California. The federation vigorously protested the inadequacy of Indian policy in California and soon incurred the wrath of federal officials. In 1922 some fifty-seven Indian members of the federation were indicted by the Department of Justice for conspiring against the government.[5]

Meanwhile, in northern California similar humanitarian work was undertaken by a variety of secular and religious organizations. The Northern California Indian Association purchased a small tract of land for a band of homeless Pomos in 1902. The secretary of the association, C. E. Kelsey, later persuaded Congress to appropriate $100,000 for additional lands and services for California Indians. Perhaps the most effective and controversial organization for the benefit of California natives was the Indian Board of Cooperation, organized in 1913 by a Methodist minister, Frederick G. Collett. The Indian Board concentrated its early efforts on improving educational opportunities for Indian children and on supporting a test case that eventually won citizenship rights for most California Indians. In 1922, the Reverend Mr. Collett launched a campaign to win compensation for the lands that had been promised but never given to the Indians in the unratified treaties of 1851–52. Collett levied "dues" on each northern California native to support his efforts on their behalf and traveled to Washington to urge Congress to appropriate a per capita cash settlement for the California tribes. Collett's work was later beset by scandal, and after indictment for mail fraud he lost the support of many of his "Indian auxiliaries." Disgruntled Indian members of the board formed in 1926 the first all-Indian welfare and intertribal organization, the California Indian

Brotherhood. This new organization continued to press for additional lands, educational opportunities, and material relief for the Indians of California.[6]

During the 1920s the Mission Indian Federation, the Indian Board of Cooperation, and the Indian Brotherhood were joined by a host of influential civic organizations, such as the Commonwealth Club of San Francisco, the Federated Women's Clubs, the Natives Sons of the Golden West, and the Women's Christian Temperance Union, in a campaign for passage of legislation to compensate the California Indians for the 1851–52 treaty lands. Some of those groups, notably the Commonwealth Club, had supported such legislation for years. In 1927 the California legislature authorized the state attorney general to act on behalf of the California Indians and to sue the federal government for compensation. In the following year Congress passed the California Indians' Jurisdictional Act inviting such a suit. The resulting litigation in the United States Court of Claims was extraordinarily complex and took sixteen years to reach a final settlement. On December 4, 1944, the court awarded the Indians of California $17 million for the reservations that had been promised in the treaties signed nearly a century earlier. To be deducted from that amount, however, were "off-sets" totalling $12 million for goods and services that had been provided to the Indians over the years by the federal government. The remaining sum, more than $5 million, was to be distributed to those Indians of California who had been residents of the state in 1852 and their descendants. In the 1950s, Congress authorized a per capita payment of about $150 to the more than 36,000 California Indians whose names appeared on a roll approved by the secretary of the interior.[7]

The rather modest settlement of the 1928 claims case satisfied neither the California Indians nor their white allies. The Commonwealth Club and other groups pressed for compensation for the remaining ninety-one million acres of California that were not included in the 1851–52 reservations. In 1946, Congress created the Indian Claims Commission, and during the next decade groups of California Indians filed more than twenty separate petitions for compensation. In 1963 the Indians of California and the commission agreed to a compromise settlement involving most of those claims. The settlement provided for payment of about $29 million for 64,425,000 acres—the amount of land remaining in California after deducting reservation lands, Spanish and Mexican land grants, and other parcels. A new list of eligible recipients was prepared by the secretary

210

of the interior, and by 1972 a list of more than 69,000 California Indians had been approved to receive payments of less than $700 each.[8]

In addition to receiving compensation, however meager, for the lost lands, the California Indians also gradually obtained additional reservation lands. In 1875 several small executive-order reserves were set aside by President Grant for the Indians of southern California. Those reserves and others were given trust-patent status by the Act for the Relief of Mission Indians in 1891. Meanwhile, in northern California a small portion of the Indian population continued on the reservations that remained of those that Congress had provided in the 1850s. The reservation at Round Valley, for example, reported 1,144 residents in 1875, but only 534 Indians were there five years later. Beginning in 1906, Congress initiated a series of acts to provide additional reserves for California Indians, and by 1930 thirty-six small "rancherias" had been set aside in sixteen northern California counties.[9]

Indians on the California reserves were subject to the vicissitudes of national Indian policy. During the late nineteenth century Indian agents, teachers, and missionaries continued their efforts at acculturation while, under provisions of the Dawes Allotment Act of 1887, the Bureau of Indian Affairs proceeded to divide reservation lands into tracts to be owned by individual Indians. Nationally the allotment policy had a devastating impact on American Indians: within fifty years they lost nearly two-thirds of their former reservation lands, and tribal governments gravely deteriorated. In California, however, less than one-fourth of the reservation land was taken out of trust, and much of the allotted land was retained by Indian owners.

In the 1930s under the leadership of John Collier, director of the Bureau of Indian Affairs, federal Indian policy underwent a fundamental shift. The 1934 Indian Reorganization Act prohibited further allotments of reservation land and encouraged tribes to reestablish themselves as corporate entities. Several California reservations and rancherias reconstituted themselves along the lines suggested by the Reorganization Act, and Congress once again began to provide additional land for California Indians. By 1950 a total of 117 Indian communities had been established by the federal government, either on lands set aside from the public domain or on lands purchased by federal funds. These reservations varied in size from a one-acre plot in Strawberry Valley, Yuba County, to the Hoopa Reservation in Humboldt County with over 116,000 acres.[10]

In the 1950s federal policy shifted again. The Bureau of Indian Affairs announced its intention to "terminate" most government services to Indians and to divide their tribal assets among individuals. In 1955 the BIA ended all health services for California Indians and subsequently withdrew vocational education and economic development programs, water and sanitation development projects, and other services. It was expected that henceforth California Indians would be as eligible as other citizens for local, county, and state aid programs. Unfortunately, confusion among government officials and the Indian people was very great, and the transfer of responsibility was far from painless. In 1958, Congress authorized the termination of California reservations, and eventually thirty-six rancherias voted to terminate.[11]

In the 1960s some new federal aid programs became available to American Indians under such agencies as the Office of Economic Opportunity and the Economic Development Administration. New interreservation organizations, including the Inter-Tribal Council of California and the California Rural Indian Health Program, were created to win further benefits. In the 1960s and 1970s, as the termination policy itself was terminated, the Bureau of Indian Affairs restored certain services to California Indians, including vocational and college scholarship programs.

What of the Indian peoples themselves? How have they fared in the more than one hundred years since publication of Stephen Powers's pioneer ethnographies and the grisly conclusion of the Modoc War?

In the 1870s only scattered remnants of the aboriginal populations were still alive, and those who had survived the maelstrom of the preceding quarter century were dislocated, demoralized, and impoverished. In 1870, Tavivo, a Paiute shaman in western Nevada, announced that he had received a vision in which the world was to be returned to the Indians, all whites would be destroyed, and the dead would be returned to life. Word of the vision spread throughout the Far West and became the basis of the revivalistic movement known as the Ghost Dance. Followers of the new gospel gathered in large semisubterranean dance houses and engaged in ritual dances. In California the Ghost Dance won converts among those tribes who had suffered most from the catastrophic events of the gold rush. The Pomos, for example were easy converts to the movement. They had lost 99 percent of their homeland and were suffering from severe social, economic, and political anomie. Similarly, many Southern

212

Maidus and Southern Valley Yokuts, living a demoralized hand-to-mouth existence, found the vision of the Paiute prophet irresistible. Through the movement the shattered California bands reestablished some of their social systems, gained strength from a shared ritual, and found spiritual reassurance.[12]

During the late nineteenth century the majority of California Indians subsisted on the fringes of white settlements, where they continued to work as general farm laborers, herdsmen, grain harvesters, fruit pickers, and domestic servants. Their work often was seasonal, and their wages were generally low. Some families remained in isolated enclaves on lands undesired by whites, where they lived by hunting and gathering, which was supplemented often by farming as well. It was from one such isolated retreat that Ishi, the sole survivor of the Yahis, emerged in 1911.[13] Only a minority of the California natives (perhaps only one-fourth) remained on the old federal reserves. As new reservations were set aside, Indians were able to become self-supporting as farmers and ranchers, planting crops and orchards and raising livestock and poultry for cash sale. In the early twentieth century, especially on the new reserves in southern California, Indian farm production was comparable to that of neighboring white communities.[14]

During the twentieth century the material situation of the California Indians improved slowly, though by most indices their condition did not reach the level of the general population. Some tribes became relatively prosperous. The tribal revenues of the Hupas in northern California, for example, totaled $1 million in 1970 from timber leases and concessions. Overall, however, the Indians still had the highest unemployment rate of any group in the state. The California State Advisory Commission on Indian Affairs reported in 1966 that the median income for reservation Indians was $2,268 per family. Housing on the reservations was described as inadequate: as many as half of the homes needed replacement in 1966; between 60 and 70 percent of them had inadequate sewage systems; and about 40 percent had contaminated water. Meanwhile, more than 40 percent of all rural and reservation Indians had not gone beyond the eighth grade, and the school dropout rate of Indians was three times that of non-Indians.[15]

According to the United States census, the size of the California Indian population has risen steadily during the twentieth century. By 1980 California had the largest Indian population of any state in the nation:

Census	Indian Population
1900	15,377
1910	16,371
1920	17,360
1930	19,212
1940	18,675
1950	19,947
1960	39,014
1970	91,018
1980	198,095

The population increase reflected changing conditions. Indian resistance to diseases that originated in Europe has improved so that it is now on a par with that of other ethnic groups in the American population. In nutrition and food preparation the California tribes shifted almost entirely to contemporary methods and requirements. The vital statistics of the Indian population indicate an overall movement upward of the birth rate and downward of the death rate. The rate of infant deaths steadily decreased in the twentieth century, and in recent years the decline has been extraordinary. By 1970 the infant mortality rate among California Indians had dropped below that of the general population.[16]

The most important factor in the growth of the Indian population in California after 1950 was immigration. During and after World War II many American Indians migrated to California from reservations in the Dakotas, Oklahoma, and the Southwest generally. Also, beginning in the 1960s, the BIA provided vocational training and job assistance for reservation Indians who wished to relocate to urban areas. By the 1980s more than half of all the relocated Indians in the United States had chosen to resettle in Los Angeles or the San Francisco Bay area. The significance of Indian immigration can be gauged by comparing the census figures with the number of Indians who enrolled for settlement of the land-claims cases. The 1970 census reported more than 91,000 Indians in California, whereas the 1970 enrollment had contained the names of only 69,911 people who were descendants of the Indians living in the state in 1848. It is not known how many of those nearly 70,000 California Indians were of purely Indian ancestry. Only the preliminary tribal enrollment of 1928 indicates the "degree of blood" of the Indians. At that time only 19 percent of the Mission Indians were full-bloods, while 36 percent of the non-Mission Indians were of purely Indian origin.

It is likely that in the succeeding years intermarriage between whites and Indians increased, and thus the "degree of blood" among enrolled California natives probably diminished further. Sherburne F. Cook has predicted that in the future the rate of racial fusion will increase as both whites and Indians undergo further urbanization: "In the end the Indian race in its California aspect will almost have vanished as an independent genetic entity."[17]

Whatever the prospects for the survival of the California Indians as an "independent genetic entity," their cultural survival is ensured. In the 1960s, 1970s, and 1980s Indian people throughout the state demonstrated a growing interest in the revival, preservation, and demonstration of their past native cultures. This resurgence of interest has produced some remarkable results despite formidable obstacles. Many of the old cultures had entirely disappeared. The Gabrielinos, once one of the most populous and powerful tribes in southern California, had ceased to exist as a culturally identifiable group as early as 1900. Although there remain a few genetic descendants of the Salinan Indians, who once inhabited the coastal valleys south of Monterey, Salinan culture long has been ethnologically extinct. Of the tribes of California that have survived, many members today live in a typical rural Californian fashion. Their way of life is scarcely distinguishable from that of their white neighbors.

Generally, the tribes that have been able to remain on at least a portion of their traditional lands, have been the most successful in retaining elements of their aboriginal way of life. The Cahuillas, for example, have been able to remain on their own land in south-central California during more than two hundred years of white contact. Through the centuries the tribe has employed different strategies to deal with Anglo-Americans and has maintained a degree of political and economic autonomy. Today traditional foods are still used by the Cahuillas at ritual or social events, kin relationships remain important, precontact songs and dances continue in use, traditional practices are common at funerals, and personal rituals are still observed. Until recently Cahuilla was a dying language that only a few older tribesmen spoke fluently. Now new interest among the younger generation has sparked a revival. Language classes have started in some communities, and a few families are teaching the native language to their children. On the Morongo reservation the Cahuillas have established the Malki Museum, which offers language classes and serves as a repository for Cahuilla artifacts and ethnographic information.[18]

215

In northern California the Hupas have experienced an unusual history of uninterrupted occupancy of their homeland. In 1864 a large portion of their ancestral territory was set aside by Congress for a reservation, and today the Indian community there is the largest and most prosperous in the state. The Hupas now live much as their white neighbors do, but they still retain a strong sense of ethnic identity. Although most speakers are more at ease in English, the Hupa language continues to be spoken. Among the Hupas, young and old alike, there is a growing concern for the perpetuation of traditional beliefs and activities.[19] It is appropriate that the first California tribal history to be written by a Native American should come from a gifted young Hupa historian, Byron Nelson.[20]

Even among those tribes that were removed from their lands, the old ways have not disappeared entirely. The territory of the Kashaya Pomos, for example, was overrun in the early years of American contact. Yet today Pomo tribal leaders still maintain traditional philosophical and religious principles, and rancheria schools perpetuate ceremonial dances and songs. Several Pomo shamans, using the ancient curing practices of sucking, dreaming, and singing and herbal medicines, are known and sought after throughout California. Pomo leaders have long been active in such organizations as the Indian Board of Cooperation and the Inter-Tribal Council of California. Typical of Pomo vitality is the Ya-Ka-Ama project, which was founded in the 1970s in Sonoma County and funded by the United States Department of Labor. The project trains Indian people in modern agricultural techniques and hosts an annual springtime festival featuring traditional dances, games, costumes, and foods.[21]

The Achumawis, whose homeland once extended along the Pit River north of Mount Lassen, suffered the same assaults on their territory and lives as did other tribes in northern California. In spite of the immigration of a much larger white population into their territory, the Achumawis have maintained an extensive knowledge and use of aboriginal medicines, foods, and rituals. Their faith in their shamans remains strong and they still know the location of "power places," isolated spots in their traditional territory, where one may go to seek supernatural power. The Achumawis take pride in their history and culture, but they also have been active in defending their interests in the contemporary world. They have been in the forefront of controversies involving the land-claims cases, and in the 1970s Achumawis engaged in sit-ins and court action to regain tribal land bought by the Pacific Gas and Electric Company.[22]

216

This epilogue opened with an Achumawi creation myth, the story of Silver Fox and Coyote. The preceding chapters had traced the evolution of American images of the California Indians, the evidence of white attitudes, and their impact on Indian people. We have now seen that, although entire tribes became extinct, in more recent times the California Indian population has grown, not diminished. Although the world of the Achumawis and other California tribes has changed radically, remnants of the aboriginal peoples remain. The determination voiced by Silver Fox in that ancient myth reflects the determination of a resurgent Indian people today: "Here is solid ground. I am going ashore, and am going to live here."

Notes

Prologue

1. J. H. Parry, "Spanish Indian Policy in Colonial America: The Ordering of Society," in John J. TePaske, ed., *Three American Empires*, p. 111; James Lang, *Conquest and Commerce: Spain and England in the Americas*, p. 7.

2. Parry, "Spanish Indian Policy," in TePaske, ed., *Three American Empires*, pp. 113, 122-24; Clarence Henry Haring, *The Spanish Empire in America*, pp. 40, 59, 63; Charles Gibson, *Spain in America*, p. 52; Charles Gibson, *The Aztecs Under Spanish Rule*, p. 58; Woodrow Borah, *New Spain's Century of Depression*, p. 11; Lesley Byrd Simpson, *The Repartimiento System of Native Labor in New Spain and Guatemala*, pp. 94-96; Sanford A. Mosk, "Latin America versus the United States," in Lewis Hanke, ed., *Do the Americas Have a Common History? A Critique of the Bolton Theory*, p. 167; Lang, *Conquest and Commerce*, pp. 19-21.

3. Mosk, "Latin America," in Hanke, ed., *Common History*, p. 167; Almon Wheeler Lauber, *Indian Slavery in Colonial Times Within the Present Limits of the United States*, pp. 49-59; Parry, "Spanish Indian Policy," in TePaske, ed., *Three American Empires*, p. 111.

4. Parry, "Spanish Indian Policy," in TePaske, ed., *Three American Empires*, p. 112.

5. Lewis Hanke, "Indians and Spaniards in the New World: A Personal View," in Howard Peckham and Charles Gibson, eds., *Attitudes of Colonial Powers Toward the American Indian*, p. 3; Lang, *Conquest and Commerce*, p. 22; Parry, "Spanish Indian Policy," in TePaske, ed., *Three American Empires*, p. 126; Mosk, "Latin America," in Hanke, ed., *Common History*, p. 168.

6. Parry, "Spanish Indian Policy," in TePaske, ed., *Three American Empires*, p. 124; Gibson, *Spain in America*, p. 41; Haring, *Spanish Empire in America*, pp. 5-6, 40-41; Lauber, *Indian Slavery*, pp. 49-50.

7. Haring, *Spanish Empire in America*, pp. 166, 169, 172.

8. Sherburne F. Cook, *The Population of the California Indians, 1769-1970*, pp. 1-43; Robert F. Heizer, "The California Indians: Archaeology, Varieties of Culture, Arts of Life," *California Historical Society Quarterly*, 41 (March, 1962): 2-4; Robert F. Heizer, "Introduction," in Heizer, ed., *California*, vol. 8 of *Handbook of North American Indians*, p. 3; Alfred L. Kroeber, "Elements of Culture in Native California," in Robert F. Heizer and M. A. Whipple, eds., *The California Indians: A Source Book*, p. 25.

219

9. Heizer, "California Indians," p. 4; Heizer, "Introduction," *California*, pp. 1-3. For an excellent summary see Robert F. Heizer and Albert B. Elsasser, *The Natural World of the California Indians.*

10. Heizer, "California Indians," p. 12.

11. Campbell Grant, "Eastern Coastal Chumash," in Heizer, ed., *California*, pp. 517-18.

12. Heizer, "California Indians," p. 13.

13. Kroeber, "Elements of Culture," in Heizer and Whipple, eds., *California Indians*, pp. 3-7, 39; Theodora Kroeber and Robert F. Heizer, *Almost Ancestors: The First Californians*, ed. David Hales, pp. 28-29, 35-37; Heizer, "Introduction," *California*, p. 10.

14. Heizer, "California Indians," pp. 6-8; Kroeber and Heizer, *Almost Ancestors*, p. 52.

15. Ibid., p. 17; Heizer, "Introduction," *California*, p. 3.

16. Heizer, "California Indians," p. 17.

17. Ibid., pp. 14-17; Jack D. Forbes, *Warriors of the Colorado: The Yumas of the Quechan Nation and Their Neighbors.*

18. For a discussion of the process of "invention," see Robert F. Berkhofer, Jr., *The White Man's Indian: Images of the American Indian from Columbus to the Present*, pp. 3-31.

19. Herbert Eugene Bolton, "The Mission as a Frontier Institution in the Spanish American Colonies," in John Francis Bannon, ed., *Bolton and the Spanish Borderlands*, pp. 194-95, 198-201.

20. Sherburne F. Cook, *The Conflict Between the California Indian and White Civilization: The Indian Versus the Spanish Mission*, p. 5; Edward D. Castillo, "The Impact of Euro-American Exploration and Settlement," in Heizer, ed., *California*, p. 105.

21. Bolton, "Mission as a Frontier Institution," in Bannon, ed., *Spanish Borderlands*, pp. 200-201. Whether force was used to gather non-Christian Indians to the missions is a matter of dispute. See Francis F. Guest, "An Examination of the Thesis of S. F. Cook on the Forced Conversion of Indians in the California Missions," *Southern California Quarterly*, 61 (Spring, 1979): 2.

22. Jack D. Forbes, *Native Americans of California and Nevada*, p. 29.

23. Ibid.; Ira B. Cross, *A History of the Labor Movement in California*, p. 4; Castillo, "Impact," in Heizer, ed., *California*, pp. 99-104.

24. Frank Adams, "The Historical Background of California Agriculture," in Claude B. Hutchison, ed., *California Agriculture*, pp. 7-15; Robert Glass Cleland and Osgood Hardy, *March of Industry*, p. 3; Edith Buckland Webb, *Indian Life at the Old Missions;* Bolton, "Mission as a Frontier Institution," in Bannon, ed., *Spanish Borderlands*, p. 209.

25. Cook, *Conquest: Spanish Mission*, pp. 1-5, 12, 134; Robert Archibald, *The Economic Aspects of the California Missions*, pp. 184-185.

26. Kroeber, quoted in Joseph H. Engbeck, Jr., *La Purisima Mission State Historic Park*, p. 16.

27. Cook, *The Conflict Between the California Indian and White Civilization: The American Invasion, 1848-1870*, pp. 47-48.

28. Ibid., p. 50. See also George Harwood Phillips, "Indians and the Break-

down of the Spanish Mission System in California," in David J. Weber, ed., *New Spain's Far Northern Frontier: Essays on Spain in the American West, 1540–1821*, p. 267.

29. Cook, *Conflict: American Invasion*, pp. 48–50; Cross, *Labor Movement*, pp. 6–7; Robert F. Heizer and Alan J. Almquist, *The Other Californians: Prejudice and Discrimination Under Spain, Mexico, and the United States to 1920*, pp. 18–20.

30. Hubert Howe Bancroft, *History of California* 2: 420–21; Bancroft, *California Pastoral, 1769–1848*, pp. 347–48, 438; Cross, *Labor Movement*, pp. 6–9.

CHAPTER 1. *Prophetic Patterns*

1. As quoted in Robert F. Heizer, ed., *California*, vol. 8 of *Handbook of North American Indians*, p. 509.

2. As quoted in Robert F. Heizer, *Elizabethan California: A Brief and Sometimes Critical Review of Opinions on the Location of Francis Drake's Five Weeks' Visit with the Indians of Ships Land in 1579*, pp. 86–87.

3. See Cecilia Imelda Azevedo, "Descriptions of California Indians by Early Voyagers" (M.A. thesis, University of California, Berkeley, 1946).

4. Heizer, "Introduction," *California*, p. 6.

5. Gerónimo Boscana, "Chinigchinich," in Alfred Robinson, *Life in California: During a Residence of Several Years in That Territory, Comprising a Description of the Country and the Missionary Establishments*, ed. Doyce B. Nunis, Jr., pp. 242–84, 335. See also Maynard Geiger and Clement W. Meighan, eds., *As the Padres Saw Them: California Indian Life and Customs as Reported by the Franciscan Missionaries, 1813–1815*.

6. Jean François Galaup de La Pérouse, *A Voyage Round the World in the Years 1785, 1786, 1787, and 1788*, ed. M. L. A. Milet-Mureau, 2:195–96, 202.

7. Ibid., 2:203–204, passim. See also Claude François Lambert, *Curious Observations upon the Manners, Customs, Usages . . . of the Several Nations of Asia, Africa, and America* 1:123–33; George Verne Blue, ed., "The Report of Captain La Place on His Voyage to the Northwest Coast and California in 1839," *California Historical Society Quarterly*, 18 (March, 1939): 319–23; Abel Du Petit-Thouars, *Voyage of the Venus: Sojourn in California*, trans. Charles N. Rudkin, pp. 33–37; William Finley Shepard, ed., "California Prior to Conquest: A Frenchman's Views," *California Historical Society Quarterly* 37 (March, 1958): 71; August C. Mahr, *The Visit of the "Rurik" to San Francisco in 1816*, pp. 77–79; Georg Heinrich von Langsdorff, *Langsdorff's Narrative of the Rezanov Voyage to Nueva California in 1806*, ed. and trans. Thomas C. Russell, pp. 62–64; Frederick William Beechey, *Narrative of a Voyage to the Pacific and Beering's Strait . . . in the Years 1825, 26, 27, 28* 2:66–67; Francis Guillemard Simpkinson and Edward Belcher, *H.M.S. Sulphur at California, 1837 and 1839*, ed. Richard A. Pierce and John W. Winslow, pp. 21–22; Albert M. Gilliam, *Travels in Mexico During the Years 1843 and 44*, p. 288; Alejandro Malaspina, *Malaspina in California*, ed. Donald C. Cutter, p. 53.

8. Beechey, *Narrative of a Voyage* 2:66–67; Gilliam, *Travels in Mexico*, p. 288. On the growing imperial interest in California see Robert Glass Cleland, *The*

Early Sentiment for the Annexation of California: An Account of the Growth of American Interest in California from 1835 to 1846; Abraham P. Nasatir, *French Activities in California: An Archival Calendar Guide;* Rufus Kay Willys, "French Imperialists in California," *California Historical Society Quarterly* 8 (June, 1929): 166–219; and the several articles on Russian interest in the same journal, vol. 12 (September, 1933).

9. As quoted in Blue, "The Report of Captain La Place," pp. 319, 323.

10. As quoted in Shepard, "California Prior to Conquest," p. 71.

11. Simpkinson, *H.M.S. Sulphur at California,* pp. 21–22.

12. La Pérouse, *Voyage Round the World* 2:197. See also Simpkinson, *H.M.S. Sulphur at California,* p. 17; Adelbert von Chamisso in Mahr, ed., *Visit of the "Rurik,"* p. 83; Malaspina, *Malaspina in California,* p. 53; Eugene Duflot de Mofras, *Duflot de Mofras' Travels on the Pacific Coast,* ed. and trans. Marguerite Eyer Wilbur, vol. 2, p. 188.

13. George Vancouver, *Vancouver in California, 1792–1794: The Original Account of George Vancouver,* ed. Marguerite Eyer Wilbur, pp. 11, 26, 42.

14. See, for example, Beechey, *Narrative of a Voyage* 2:17, 51, 77; Langsdorff, *Langsdorff's Narrative,* pp. 55–57; Simpkinson and Belcher, *H.M.S. Sulphur at California,* pp. 17, 39, 45; Edmond Le Netrel, *Voyage of the Héros Around the World with Duhaut-Cilly in the Years 1826, 1827, 1828 & 1829,* trans. Blanche Collet Wagner, p. 39. Alfred Kroeber has noted that in many parts of California "all men went wholly naked except when the weather enforced protection" (Kroeber, *Elements of Culture in Native California,* p. 260).

15. Vancouver, *Vancouver in California,* pp. 11, 26–28, 65.

16. La Pérouse, *Voyage Round the World* 2:211.

17. Beechey, *Narrative of a Voyage* 2:57, 75; Chamisso and Louis Choris, in Mahr, ed., *Visit of the "Rurik,"* pp. 85, 99–101; Langsdorff, *Langsdorff's Narrative,* p. 58; Du Petit-Thouars, *Voyage of the Venus,* pp. 48–49; Kirill T. Khlebnikov, "Memoirs of California," trans. Anatole G. Mazour, *Pacific Historical Review* 9 (Sept., 1940): 333; August Bernard Duhaut-Cilly, "Duhaut-Cilly's Account of California in the Years 1827–1828," trans. Charles F. Carter, *California Historical Society Quarterly,* 8 (December, 1929): 314; Alexander Markoff, *The Russians on the Pacific Coast,* trans. Ivan Petroff, p. 60.

18. Langsdorff, *Langsdorff's Narrative,* pp. 57–59. Cf. Beechey, *Narrative of a Voyage* 2:74–77.

19. Vancouver, *Vancouver in California,* p. 26; Duhaut-Cilly, "Duhaut-Cilly's Account of California," pp. 313–14; Otto von Kotzebue, in Mahr, ed., *Visit of the "Rurik,"* p. 61.

20. Camille de Roquefeuil, *Camille de Roquefeuil in San Francisco, 1817–1818,* ed. and trans. Charles N. Rudkin, p. 71.

21. Du Petit-Thouars, *Voyage of the Venus,* pp. 48–49.

22. Langsdorff, *Langsdorff's Narrative,* p. 57.

23. Langsdorff, *Langsdorff's Narrative,* pp. 62–63.

24. For a discussion of "environmentalism" see Robert F. Berkhofer, Jr., *The White Man's Indian: Images of the American Indian from Columbus to the Present,* pp. 38–44.

25. See, for example, Malaspina, *Malaspina in California,* p. 53; José Bandini,

A Description of California in 1828, trans. Doris Marion Wright, p. 18.

26. Lambert, *Curious Observations* 1:128–31.

27. Khlebnikov, "Memoirs of California," p. 333.

28. Vancouver, *Vancouver in California*, pp. 93–104, 139, 148–49; Du Petit-Thouars, *Voyage of the Venus*, p. 83; Beechey, *Narrative of a Voyage* 2:13, 19, 21, 24, 29–34; George Simpson, *Narrative of a Voyage to California Ports in 1841–42*, pp. 53–54, 60–67, 132.

29. Du Petit-Thouars, *Voyage of the Venus*, p. 77.

30. La Pérouse, *Voyage Round the World* 2:201–206, 212–14, 218–20.

31. Ibid., 2:205, 213–16, 220, 225.

32. Chamisso, in Mahr, ed., *Visit of the "Rurik,"* p. 81; Du Petit-Thouars, *Voyage of the Venus*, p. 40; Rosamel, in Shepard, "California Prior to Conquest," p. 66; Heinrich Künzel, *Upper California*, trans. Anthony and Max Knight, p. 45.

33. Duhaut-Cilly, "Duhaut-Cilly's Account of California," pp. 214–15, 242, 317.

34. Ibid., 215, 242.

35. Ibid., 215, 317.

36. Kotzebue, Chamisso, and Choris, in Mahr, ed., *Visit of the "Rurik,"* pp. 61–63, 81–83, 95; Khlebnikov, "Memoirs of California," pp. 312, 334; Langsdorff, *Langsdorff's Narrative*, pp. 47–48, 66–68; Beechey, *Narrative of a Voyage* 2:17–19, 21–33; Thomas Coulter, *Notes on Upper California: A Journey from Monterey to the Colorado River in 1832*, pp. 24–27.

37. John Coulter, *Adventures on the Western Coast of South America and in the Interior of California* 1:168–70.

38. Vassilli Petrovitch Tarakanoff, *Statement of My Captivity Among the Californians*, trans. Ivan Petroff, pp. 15–18.

39. Kotzebue and Chamisso, in Mahr, ed., *Visit of the "Rurik,"* pp. 59, 79; Khlebnikov, "Memoirs of California," p. 333; Duhaut-Cilly, "Duhaut-Cilly's Account of California," pp. 159–316; Du Petit-Thouars, *Voyage of the Venus*, p. 46; Beechey, *Narrative of a Voyage* 2:18; Simpson, *Narrative of a Voyage*, pp. 66, 132.

40. Chamisso, in Mahr, ed., *Visit of the "Rurik,"* p. 83.

41. Beechey, *Narrative of a Voyage*, 2:22.

42. Coulter, *Notes on Upper California*, p. 26; Le Netrel, *Voyage of the Héros*, pp. 36–37; Kotzebue, in Mahr, ed., *Visit of the "Rurik,"* p. 59; Duhaut-Cilly, "Duhaut-Cilly's Account of California," p. 228; Beechey, *Narrative of a Voyage* 2:71; Roquefeuil, *Camille de Roquefeuil in San Francisco* 2:18, 71.

43. Du Petit-Thouars, *Voyage of the Venus*, p. 85; Beechey, *Narrative of a Voyage* 2:71, 78.

44. Roquefeuil, *Camille de Roquefeuil in San Francisco*, p. 21; Coulter, *Notes on Upper California*, p. 26; Simpson, *Narrative of a Voyage*, p. 67; Belcher, *H.M.S. Sulphur at California*, p. 46; Kotzebue, Chamisso, and Choris, in Mahr, ed., *Visit of the "Rurik,"* pp. 61–63, 83, 99; Duhaut-Cilly, "Duhaut-Cilly's Account of California," p. 316.

45. Cutter, "Introduction," *Malaspina in California*, p. v.

46. Malaspina, *Malaspina in California*, pp. 50, 53, 58, 62–65.

47. Le Netrel, *Voyage of the Héros*, p. 36.

48. Rosamel, in Shepard, "California Prior to Conquest," pp. 66–67.

49. Philip Wayne Powell, *Tree of Hate: Propaganda and Prejudice Affecting United States Relations with the Hispanic World*, p. 11.

50. Charles Gibson, *Spain in America*, pp. 136–37; John Francis Bannon, Robert Ryal Miller, and Peter Masten Dunne, *Latin America*, pp. 125–26.

CHAPTER 2. *The Vanguard*

1. Franklin Walker, *A Literary History of Southern California*, p. 7.

2. James Cook, *A Voyage to the Pacific Ocean, Undertaken by the Command of His Majesty . . . in the Years 1776, 1777, 1778, 1779, and 1780*, 3 vols.; Adele Ogden, *The California Sea Otter Trade, 1784–1848*, pp. 1–3.

3. Hubert Howe Bancroft, *History of California* 2:37, 267. A sampling of logbooks of vessels engaged in hunting along the California coast produced little useful information on California Indians. Consulted were the logbooks of the *Eagle* (1820–22), the *Arab* (1821–25), the *Rover* (1822–26), the *Mentor* (1824–25), the *Courier* (1825–29), and the *Waverly* (1828–29), all in the Bancroft Library, University of California, Berkeley.

4. Ogden, *Sea Otter Trade*, pp. 2, 16, 21–22, 35.

5. Ibid., pp. 43–44.

6. William Heath Davis, *Sixty Years in California: A History of . . . the Events Described*, p. 371. See also Ogden, *Sea Otter Trade*, pp. 101, 107, 111, 133–36; Job F. Dye, "Recollections of a Pioneer of California," *Santa Cruz Sentinel*, 15 May 1869; Henry J. Dally, "Narrative of His Life and Events in California Since 1843," pp. 20–21, Bancroft Library, University of California, Berkeley.

7. See, for example, the sentiments of George Nidever, *The Life and Adventures of George Nidever*, ed. William Henry Ellison, p. 56.

8. William Dane Phelps, "Solid Men of Boston in the Northwest," pp. 14, 20, 22, Bancroft Library, University of California, Berkeley; Nicholas Dawson, *California in '41. Texas in '51*, pp. 57, 112–14; Bancroft, *History of California* 2:63–64.

9. Nidever, *Life and Adventures*, p. 44. See also Hugo Reid, *The Indians of Los Angeles County: Hugo Reid's Letters of 1852*, ed. Robert F. Heizer, pp. 100–101.

10. Phelps, "Solid Men of Boston," p. 22.

11. Bancroft, *History of California* 2:23. Thus Shaler's journal was also the first American account of the California Indians to be published in the United States.

12. Richard J. Cleveland, *A Narrative of Voyages and Commercial Enterprises* 1:213–16.

13. William Shaler, *Journal of a Voyage Between China and the Northwestern Coast of America . . . by William Shaler*, pp. 27–28, 35–36.

14. Ibid., pp. 27–28, 30, 37. Raymond A. Rydell has concluded that the otter hunters faced "almost constant danger" from Northwest Indians (Rydell, *Cape Horn to the Pacific: The Rise and Decline of an Ocean Highway*, p. 30).

15. Shaler, *Journal of a Voyage*, pp. 34–35, 56–57.

16. Cleveland, *Narrative of Voyages* 1:210. It is difficult to account for Cleveland's judgment here. Alfred Kroeber has described the Gabrielinos, who inhabited parts of the southern coast and the islands of San Clemente and Santa Catalina, as "the most advanced group south of Tehachipi, except perhaps the Chumash" (Kroeber, *Handbook of the Indians of California*, p. 621).

17. Dale L. Morgan, *Jedediah Smith and the Opening of the West*, p. 201; Joseph J. Hill, "Ewing Young in the Fur Trade of the Far Southwest, 1822–1834," *Oregon Historical Society Quarterly* 24 (March, 1923): 5.

18. Thomas N. Layton, however, has recently suggested that California Indians may have driven horses through the Sierra to the Humboldt Sink area of Nevada. There the California natives may have engaged in horse-trading activity with white trappers and natives of the Great Basin. (Layton, "Traders and Raiders: Aspects of Trans-Basin and California-Plateau Commerce, 1800–1830," *Journal of California and Great Basin Anthropology* 3 [Summer, 1981]: 127–37).

19. Lewis O. Saum, "The Fur Trader and the Noble Savage," *American Quarterly* 15 (Winter, 1963): 554–71. See also Saum, "Frenchmen, Englishmen, and the Indian," *American West* 1 (Fall, 1964): 4; Alvin M. Josephy, Jr., "By Fayre and Gentle Means: The Hudson's Bay Company and the American Indian," *American West* 9 (Sept., 1972): 4–12.

20. Virginia Cole Trenholm and Maurine Carley, *The Shoshonis: Sentinels of the Rockies*, p. 5. California natives of the Shoshonean family also employed a digging stick in gathering roots for baskets and, perhaps less commonly, in harvesting wild vegetables (Kroeber, *Handbook*, pp. 563, 736, 935).

21. Thomas Jefferson Farnham, *Travels in the Californias and Scenes in the Pacific Ocean*, p. 58. See also Farnham, *Life and Adventures in California and Scenes in the Pacific Ocean*, p. 376; Hiram M. Chittenden, *The American Fur Trade of the Far West: A History of . . . Santa Fe* 1:10.

22. Jedediah Strong Smith, "The Smith Narrative," in Harrison Clifford Dale, ed., *The Ashley-Smith Explorations and the Discovery of a Central Route to the Pacific, 1822–1829*, p. 190.

23. George C. Yount, "The Chronicles of George C. Yount," ed. Charles L. Camp, *California Historical Society Quarterly* 2 (April, 1923): 38–39. See also Frances Auretta Fuller Barrett Victor, *The River of the West: Life and Adventures . . . of the Fur Traders*, pp. 121–23.

24. Maurice S. Sullivan, *The Travels of Jedediah Smith: A Documentary Outline Including the Journal of the Great American Pathfinder*, pp. 72–73. See also Smith, in Dale, ed., *Ashley-Smith Explorations*, p. 187.

25. See, for example, Charles Alexander, *The Life and Times of Cyrus Alexander*, ed. George Shochat, pp. 44, 47–48, 85.

26. Zenas Leonard, *Narrative of the Adventures of Zenas Leonard*, ed. Milo Milton Quaife, pp. 143–44, 149, 156, 198–99.

27. Hill, "Ewing Young," pp. 23–24; Victor, *River of the West*, p. 152; Leonard, *Narrative of the Adventures*, pp. 141–42; Nidever, *Life and Adventures*, p. 35; Albert Ferdinand Morris, "The Journal of a 'Crazy Man.' Travels and Scenes in California From the Year 1834 to the American Conquest: The Nar-

rative of Albert Ferdinand Morris," ed. Charles L. Camp, *California Historical Society Quarterly* 15 (June, 1936): 103–38 (Sept., 1936): 224–47.

28. Sullivan, *Travels of Jedediah Smith*, pp. 60–66, 82, 99; Smith, in Dale, ed., *Ashley-Smith Explorations*, pp. 248–51, 254–61, 276.

29. Rogers, "The Second Journal of Harrison G. Rogers," in Dale, ed., *Ashley-Smith Explorations*, pp. 245–46; Sullivan, *Travels of Jedediah Smith*, pp. 56–58, 69.

30. Yount, "Chronicles," p. 35.

31. Adele Ogden, "Boston Hide Droghers Along California Shores," *California Historical Society Quarterly* 8 (Dec., 1929): 290.

32. Richard Henry Dana, *Two Years Before the Mast: A Personal Narrative of Life at Sea* 1:100–101.

33. Ibid., 1:122.

34. Faxon Dean Atherton, *The California Diary of Faxon Dean Atherton, 1836–1839*, ed. Doyce B. Nunis, Jr., pp. 52–53.

35. Ibid., pp. 58–59.

36. William H. Thomes, *On Land and Sea: Or, California in the Years 1843, '44, and '45*, pp. 5–6. See also George R. Stewart, *Take Your Bible in One Hand: The Life of William Henry Thomes*.

37. Thomes, *On Land and Sea*, pp. 329–30.

38. Ibid., p. 417. See also pp. 329–33.

39. Cleveland, *Narrative of Voyages* 1:220.

40. Shaler, *Journal of a Voyage*, pp. 57–59, 61; Bancroft, *History of California* 2: 23.

41. Shaler, *Journal of a Voyage*, pp. 59–60, 75–78.

42. Morgan, *Jedediah Smith*, pp. 236–55.

43. James Ohio Pattie, *Personal Narrative of James O. Pattie*, ed. William Goetzmann. It has never been determined how much of Pattie's narrative was actually written or invented by its original editor, Timothy Flint (Goetzmann, Introduction, p. ix).

44. Morris, "Journal of a 'Crazy Man,'" p. 109.

45. Leonard, *Narrative of the Adventures*, pp. 136, 166.

46. Washington Irving, *The Adventures of Captain Bonneville, U.S.A., in the Rocky Mountains and the Far West*, ed. Edgeley W. Todd, p. 290.

47. Pattie, *Personal Narrative*, pp. 194–95, 202, 216–17. Pattie's charge of involuntary conversions should be balanced against the argument of Francis F. Guest, "An Examination of the Thesis of S. F. Cook on the Forced Conversion of Indians in the California Missions," *Southern California Quarterly* 61 (Spring, 1979): 1–78.

48. Rogers, "Second Journal," in Dale, ed., *Ashley-Smith Explorations*, pp. 195–206, 222.

49. Jean François Galaup de La Pérouse, *A Voyage Round the World, in the Years 1785, 1786, 1787, and 1788*, ed. M. L. A. Milet-Mureau, 2: 201–206.

50. Rogers, "Second Journal," in Dale, ed. *Ashley-Smith Explorations*, pp. 196, 200–208, 217, passim.

51. Leonard, *Narrative of the Adventures*, pp. 190–91.

52. Irving, *Adventures of Captain Bonneville*, p. 295. Cf. Jack D. Forbes,

Native Americans in California and Nevada, p. 44.

53. James D. Hart, *American Images of Spanish California,* p. 5. This, of course, is not Hart's own view; it is his ironic comment on the conclusions of Washington Irving.

54. See Sherburne F. Cook, *Expeditions to the Interior of California: Central Valley, 1820–1840,* pp. 151–213.

55. Leonard, *Narrative of the Adventures,* pp. 178–86; Morris, "Journal of a 'Crazy Man,'" pp. 231–32.

56. Morris, "Journal of a 'Crazy Man,'" pp. 232–33. See also Charles F. Brown, "Statement of Recollections of Early Events in California," pp. 12–19, Bancroft Library, University of California, Berkeley; Yount, "Chronicles," p. 54.

57. Dana, *Two Years Before the Mast* 1:84, 168.

58. Ibid., 1: 87, 170–71.

59. Ibid., 1: 172.

60. Atherton, *California Diary,* pp. 58–59, 67.

61. Robert B. Forbes, *Personal Reminiscences,* pp. 95–96, 335–36. I know of only one contemporary account of the branding of neophytes: Benjamin David Wilson, "Observations on Early Days in California and New Mexico," *Annual Publication of the Historical Society of Southern California* (1934), p. 90. See also Jack Forbes, *Native Americans of California and Nevada,* p. 29.

62. Jonathan S. Green, *Journal of a Tour on the North West Coast of America in the Year 1829,* pp. 94–97, 103–105.

63. Farnham, *Life and Adventures,* pp. 99–100, 110–12, 350–51, 363.

CHAPTER 3. *Shifting Perspectives*

1. Andrew F. Rolle, *An American in California: The Biography of William Heath Davis, 1822–1909,* p. 29.

2. William Heath Davis, *Sixty Years in California: A History of Events and Life in California,* pp. 9, 34, 72, 242–43, 334–35.

3. Rolle, *American in California,* pp. 29, 56.

4. Hubert Howe Bancroft, *History of California* 3:777; Adele Ogden, "Hides and Tallow: McCullough, Hartnell and Company, 1822–1828," *California Historical Society Quarterly* 6 (Sept., 1927): 254–64. See also Susanna Bryant Dakin, *The Lives of William Hartnell.*

5. Dakin, *Lives of William Hartnell,* pp. 72, 76, 121, 155, 157–58, 181.

6. Bancroft, *History of California* 4:706–707. See also Reuben L. Underhill, *From Cowhides to Golden Fleece . . . California's Only American Consul.*

7. Thomas Oliver Larkin, "Description of California, June 15, 1846," in Charles W. Hackett et al., eds., *New Spain and the Anglo-American West: Historical Contributions Presented to Herbert Eugene Bolton* 2:108–109.

8. Bancroft, *History of California* 5:698; Adele Ogden, "Alfred Robinson, New England Merchant in Mexican California," *California Historical Society Quarterly* 23 (Sept., 1944): 202; James D. Hart, *American Images of Spanish California,* p. 22.

9. Alfred Robinson, "Journal on the Coast of California, on Board the

Ship *Brookline,* Year 1829," *California Historical Society Quarterly* 23 (Sept., 1944): 203, 208.

10. Alfred Robinson, *Life in California . . . and the Missionary Establishments,* ed. Doyce B. Nunis, Jr., p. 226.

11. Ibid., pp. 24, 26, 32, 44–45, 49–50, 58, 75, 81.

12. "Business Letters of Alfred Robinson," ed. Adele Ogden, *California Historical Society Quarterly* 23 (Dec., 1944): 305. Robinson was referring to the abortive secularization plan of Governor José María Echeandía of 6 January 1831. See Bancroft, *History of California* 3:305–306.

13. Robinson, *Life in California,* p. 217–19, passim.

14. Bancroft, *History of California* 4:730–31.

15. John Marsh, "Letter of John Marsh to Hon. Lewis Cass," *California Historical Society Quarterly* 23 (Dec., 1943): 316–18.

16. John Bidwell, *A Journey to California,* pp. 21, 23–26; Bancroft, *History of California* 2:719–20.

17. Bidwell, *Journey to California,* p. 26.

18. Belden, *Josiah Belden, 1841 California Overland Pioneer: His Memoir and Early Letters,* ed. Doyce B. Nunis, Jr., pp. 54, 58, 88.

19. Marsh, "Letter of John Marsh," p. 320.

20. Ibid., pp. 317, 320–21.

21. Ibid., p. 321.

22. George D. Lyman, *John Marsh, Pioneer: The Life Story of a Trail-blazer on Six Frontiers,* pp. 218–20, 277. For accounts of other California pioneers who adopted the Hispanic model of Indian labor exploitation, see Ruby Johnson Swartzlow, "Peter Lassen: Northern California's Trail-Blazer," *California Historical Society Quarterly* 18 (Dec., 1939): 297; T. Vogel-Jorgensen, "Peter Lassen of California," trans. Helge Norrung, pp. 23, 24, 72; Charles Alexander, *The Life and Times of Cyrus Alexander,* ed. George Shochat, pp. 44–55, 61, 85; John Yates, *A Sailor's Sketch of the Sacramento Valley in 1842,* ed. Ferol Egan, pp. 17, 20–21.

23. Sutter's story has often been told. See, for example, James P. Zollinger, *Sutter: The Man and His Empire;* Richard Dillon, *Fool's Gold: The Decline and Fall of Captain John Sutter of California.*

24. Walton Bean and James J. Rawls, *California: An Interpretive History,* p. 65.

25. See John Chamberlain, "Memoirs of California Since 1840," p. 16, Bancroft Library, University of California, Berkeley; Titian Ramsay Peale, *Titian Ramsay Peale, 1799–1855, and His Journals of the Wilkes Expedition,* ed. Jessie Poesch, p. 196; George N. Colvocresses, *Four Years in a Government Exploring Expedition,* pp. 301–302; Yates, *Sailor's Sketch,* pp. 6, 18; Jacob Wright Harlan, *California '46 to '88,* pp. 75–76; [Washington Allon Bartlett], "Letters from California (1846)," *Magazine of History with Notes and Queries* 24 (1923): 78.

26. Edwin Bryant, *What I Saw in California: Being the Journal of a Tour . . . in the Years 1846, 1847,* pp. 267–68.

27. John C. Frémont, *Narrative of the Exploring Expedition to . . . North California in the Years 1843–1844,* pp. 262–65.

28. Bancroft, *History of California,* 3:778–79, 355–56, 396–99. Cf. Thomas F. Andrews, "Lansford W. Hastings and the Promotion of the Salt Lake Desert

Cutoff: A Reappraisal," *Western Historical Quarterly* 4 (April, 1973): 133–50.

29. Lansford W. Hastings, *The Emigrants' Guide to Oregon and California: Containing Scenes . . . and the Methods of Travelling*, p. 133. See also James C. Ward, "Extracts from the Diary of an Early Californian," *Argonaut* (San Francisco), 10 August 1878; Samuel C. Damon, "A Trip from the Sandwich Islands to Lower California and Upper California," *Magazine of History with Notes and Queries* 25 (1923): 74; J. M. Shively, *Route and Distances to Oregon and California: With a Description of Watering-places, Crossings, Dangerous Indians, &c. &c.*, p. 14.

30. Hastings, *Emigrants' Guide*, p. 132.

31. Ibid.

CHAPTER 4. *To Make Them Useful*

1. See Sherburne F. Cook, *The Population of the California Indians, 1769–1970*, pp. 44, 60.

2. *California Star* (Yerba Buena and San Francisco), 11 Dec. 1847. See also Thomas Oliver Larkin, *The Larkin Papers: Personal, Business and Official Correspondence of Thomas Oliver Larkin*, ed. George P. Hammond, 7:125.

3. *California Star*, 11 Dec. 1847. See also Joseph Warren Revere, *Naval Duty in California*, pp. 71, 103.

4. *California Star*, 15 Jan. 1848.

5. *Californian* (Monterey), 7 Nov. 1846.

6. Ibid., 16 Jan. 1847. For the concern later over "enticement," see California Legislature, Joint Committee on the Mendocino War, *Majority and Minority Reports*, p. 11; *Sacramento Union*, 9 Sept. 1860; *San Francisco Bulletin*, reprinted in *Sacramento Union*, 29 Sept. 1860.

7. U.S. Congress, Senate, *Executive Documents*, 31st Cong., 1st sess., doc. 18, pp. 334–35.

8. *California Star*, 18 Sept. 1847. See also same newspaper, 11 Dec. 1847.

9. J. Ross Browne, *Report of the Debates in the Convention of California*, pp. 63–68. The delegates also provided that Indians in the future could be granted the suffrage by a concurrent two-thirds vote of the legislature.

10. California Legislature, *Statutes of California*, 1st sess., chap. 133 (1850), pp. 408–10. For the effects of the "bail-out" provision see Horace Bell, *Reminiscences of a Ranger: Or, Early Times in Southern California*, pp. 47–49; William W. Robinson, *The Indians of Los Angeles: Story of the Liquidation of a People*, pp. 1–3.

11. *Statutes of California*, 1st sess., chap. 133 (1850), p. 408.

12. Sherburne F. Cook, *The Conflict Between the California Indians and White Civilization: The American Invasion, 1848–1870*, p. 54.

13. California Senate, *Journal of the Senate*, 1st sess. (1850), pp. 217, 223, 228–29, 257. For Bidwell's dependence on Indian labor see Dorothy Hill, *The Indians of Chico Rancheria*, pp. 27–33.

14. California Assembly, *Journal of the Assembly*, 1st sess. (1850), pp. 1205, 1233. On Brown, see *History of Contra Costa County . . . and Representative Men*, pp. 515–31.

15. [W. F. Wallace], ed., *History of Napa County . . . and Principal Inhabitants*, p. 96; *An Illustrated History of San Joaquin County . . . Together with Glimpses of Its Future Prospects*, p. 47.

16. California, *Journal of the Senate*, 1st sess. (1850), pp. 366–67, 369, 384; *Journal of the Assembly*, 1st sess. (1850), p. 1284.

17. *San Francisco Bulletin*, 29 June 1857; U.S. Interior Department, Office of Indian Affairs, *Report of the Commissioner . . . for . . . 1858*, pp. 9–11; *Tulare Times*, 1860. (A copy of the *Tulare Times* article is pasted in Hubert Howe Bancroft's Newspaper Scrapbooks, vol. 36, p. 15, in the Bancroft Library, University of California, Berkeley. The scrapbooks are hereafter cited as Bancroft Scraps.)

18. *Marysville Herald*, Nov., 1856, reprinted in Robert F. Heizer, ed., *They Were Only Diggers: A Collection of Articles from California Newspapers, 1851–1866, on Indian and White Relations*, p. 72.

19. *Sacramento Standard*, in *San Francisco Alta California*, 17 March 1860.

20. California Legislature Joint Committee on the Mendocino War, *Majority and Minority Reports*, p. 11.

21. California, *Journal of the Senate*, 11th sess. (1860), p. 196; Richard Lambert, comp., *Homographic Chart of the State Officers, Senators, Representatives of the Eleventh Session of the California Legislature*, p. 1.

22. *Statutes of California*, 11th sess., chap. 231 (1860), pp. 196–97.

23. Robert F. Heizer, ed., *The Destruction of California Indians: A Collection of Documents . . . of the Things that Happened to Some of the Indians of California*, p. 219.

24. *Sacramento Union*, 4 Feb. 1861. See also *San Francisco Bulletin*, 2 March 1861; *Humboldt Times*, 23 Feb. 1861; *Columbia Times*, 10 Jan. 1861; *Red Bluff Independent*, in *Marysville Appeal*, 4 Jan. 1861.

25. *Sacramento Union*, 4 Feb. 1861.

26. *Humboldt Times*, 23 Feb. 1861, in *San Francisco Bulletin*, 2 March 1861.

27. *Marysville Appeal*, 4 Jan. 1861, reprinted in Heizer, ed., *Destruction of California Indians*, p. 240. See also *Marysville Appeal*, 22 March 1861.

28. *Sacramento Union*, 31 July 1860.

29. Ibid.

30. *Constitution of the State of California* (1849) sec. 18, art. 1.

31. James Delavan, *Notes on California and the Placers: How to Get There and What to do Afterwards*, p. 54. See also *Columbia Times*, 10 Jan. 1861.

32. *Yreka Semi-Weekly Union*, 28 Sept. 1864, reprinted in Heizer, ed., *They Were Only Diggers*, pp. 94–95.

33. U.S. Office of Indian Affairs, *Report of Commissioner . . . for . . . 1861*, pp. 149–50.

34. U.S. Office of Indian Affairs, *Report of Commissioner . . . for . . . 1862*, p. 315.

35. Cook, *Conflict: American Invasion*, p. 57.

36. Ibid., p. 61. Edward D. Castillo, "The Impact of Euro-American Exploration and Settlement," in Robert F. Heizer, ed., *California*, p. 109.

37. *San Francisco Alta California*, 2 Oct. 1854; correspondence dated 31 Aug.

1862 to *Sacramento Union*, in Bancroft Scraps, 36: 101; *San Francisco Alta California*, 5 Oct. 1862.

38. Quoted in Heizer, ed., *Destruction of California Indians*, pp. 232–33.

39. *Ukiah Herald*, in *San Francisco Alta California*, 14 April 1862.

40. Correspondence dated 15 July 1862 to the *Sacramento Union*, a copy of which is pasted in Benjamin Hayes's Scrapbooks, 42:219, Bancroft Library, University of California, Berkeley. The Hayes scrapbooks are hereafter cited as Hayes Scraps.

41. Henry Clay Bailey, "Indian Life in the Sacramento Valley," *San Bernardino County Museum Quarterly* 7 (Fall, 1959): 17.

42. *Marysville Appeal*, 6 Dec. 1861; *Humboldt Times*, 5 May 1855.

43. Bailey, "Indian Life," p. 18.

44. *Marysville Appeal*, in *San Francisco Alta California*, 21 Oct. 1861.

45. *Ukiah Herald*, in *San Francisco Alta California*, 14 April 1862.

46. Correspondence dated 15 July 1862 to the *Sacramento Union*, in Hayes Scraps, 42:219.

47. Quoted in correspondence dated 31 Aug. 1862 to *Sacramento Union*, in Bancroft Scraps, 36:101.

48. *San Francisco Alta California*, 2 Oct. 1854; *Sacramento Union*, 13 Sept. 1854.

49. *Butte Record*, 23 May 1857, quoted in Cook, *Conflict: American Invasion*, p. 57.

50. *San Francisco Alta California*, 5 Oct. 1862.

51. U.S. Senate, *Executive Documents*, 32d Cong., 2d sess., doc. 57, pp. 9–10; Cook, *Conflict: American Invasion*, p. 57; Bailey, "Indian Life," p. 17.

52. *San Francisco Bulletin*, 2 Jan. 1858.

53. William H. Brewer, *Up and Down California in 1860–1864: The Journal of William H. Brewer*, ed. Francis P. Farquhar, p. 493.

54. Isaac Cox, *The Annals of Trinity County*, pp. 102, 112, 114.

55. *Sacramento Union*, 31 July 1860. See also same newspaper, 8 May 1857.

56. *Marysville Appeal*, 6 Dec. 1861. See also *San Francisco Alta California*, 17 Jan. 1858.

57. *Marysville Appeal*, reprinted in *San Francisco Alta California*, 21 Oct. 1861; *San Francisco Bulletin*, reprinted in *Hutchings' California Magazine* 5 (1860): 48.

58. *Marysville Appeal*, 6 Dec. 1861.

59. *Sacramento Union*, 31 July 1860.

60. Bailey, "Indian Life," p. 18.

61. *San Francisco Bulletin*, 2 Sept. 1856; *San Francisco Alta California*, 28 May 1868; *Yreka Journal*, 28 May 1873; *San Francisco Chronicle*, 19 and 26 Sept. 1897.

62. Franklin A. Buck, *A Yankee Trader in the Gold Rush: The Letters of Franklin A. Buck*, ed. Katherine A. White, pp. 117–18.

63. *Sacramento Union*, 20 May 1857.

64. Correspondence dated 15 July 1862 to *Sacramento Union*, in Hayes Scraps, 42:219.

65. Bailey, "Indian Life," p. 18.

66. Correspondence dated 15 July 1862 to *Sacramento Union*, in Hayes Scraps, 42:219.

67. Elijah Renshaw Potter, "Reminiscences of the Early History of Northern California and of the Indian Troubles," pp. 8–9, Bancroft Library, University of California, Berkeley. The most notable resistance to the conditions of forced labor occurred in Lake County in 1849. See William Ralganal Benson, "The Stone and Kelsey 'Massacre' on the Shores of Clear Lake in 1849," *California Historical Society Quarterly* 11 (Sept., 1932): 266–73.

68. Robert A. Anderson, *Fighting the Mill Creeks: Being a Personal Account of Campaigns Against Indians of the Northern Sierras*, pp. 80, 84–85; Sim Moak, *The Last of the Mill Creeks and Early Life in Northern California*, p. 24.

69. Cox, *Annals of Trinity County*, p. 114.

70. *San Francisco Alta California*, 5 Oct. 1862.

71. Correspondence dated 1 June 1860 to *San Francisco Bulletin*, reprinted in *Hutchings' California Magazine* 5 (1860): 48.

72. *Sacramento Union*, 20 May 1857; *San Francisco Alta California*, 7 April 1855, 5 Oct. 1862, 24 Jan. 1863, 20 Sept. 1863; *Humboldt Times*, 5 May 1855; Office of Indian Affairs, *Report of Commissioner . . . for . . . 1862*, p. 315; Cox, *Annals of Trinity County*, p. 102; Bell, *Reminiscences of a Ranger*, p. 115; Bailey, "Indian Life," p. 17; correspondence dated 15 July 1862 to *Sacramento Union*, in Hayes Scraps, 42:219.

73. Correspondence dated 31 Aug. 1862 to *Sacramento Union*, in Bancroft Scraps, 36:101.

74. *Sacramento Union*, 7 March 1861; *San Francisco Herald*, 14 Feb. 1860.

75. *Ukiah Herald*, in *San Francisco Alta California*, 14 April 1862. See also *San Diego Union*, 1 Jan. 1863; Carl Meyer, *Bound for Sacramento: Travel Pictures of a Returned Wanderer*, trans. Ruth Frey Axe, pp. 172–73.

76. Quoted in Heizer, ed., *Destruction of California Indians*, p. 233. See also *San Francisco Bulletin*, 1 June 1860.

77. See Heizer, ed., *Destruction of California Indians*, p. 26.

78. Ibid., pp. 234–36.

79. U.S. Office of Indian Affairs, *Report of Commissioner . . . for . . . 1862*, p. 315. See also Office of Indian Affairs, *Report of Commissioner . . . for . . . 1861*, p. 150.

80. U.S. Office of Indian Affairs, *Report of Commissioner . . . for . . . 1862*, p. 315.

81. See, for example, the case of three kidnappers described in Heizer, ed., *Destruction of California Indians*, pp. 238–39; and the case of George Woodman in the *San Francisco Bulletin*, 3 Feb. 1860 and 27 March 1861, and *Sacramento Union*, 13 and 26 March 1863.

82. Quoted in Heizer, ed., *Destruction of California Indians*, p. 229.

83. *Sacramento Union*, 31 Aug. 1862.

84. *Sacramento Union*, 5 May 1862.

85. Robert F. Heizer and Alan J. Almquist, *The Other Californians: Prejudice and Discrimination under Spain, Mexico and the United States to 1920*, p. 58.

86. *Sacramento Union*, 19 Aug. 1865.

87. *California Police Gazette*, 26 Sept. 1865.

88. U.S. Office of Indian Affairs, *Report on Indian Affairs . . . for . . . 1867*, p. 117.

89. Almon Wheeler Lauber, *Indian Slavery in Colonial Times Within the Present Limits of the United States*, pp. 291-95, 311-14; Wilbur R. Jacobs, "British-Colonial Attitudes and Policies Toward the Indians in the American Colonies," in Howard Peckham and Charles Gibson, eds., *Attitudes of Colonial Powers Toward the American Indian*, p. 97.

90. Lauber, *Indian Slavery*, pp. 295-98, 303-11.

91. Winthrop D. Jordan, *White Over Black: American Attitudes Toward the Negro, 1550-1812*, pp. 21-25.

92. Sanford A. Mosk, "Latin America Versus the United States," and Charles C. Griffen, "Unity and Variety in American History," in Lewis Hanke, ed., *Do the Americas Have a Common History? A Critique of the Bolton Theory*, pp. 178-79, 258; Clarence Henry Haring, *The Spanish Empire in America*, pp. 28-29.

93. John Hope Franklin, *Reconstruction After the Civil War*, pp. 48-49.

94. Kenneth M. Stampp, *The Era of Reconstruction, 1865-1877*, p. 80.

95. Ibid., pp. 80-81; Franklin, *Reconstruction*, pp. 48-49.

96. Stampp, *Era of Reconstruction*, pp. 80-81.

CHAPTER 5. *The Varieties of Exploitation*

1. Ira B. Cross, *A History of the Labor Movement in California*, pp. 10-13.

2. John W. Caughey, ed., *The Indians of Southern California in 1852: The B. D. Wilson Report and a Selection of Contemporary Comment*, pp. 16, 21. On the importance of Indian labor in Los Angeles see George Harwood Phillips, "Indians in Los Angeles, 1781-1875: Economic Integration, Social Disintegration," *Pacific Historical Review* 49 (August 1980): 427-51.

3. William Robert Garner, *Letters from California, 1846-1847*, ed. Donald Munro Craig, p. 18; *Sacramento Union*, 28 October 1871; Sherburne F. Cook, *The Conflict Between the California Indian and White Civilization: The American Invasion, 1848-1870*, p. 64.

4. Howard C. Gardiner, *In Pursuit of the Golden Dream: Reminiscences of San Francisco and the Northern and Southern Mines, 1849-1857*, ed. Dale L. Morgan, pp. 190-91, 193; Mrs. D. B. Bates, *Incidents on Land and Water: Or Four Years on the Pacific Coast*, pp. 80-88.

5. Frank Adams, "The Historical Background of California Agriculture," in Claude B. Hutchison, ed., *California Agriculture*, p. 27.

6. Quoted in Robert F. Heizer, ed., *The Destruction of California Indians: A Collection of Documents . . . of the Things that Happened to Some of the Indians of California*, pp. 31-32.

7. James Mason Hutchings, Diary, p. 179, University of California, Berkeley; Sim Moak, *The Last of the Mill Creeks and Early Life in Northern California*, p. 9.

8. Jacob D. B. Stillman, *The Gold Rush Letters of J. D. B. Stillman*, p. 63.

9. James L. Tyson, *Diary of a Physician . . . and Observations on the Climate, Soil, Resources of the Country, Etc.*, p. 83.

10. George Gibbs, "Journal of the Expedition of Redick M'Kee, United States Indian Agent, Through Northwestern California in the Summer and Fall of 1851," in Henry Rowe Schoolcraft, *Archives of Aboriginal Knowledge: Containing All . . . of the Indian Tribes of the United States* 3:100–102.

11. Adams, "Historical Background," in Hutchison, ed., *California Agriculture*, p. 27; Carey McWilliams, *Factories in the Field: The Story of Migratory Farm Labor in California*, pp. 62–63.

12. Cross, *History of the Labor Movement*, pp. 29–30.

13. Cook, *Conflict: American Invasion*, p. 61.

14. U.S. Interior Department, Office of Indian Affairs, *Report of the Commissioner . . . for . . . 1865*, p. 119.

15. U.S. Office of Indian Affairs, *Report of the Commissioner . . . on . . . 1869*, pp. 194–95.

16. Correspondence to the *New York Tribune*, 6 May 1872. Cf. *Sacramento Bee*, 5 May 1875.

17. U.S. Office of Indian Affairs, *Report of the Commissioner . . . for . . . 1871*, p. 329.

18. *San Diego Union*, 21 Oct. 1874.

19. *San Francisco Alta California*, 26 Feb. 1875.

20. Quoted in *Sacramento Union*, 22 Nov. 1879. See also Florence C. Shipek, "History of Southern California Mission Indians," in Robert F. Heizer, ed., *California*, vol. 8 of *Handbook of North American Indians*, pp. 610–18.

21. McWilliams, *Factories in the Field*, pp. 55–56.

22. Ibid., p. 65.

23. *Sacramento Union*, 17 July 1865; Cook, *Conflict: American Invasion*, pp. 63–64.

24. Quoted in Cook, *Conflict: American Invasion*, p. 63.

25. U.S. Office of Indian Affairs, *Report on Indian Affairs . . . for . . . 1867*, p. 117.

26. *San Francisco Bulletin*, 7 July 1862.

27. U.S. Office of Indian Affairs, *Report on Indian Affairs . . . for . . . 1867*, p. 117.

28. U.S. Congress, House, *Executive Documents*, 31st Cong., 1st sess., doc. 59, p. 8; U.S. Office of Indian Affairs, *Report of the Commissioner . . . for . . . 1865*, p. 119; Garner, *Letters from California*, p. 91; John Strother Griffen, *A Doctor Comes to California . . . 1846–1847*, p. 43; James Mason Hutchings, *Scenes of Wonder and Curiosity in California . . . the Yosemite Valley*, pp. 191–92; Bates, *Incidents on Land and Water*, pp. 80–88.

29. Jessie Benton Frémont, *A Year of American Travel: A Narrative of Personal Experience*, pp. 71, 91; Frémont, *Mother Lode Narratives*, ed. Shirley Sargent, pp. 102–103.

30. U.S. House, *Executive Documents*, 30th Cong., 2d sess., doc. 1, p. 60. For a recent account of the importance of Indian labor in the mines, see J. S. Holliday, *The World Rushed In: The California Gold Rush Experience*, pp. 38–41, 328.

31. E. Gould Buffum, *The Gold Rush: An Account of Six Months in the California Diggings*, ed. Oscar Lewis, p. 80.

32. Quoted in G. G. Foster, ed., *The Gold Regions of California: Being a Succinct Description . . . of California*, pp. 30–31.

33. B. Schmölder, *The Emigrant's Guide to California: Describing its Geography, Agricultural and Commercial Resources*, pp. 51–53.

34. William G. Johnston, *Experiences of a Forty-Niner*, p. 240; Peter Decker, *The Diaries of Peter Decker: Overland to California in 1849 and Life in the Mines, 1850–51*, ed. Helen S. Giffen, pp. 19, 190; James H. Carson, *Recollections of the California Mines: An Account . . . of the Great Tulare Valley*, p. 59.

35. Henry I. Simpson, *Three Weeks in the Gold Mines: Or Adventures with the Gold Diggers of California . . . with a Map and Illustrations*, p. 6. Although Simpson's book was something of a hoax, it was based on contemporary sources that were themselves fairly accurate. See William M'Collom, *California as I Saw It: Pencillings by the Way of Its Gold and Gold Diggers*, ed. Dale L. Morgan, p. 11; Carl I. Wheat, *Books of the California Gold Rush: A Centennial Selection*, p. 189; Douglas S. Watson, "Spurious Californiana," *California Historical Society Quarterly* 11 (March, 1932): 65–68.

36. Bayard Taylor, *Eldorado: Or, Adventures in the Path of Empire . . . and Experiences of Mexican Travel* 1:85.

37. *San Francisco Alta California*, 31 May 1850.

38. Johnston, *Experiences of a Forty-Niner*, p. 240.

39. James Clyman, "James Clyman: His Diaries and Reminiscences," ed. Charles L. Camp, *California Historical Society Quarterly* 6 (March, 1927): 62.

40. Albert Lyman, *Journal of a Voyage to California and . . . the Sandwich Islands*, p. 142.

41. U.S. House, *Executive Documents*, 30th Cong., 2d sess., doc. 1, p. 60.

42. See, for example, James Wyld, *A Guide to the Gold Country of California: An Authentic and Descriptive Narrative of the Latest Discoveries in that Country;* Joseph Warren Revere, *A Tour . . . of the Gold Region*, ed. Joseph N. Balestier; J. Ely Sherwood, *California: And the Way to Get There . . . with the Subject;* J. Ely Sherwood, *The Pocket Guide to California . . . Practical Advice to Voyagers;* John T. Hughes, *California: Its History, Population, Climate, Soil, Productions, and Harbors;* Foster, *Gold Regions of California;* Schmölder, *Emigrant's Guide to California*.

43. U.S. House, *Executive Documents*, 30th Cong., 2d sess., doc. 1, pp. 58–62. The wide-brimmed, tightly woven baskets of the California Indians were easily converted from their original functions to serve as basins for panning placer gold by Indian and white miners. This instance of white adoption of Indian materials should be added to the list in A. Irving Hallowell, "The Impact of the Indian on American Culture," *American Anthropologist* 59 (April, 1957).

44. U.S. House, *Executive Documents*, 30th Cong., 2d sess., doc. 1, pp. 58–62. Mason or the government typesetter incorrectly rendered the name "Suñol" as "Lunol" and "Daylor" as "Daly."

45. [John M. Letts], *California Illustrated: Including a Description of the Panama and Nicaragua Routes*, p. 63.

46. Hubert Howe Bancroft, *History of California* 5:738.

47. Simpson, *Three Weeks in the Gold Mines*, p. 8.

48. Antonio Francisco Coronel, "Cosas de California," Bancroft Library, University of California, Berkeley; William Perkins, *Three Years in California: William Perkins' Journal of Life at Sonora, 1849–1852*, ed. Dale L. Morgan and James R. Scobie, pp. 22–23.

49. Leonard Pitt, *The Decline of the Californios: A Social History of the Spanish-Speaking Californians, 1846–1890*, p. 50.

50. Buffum, *Gold Rush*, p. 109; Bancroft, *History of California* 5:770. For an account of Weber's use of Indian labor see George P. Hammond, *The Weber Era in Stockton History*, pp. 87–93.

51. *San Andreas Independent*, in *Sacramento Union*, 31 Jan. 1857; Bancroft, *History of California* 6:75–76; *An Illustrated History of San Joaquin County, California*, p. 61.

52. Carson, *Recollections of the California Mines*, pp. 5–8.

53. Bancroft, *History of California* 4:749; Erwin G. Gudde, *California Place Names: The Origin and Etymology of Current Geographical Names*, p. 215; J. Heckendorn, *Miners and Business Men's Directory*, p. 96, cited in Cook, *Conflict: American Invasion*, p. 66.

54. Walter Colton, *Three Years in California*, p. 277.

55. Wyld, *Guide to the Gold Country*, p. 43; Sherwood, *Pocket Guide to California*, p. 36. See also Theodore T. Johnson, *Sights in the Gold Region, and Scenes by the Way*, pp. 209, 218; Bancroft, *History of California* 5:721; Henry Vizetelly [J. Tyrwhitt Brooks, M.D.], *Four Months Among . . . the Gold Districts*, p. 22. Like Simpson's *Three Weeks*, Vizetelly's *Four Months* was a spurious "first-hand" account of California based on various contemporary sources.

56. George D. Lyman, *John Marsh, Pioneer: The Life Story of a Trail-blazer on Six Frontiers*, p. 277.

57. Henry P. De Groot, *Recollections of California Mining Life*, p. 8; Bancroft, *History of California* 6:69.

58. John E. Ross, "Narrative of an Indian Fighter," p. 11, Bancroft Library, University of California, Berkeley.

59. Quoted in Isaac Cox, *The Annals of Trinity County*, p. 2. See also De Groot, *Recollections*, p. 8.

60. U.S. House, *Executive Documents*, 30th Cong., 2d sess., doc. 1, p. 60.

61. John A. Sutter, "The Discovery of Gold in California," *Hutchings' Illustrated California Magazine* 2 (Nov., 1857): 197; Carson, *Recollections of the California Mines*, p. 5; Joseph A. McGowan, *History of the Sacramento Valley*, p. 50; Bancroft, *History of California* 4:103–105.

62. James Delavan, *Notes on California and the Placers: How to Get There and What to Do Afterwards*, p. 55; Johnston, *Experiences of a Forty-Niner*, p. 240.

63. John A. Swan, *A Trip to the Gold Mines of California in 1848*, ed. John A. Hussey, p. 7; M'Collom, *California As I Saw It*, p. 156; Ryan, *Personal Adventures* 2:41–42; Simpson, *Three Weeks in the Gold Mines*, p. 7; Decker, *Diaries*, p. 174; Johnson, *Sights in the Gold Region*, p. 206; *Sacramento Union*, 24 June 1851; Luther M. Schaeffer, *Sketches of Travels in South America, Mexico and California*, p. 170; Carson, *Recollections of the California Mines*, p. 60.

64. Buffum, *Gold Rush*, p. 110–11.

65. Annie R. Mitchell, "Major James D. Savage and the Tulareños," *Cali-*

fornia Historical Society Quarterly, 28 (Dec., 1949): 323–41; Benjamin Butler Harris, *The Gila Trail: The Texas Argonauts and the California Gold Rush*, ed. Richard H. Dillon, pp. 20–21, 146–47; Robert Eccleston, *The Mariposa Indian War, 1850–1851: Diaries of Robert Eccleston*, ed. C. Gregory Crampton, pp. iii, iv, 110; Paul E. Vandor, *History of Fresno County . . . to the Present*, p. 77.

66. Harris, *Gila Trail*, p. 147; Perkins, *Three Years in California*, p. 118. John Marsh traded sugar to the Indians for equal weights of gold dust. See Lyman, *John Marsh*, p. 277.

67. Harris, *Gila Trail*, p. 146.

68. Oliver M. Wozencraft, "Indian Affairs, 1849–1850," p. 2, Bancroft Library, University of California, Berkeley.

69. Cook, *Conflict: American Invasion*, p. 67. See, however, J. D. Borthwick, *Three Years in California*, pp. 288–89; and John Doble, *John Doble's Journal and Letters From the Mines: Mokelumne Hill, Jackson, Volcano and San Francisco*, ed. Charles L. Camp, pp. 45–46.

70. Rodman Paul, *California Gold: The Beginning of Mining in the Far West*, pp. 50–66.

71. Rudolph M. Lapp, *Blacks in Gold Rush California*, pp. 128–29; Clyde A. Duniway, "Slavery in California after 1848," *Annual Report of the American Historical Association for the Year 1905* 2:243.

72. Ralph P. Bieber, "California Gold Mania," *Mississippi Valley Historical Review* 35 (June, 1948): 3–28.

73. Quoted in Cox, *Annals of Trinity County*, p. 2; Ross, "Narrative of an Indian Fighter," p. 11.

74. Bancroft, *History of California* 6:100–101; Ross, "Narrative of an Indian Fighter," pp. 13–14.

75. George Frederic Parsons, *Life and Adventures of James W. Marshall: The Discoverer of Gold in California*, pp. 111–12.

76. Quoted in Edward E. Dunbar, *The Romance of the Age: Or, the Discovery of Gold in California*, pp. 117–18.

77. Parsons, *Life and Adventures*, pp. 112–13.

78. *San Francisco Placer Times and Transcript*, 5 May 1849, in *San Francisco Alta California*, 17 May 1849.

79. Ross, "Narrative of an Indian Fighter," p. 15; Dunbar, *Romance of the Age*, p. 118.

80. Ross, "Narrative of an Indian Fighter," p. 16.

81. Ibid., p. 17. Correspondence from William Daylor to *San Francisco Placer Times and Transcript*, 12 May 1849, in *San Francisco Alta California*, 31 May 1849.

82. Ray Howard Glassley, *Indian Wars of the Pacific Northwest*, pp. 13–38.

83. Ross, "Narrative of an Indian Fighter," p. 15. See also Glassley, *Indian Wars*, pp. 82–86; and Theodore H. Hittel, *History of California* 3:888, 4:58.

84. See M'Collom, *California As I Saw It*, pp. 147–48, 153, 156; Delavan, *Notes on California*, p. 54; Ryan, *Personal Adventures* 2:299–301; [Letts,] *California Illustrated*, p. 112; Theodore T. Johnson, *California and Oregon: Or, Sights in the Gold Region and Scenes by the Way*, p. 181; Johnson, *Sights in the Gold Region*, pp. 173, 197–98, 201.

85. Buffum, *Gold Rush,* pp. 19, 57, 66, 80, 119. See also Daniel B. Woods, *Sixteen Months at the Gold Diggings,* p. 84; Johnson, *Sights in the Gold Region,* pp. 206–208; Jill L. Cossley-Batt, *The Last of the California Rangers,* pp. 73–74, 118.

86. Delavan, *Notes on California,* p. 55.

87. Johnson, *Sights in the Gold Region,* pp. 206–209, 218; Johnson, *California and Oregon,* pp. 132, 140, 142–43.

88. Johnson, *Sights in the Gold Region,* pp. 152–53; Johnson, *California and Oregon,* p. 140.

CHAPTER 6. *Removal and Reservation*

1. James D. Richardson, ed., *A Compilation of the Messages and Papers of the Presidents, 1789–1897* 2:520–21. Jackson was not the first or only American President to express such views. Compare, for example, the 1802 remarks of John Quincy Adams: "There are moralists who have questioned the right of Europeans to intrude upon the possessions of the aborigines in any case and under any limitations whatsoever. But have they maturely considered the whole subject? . . . Shall the lordly savage . . . forbid the oaks of the forest to fall before the ax of industry and rise again transformed into the habitations of ease and elegance? Shall he doom an immense region of the globe to perpetual desolation, and to hear the howlings of the tiger and wolf silence forever the voice of human gladness?" (quoted in U.S. Interior Department, Office of Indian Affairs, *Report on Indian Affairs . . . for . . . 1867,* p. 144). Compare also the later and more familiar sentiments of Theodore Roosevelt in *The Winning of the West* 1:257–64, 331–32.

2. See Robert F. Berkhofer, Jr., *The White Man's Indian: Images of American Indians from Columbus to the Present,* pp. 113–45; Roy Harvey Pearce, *The Savages of America: A Study of the Indian and the Idea of Civilization;* Pearce, "The Metaphysics of Indian Hating," *Ethnohistory* 4 (1957): 27–37.

3. Gary B. Nash, *Red, White and Black: The Peoples of Early America,* pp. 276–97; Richard R. Johnson, "The Search for a Usable Indian: An Aspect of the Defense of Colonial New England," *Journal of American History* 64 (Dec., 1977): 625.

4. Wilbur R. Jacobs, "British-Colonial Attitudes and Policies Toward the Indian in the American Colonies," in Howard Peckham and Charles Gibson, eds., *Attitudes of Colonial Powers Toward the American Indian,* pp. 99–100; Wilcomb E. Washburn, *The Indian in America,* p. 211; Berkhofer, *White Man's Indian,* p. 133; S. Lyman Tyler, *A History of Indian Policy,* pp. 31–46.

5. Pearce, *Savages of America,* p. 11. See also the penetrating discussion in Bernard W. Sheehan, *Seeds of Extinction: Jeffersonian Philanthropy and the American Indian.*

6. Johnson, "Search for a Usable Indian," pp. 648–49.

7. Tyler, *History of Indian Policy,* pp. 28–29.

8. Francis Paul Prucha, *American Indian Policy in the Formative Years: The Indian Trade and Intercourse Acts, 1790–1834,* p. 186.

9. Ibid., p. 225.

10. Washburn, *Indian in America*, p. 165.

11. Quoted in *San Francisco Alta California*, 14 Jan. 1851.

12. William Henry Ellison, "The Federal Indian Policy in California, 1846-1860" (Ph.D. diss., University of California, Berkeley, 1918), pp. 323-24.

13. U.S. Senate, *Executive Documents*, 33d Cong., spec. sess., 1853 doc. 4, p. 82.

14. *San Francisco Alta California*, 12 Jan. 1851. See also *Alta California*, 26 July 1851, 10 Sept. 1851, 9 and 11 Feb. 1852.

15. *San Francisco Alta California*, 9 Feb. 1852. See also same newspaper, 2 March 1852.

16. *San Francisco Alta California*, 16 Jan. 1852 and 9 Feb. 1852. In 1854, Governor Bigler reemphasized his support for removal, saying that to place the Indians on reservations within the state "cannot fail to exercise a blighting influence on the future prosperity of California" (California Legislature, *Journal of the Assembly*, 5th sess., 1854, p. 28). See also *Alta California*, 26 July 1851; *Los Angeles Star*, 13 March 1852; and Hubert Howe Bancroft, *History of California* 4:645.

17. California Legislature, *Journal of the Senate*, 3d sess., 1852, pp. 44-45, 600-601.

18. California Legislature, *Journal of the Senate*, 3d sess., 1852, pp. 597-601. Compare with the similar recommendations in California Legislature, *Journal of the Assembly*, 3d sess., 1852, pp. 202-205.

19. Joseph J. Hill, *The History of Warner's Ranch and its Environs*, ed. Herbert E. Bolton, pp. 136-37. See also the excellent discussion of Warner in George Harwood Phillips, *Chiefs and Challengers: Indian Resistance and Cooperation in Southern California*, pp. 59, 65.

20. California Legislature, *Journal of the Senate*, 3d sess., 1852, pp. 602-604.

21. William Henry Ellison, *A Self-Governing Dominion: California, 1849-1860*, pp. 155-57; Ellison, "Federal Indian Policy," pp. 323-43; George E. Anderson, W. H. Ellison, and Robert F. Heizer, *Treaty Making and Treaty Rejection by the Federal Government in California, 1850-1852*.

22. U.S. Congress, Senate, *Congressional Globe*, 32d Cong., 1st sess., 1852, 3:2173; Ellison, "Federal Indian Policy," p. 341; Ellison, *Self-Governing Dominion*, p. 156; Robert F. Heizer and Alan J. Almquist, *The Other Californians: Prejudice and Discrimination Under Spain, Mexico and the United States to 1920*, p. 77.

23. California Senate, *Congressional Globe*, 32d Cong., 1st sess., 1852, app., p. 1082.

24. Ellison, "Federal Indian Policy," p. 342. This judgment is only slightly modified in Ellison's *Self-Governing Dominion*, p. 157. Compare with the similar views in Edward Everett Dale, *Indians of the Southwest: A Century of Development Under the United States*, p. 30.

25. Heizer and Almquist, *Other Californians*, pp. 68-69. George Harwood Phillips, however, has commented, "Considering that the treaties were negotiated by a colonizing power, they were quite fair and even generous to the Indians" (Phillips, *Chiefs and Challengers*, p. 172).

26. Wozencraft offered the following prescient observation in 1852: "What

will be the state of affairs with our Indian tribes if we refuse a faithful compliance with promises made them, and do not attempt to conciliate those who, as yet, have not been treated with? There can be but one answer . . . *war to extermination"* (California Senate, *Executive Documents*, 33d Cong., spec. sess., doc. 4, p. 334).

27. See Wilbur R. Jacobs, "The Fatal Confrontation: Early Native-White Relations on the Frontiers of Australia, New Guinea, and America—A Comparative Study," *Pacific Historical Review*, 40 (Sept., 1971): 283–310.

28. California Legislature, *Journal of the Assembly*, 8th sess., 1857, pp. 25–26, 645; *San Francisco Herald*, 4 May 1856; *San Francisco Alta California*, 9 Jan. 1857, 6 Jan. 1859, and 15 Nov. 1862; *San Francisco Chronicle*, 11 March 1857; *San Francisco Herald*, 4 Dec. 1861.

29. California Legislature, Joint Committee on the Mendocino War, *Majority and Minority Reports*, p. 1.

30. U.S., *Statutes at Large* 10: 2–3.

31. Alban Hoopes, *Indian Affairs and Their Administration: With Special References to the Far West, 1849–1860*, p. 47; Edward E. Hill, *The Office of Indian Affairs, 1824–1880: Historical Sketches*, p. 24. See also Stephen Bonsal, *Edward Fitzgerald Beale: A Pioneer in the Path of Empire, 1822–1903*.

32. U.S. Senate, *Executive Documents*, 33d Cong., spec. sess., doc. 4, pp. 373–74. Cf. U.S. House, *Executive Documents*, 31st Cong., 1st sess., doc. 59, p. 8.

33. Robert A. Trennert, Jr., *Alternative to Extinction: Federal Indian Policy and the Beginnings of the Reservation System, 1846–1851*, p. viii; Tyler, *History of Indian Policy*, pp. 70–75; Hill, *Office of Indian Affairs*, p. 20; Hoopes, *Indian Affairs*, pp. 35–51; Washburn, *Indian in America*, pp. 170–96.

34. U.S. Senate, *Executive Documents*, 33d Cong., spec. sess., doc. 4, p. 380.

35. John Walton Caughey, ed., *The Indians of Southern California in 1852: The B. D. Wilson Report and a Selection of Contemporary Comments*, pp. 3, 47–48; *Los Angeles Star*, 16 Oct. 1852, 20 Dec. 1852, 15 Jan. 1853, and 4 June 1853. Whether Wilson actually wrote this important report is a matter of dispute. Caughey argues convincingly that Benjamin Hayes may have ghostwritten the report for Wilson. (*Indians of Southern California in 1852*, pp. xxvi–xviii).

36. Phillips, *Chiefs and Challengers*, p. 173.

37. See, for example, *San Francisco Alta California*, 5 Sept. 1853. The controversy over this point may be traced in the *Alta California*, 5 Dec. 1850, 12 and 14 Jan. 1851, 21 Nov. 1855, 18 April 1862, 15 Nov. 1862, 22 Aug. 1868, 10 Nov. 1869, 29 Oct. 1874, and 1 Nov. 1874; *San Francisco Herald*, 14 May 1856; *Sacramento Union*, 30 Jan. 1860, 3 May 1860, 22 Nov. 1879; *Sacramento Bee*, 5 May 1875; *Los Angeles Star*, 15 Aug. 1852; *Yreka Journal*, 19 March 1873; *Humboldt Times*, 20 Nov. 1858; *Grass Valley Telegraph*, 29 March 1856. See also Harry Kelsey, "The California Indian Treaty Myth," *Southern California Quarterly* 55 (Fall, 1973): 225–35.

38. U.S. House, *Executive Documents*, 31st Cong., 1st sess., doc. 59, p. 8.

39. California Legislature, *Journal of the Senate*, 3d sess., 1852, p. 597.

40. The history of Indian title in California is complicated and has never been told in the detail that it deserves. Apparently, the United States adopted the position that, since the land of California had been purchased from Mexico,

it had no obligation to recognize Indian title; lands occupied by Indians therefore became a part of the public domain (Dale, *Indians of the Southwest,* p. 45). The Board of Land Commissioners, which was created by Congress to settle disputes arising from the Mexican land grants, did nothing for the California Indians (William W. Robinson, *Land in California: The Story of Mission Lands, Ranchos, Squatters, Mining Claims, Railroad Grants, Land Scrip Homesteads,* pp. 15-16).

41. U.S., *Statutes at Large* 10:238.

42. U.S. Senate, *Executive Documents,* 33d Cong., spec. sess., doc. 4, pp. 377-80.

43. Quoted in Hoopes, *Indian Affairs,* pp. 54-55.

44. Ibid., p. 55; Dale, *Indians of the Southwest,* p. 39; Bonsal, *Edward Fitzgerald Beale,* pp. 186-89.

45. Donald L. Hilsop, *The Nome Lackee Indian Reservation, 1854-1870.* "Nome Lackee" (or "Nomlaki") was a Wintun group name, from *nom,* "west" (Erwin G. Gudde, *California Place Names: The Origin and Etymology of Current Geographical Names,* p. 223).

46. *San Francisco Bulletin,* 29 June 1857. See also Hoopes, *Indian Affairs,* pp. 66-67.

47. For a concise summary of the reservation system in the 1860s and early 1870s, see Hill, *Office of Indian Affairs,* pp. 19-24.

48. *San Francisco Herald,* 3 May 1854, 14 May 1856, 4 Dec. 1861; *San Francisco Chronicle,* 8, 10, and 11 July 1854; *San Joaquin Republican,* reprinted in *San Francisco Alta California,* 14 July 1854; *Los Angeles Star,* 17, 24 and 25 June 1854, and 20 Oct. 1855.

49. *San Francisco Alta California,* 22 Sept. 1853.

50. *San Francisco Alta California,* 16 Nov. 1853; 25 and 27 June 1854; 2, 7, and 10 July 1854.

51. *Sacramento Union,* 1 April 1856; *San Francisco Golden Era,* 4 Sept. 1856; *San Francisco Alta California,* 9 Jan. 1857; James Mason Hutchings, Diary, pp. 180-81, Bancroft Library, University of California, Berkeley.

52. *San Francisco Placer Times and Transcript,* 30 Sept. 1854.

53. *San Francisco Alta California,* 28 May 1858, 6 Jan. 1855.

54. *San Francisco Sun,* in *Sacramento Union,* 26 Jan. 1855. See also *Union,* 2 Nov. 1857, and *San Francisco Alta California,* 13 Oct. 1855.

55. *San Francisco Bulletin,* 13 Sept. 1856. See also same newspaper 12 Sept. 1856, and *California Police Gazette,* 26 Aug. 1865.

56. Quoted in Hoopes, *Indian Affairs,* p. 64.

57. U.S. Senate, *Executive Documents,* 36th Cong., 1st sess., doc. 46, pp. 13-15. See also Office of Indian Affairs, *Report of the Commissioner . . . for . . . 1858,* pp. 298-302.

58. J. Ross Browne, "The Coast Rangers: A Chronicle of Events in California," *Harpers' New Monthly Magazine* 22 (Aug., 1861): 309, 315.

59. See, for example, *San Francisco Bulletin,* 22 July 1861, 29 April 1864, 28 May 1868, 4 June 1868, 10 Nov. 1871. The "failure" of the reservations led to the suggestion that the state should take over their administration from the federal government. See Wilcomb E. Washburn, ed., *The American Indian*

and the United States: A Documentary History 2: 1246–66.

60. *Sacramento Union,* 2 July 1860. See also same newspaper, 30 Jan. 1860.

61. *San Francisco Alta California,* 24 April 1867.

62. Ibid., 18 June 1868.

63. See the account in Loring Benson Priest, *Uncle Sam's Stepchildren: The Reformation of United States Indian Policy, 1865–1887;* and Henry E. Fritz, *The Movement for Indian Assimilation, 1860–1890.*

64. The practice of appointing agents nominated by the denominations was gradually abandoned and by 1880 had been discontinued. See Laurence F. Schmeckebier, *The Office of Indian Affairs: Its History, Activities and Organization,* p. 55; Dale, *Indians of the Southwest,* p. 82; Hill, *Office of Indian Affairs,* p. 25.

65. U.S. Office of Indian Affairs, *Report of the Commissioner . . . for . . . 1868,* p. 133; *Report of the Commissioner . . . on . . . 1869,* pp. 188, 191. If these statistics are correct, about 1,700 of the state's estimated 30,000 Indians were on reservations in 1869. Two years earlier Robert J. Stevens, appointed to investigate conditions in California, had reported that 3,000 Indians were living on the state's reservations (*Report of the Commissioner . . . for . . . 1867,* p. 132).

66. The role of the Methodists in California Indian affairs has yet to find its historian. See, however, Dale, *Indians of the Southwest,* pp. 80–84.

67. U.S. Office of Indian Affairs, *Report of the Commissioner . . . for . . . 1871,* p. 335.

68. See, for example, the correspondence dated July, 1871, to an unidentified San Francisco newspaper in Bancroft Scraps, 36:137. See also U.S. Office of Indian Affairs, *Report of the Commissioner . . . for . . . 1871,* p. 335.

69. *New York Tribune,* 8 Nov. 1871.

70. U.S. Office of Indian Affairs, *Report of the Commissioner . . . for . . . 1871,* pp. 336, 338, 341; Charles Maltby to Hubert Howe Bancroft, 10 Aug. 1872, Bancroft Library, University of California, Berkeley.

71. *San Francisco Bulletin,* 10 Nov. 1871. For an account of the Round Valley reservation, see Lynwood Carranco and Estle Beard, *Genocide and Vendetta: The Round Valley Wars of Northern California.*

72. *San Francisco Alta California,* 12 Oct. 1873.

73. Ibid., 8 June 1874. See also same newspaper, 7 June 1875.

74. Stephen Powers, "The Northern California Indians," *Overland Monthly* 8 (April, 1872): 325–26. Cf. Powers's unbridgeable "chasm" to the "Impassable Gulf" of Roy Harvey Pearce's *Savages of America.*

75. *Humboldt Times,* 17 March 1860, 14 and 21 April 1860; Owen C. Coy, *The Humboldt Bay Region, 1850–1875: A Study in the American Colonization of California,* pp. 150–51; Anthony Jennings Bledsoe, *Indian Wars of the Northwest: A California Sketch.*

76. *Humboldt Times,* 2 Oct. 1858.

77. U.S. Office of Indian Affairs, *Report of the Commissioner . . . for . . . 1863,* p. 95.

78. *Butte County Appeal,* 3 Oct. 1863.

79. *Oroville Union,* 1 Aug. 1864, in Bancroft Scraps, 36:27. See also later views regarding the Modocs: *Yreka Journal,* 15 Jan. 1873, 28 May 1873, 11 June

242

1873; and *San Francisco Alta California*, 23 April 1873.

80. *San Francisco Bulletin*, 23 Dec. 1859; *Red Bluff Beacon*, reprinted in *San Francisco Bulletin*, 24 Dec. 1859; *Humboldt Times*, in *San Francisco Alta California*, 25 April 1862; *Red Bluff Semi-Weekly Independent*, 23 Sept. 1862; W. E. Roscoe, "A History of the Mattole Valley," pp. 13-14, Bancroft Library, University of California, Berkeley; Robert A. Anderson, *Fighting the Mill Creeks: Being a Personal Account of Campaigns Against Indians of the Northern Sierras*, pp. 43-44; Theodora Kroeber, *Ishi in Two Worlds: A Biography of the Last Wild Indian in North America*, pp. 57-58; Robert F. Heizer, ed., *The Destruction of California Indians: A Collection of Documents . . . of the Things that Happened to Some of the Indians of California*, pp. 126-28.

81. Correspondence to *Mariposa Gazette*, 1858, in Hayes Scraps, 42:129.

82. Reprinted in Heizer, ed., *Destruction of California Indians*, pp. 130-31.

83. Elijah Renshaw Potter, "Reminiscences of the Early History of Northern California and of the Indian Troubles," pp. 6, 15, Bancroft Library, University of California, Berkeley.

84. Correspondence to *Sonoma Journal*, 1 Oct. 1859.

85. U.S. Senate, *Congressional Globe*, 36th Cong., 1st sess., pp. 2366-67.

86. Correspondence to *San Francisco Alta California*, 31 Jan. 1852; correspondence to *Los Angeles Star*, 15 Aug. 1852, 15 Jan. 1853; correspondence to *Mariposa Gazette*, 1858, in Hayes Scraps, 42:129; *Shasta Courier*, reprinted in *Humboldt Times*, 25 Feb. 1860.

87. Quoted in Sherburne F. Cook, *The Conflict Between the California Indian and White Civilization: The American Invasion, 1848-1880*, p. 63.

88. Ibid. Cf. U.S. Office of Indian Affairs, *Report of the Commissioner . . . on . . . 1869*, p. 185.

89. U.S. House, *Executive Documents*, 34th Cong., 3d sess., doc. 76, pp. 94-95; *Sacramento Union*, 5 May 1858; U.S. Office of Indian Affairs, *Report of the Commissioner . . . for . . . 1858*, p. 288.

90. U.S. Office of Indian Affairs, *Report of the Commissioner . . . for . . . 1856*, p. 251.

91. *Inyo Independent*, Jan. 1873, in Bancroft Scraps, 36:141.

92. *Healdsburg Enterprise*, reprinted in *San Francisco Alta California*, 29 June 1876.

93. James Beith to J. M. Light, 22 Aug. 1863, Beith Letterbook, Bancroft Library, University of California, Berkeley. See also *Sacramento Union*, 15 Sept. 1866.

94. *Red Bluff Beacon*, reprinted in *San Francisco Alta California*, 19 May 1858; Anderson, *Fighting the Mill Creeks*, p. 44; Priest, *Uncle Sam's Stepchildren*, p. 7.

95. Reprinted in Heizer, ed., *Destruction of California Indians*, pp. 137-39.

96. *Colusa Sun*, reprinted in *San Francisco Bulletin*, 6 Nov. 1862.

97. U.S. Office of Indian Affairs, *Report of the Commissioner . . . for . . . 1862*, p. 323; *Report of the Commissioner . . . for . . . 1863*, p. 92; *Marysville Appeal*, reprinted in *San Francisco Bulletin*, 7 Nov. 1862.

98. U.S. Office of Indian Affairs, *Report of the Commissioner . . . for . . . 1863*, p. 95. Similar protests characterized the history of the Mendocino reservation. See *Humboldt Times*, 12 Sept. 1857, 3 Oct. 1857, 20 Nov. 1858; U.S. Office

of Indian Affairs, *Report of the Commissioner . . . for . . . 1858*, p. 285; and Coy, *Humboldt Bay Region*, p. 153–55. Protests also accompanied the establishment of the Hoopa reservation in 1864 in Humboldt County. See, for example, the *Humboldt Times*, 1 Oct. 1864; Coy, *Humboldt Bay Region*, pp. 191–96.

99. Correspondence to *San Francisco Bulletin*, 24 Dec. 1859. For a full account of Indian-white relations in Round Valley, see Carranco and Beard, *Genocide and Vendetta*.

100. U.S. Office of Indian Affairs, *Report of the Commissioner . . . for . . . 1863*, p. 91.

101. U.S. Office of Indian Affairs, *Report of the Commissioner . . . for . . . 1862*, p. 311; *Report of the Commissioner . . . for . . . 1863*, p. 98; *Sacramento Union*, 7 Nov. 1862.

102. *Mendocino Herald*, 1862, in Bancroft Scraps, 36:103; U.S. Office of Indian Affairs, *Report of the Commissioner . . . for . . . 1863*, p. 401. See also *San Francisco Alta California*, 22 and 28 Jan. 1874, 21 Feb. 1874, 28 April 1874; *West Coast Signal*, 17 March 1875, in Bancroft Scraps, 36:40.

103. Beith to Dick Deighton, 20 Sept. 1863, Beith to James McHary, 24 Sept. 1863, Beith to J. P. Prince, 14 Feb. 1864, Beith Letterbooks, Bancroft Library, University of California, Berkeley.

104. Beith to Asa Spear, 5 June 1862, Beith Letterbooks.

105. Beith to Dick Deighton, 5 June 1862, Beith Letterbooks.

106. Hill, *Office of Indian Affairs*, p. 25. Wiley was appointed 14 April 1864; his successor, Charles Maltby, was appointed on 22 March 1865.

107. Office of Indian Affairs, *Report of the Commissioner . . . for . . . 1864*, pp. 128–30.

108. Ibid., pp. 131–32.

109. *San Francisco Bulletin*, 29 April 1864, 9 July 1864, 9 Jan. 1865. See also *Sacramento Bee*, 7 Jan. 1876.

CHAPTER 7. *Extermination*

1. The exact number will never be known. See Sherburne F. Cook, *The Conflict Between the California Indian and White Civilization: The American Invasion, 1848–1870*, pp. 5–13, 111; and Cook, *The Population of the California Indians, 1769–1970*, pp. 44, 60.

2. See, for example, Thomas Butler King, "Report on California," in *Message from the Pesident* [*sic*] *of the United States, Transmitting the Report of T. Butler King*, pp. 7–8; Franklin A. Buck, *A Yankee Trader in the Gold Rush: The Letters of Franklin A. Buck*, ed. Katherine A. White, p. 100; and Titus Fey Cronise, *The Natural Wealth of California*, p. 22.

3. E. Gould Buffum, *The Gold Rush: An Account of Six Months in the California Diggings*, ed. Oscar Lewis, p. 119.

4. Horace Bell, *Reminiscences of a Ranger: Or, Early Times in Southern California*, p. 313.

5. Stephen Powers, "The Northern California Indians," *Overland Monthly* 8 (April, 1872): 325.

6. "The World in California," *Hutchings' Illustrated California Magazine* 1 (Feb., 1857): 338.

7. Indians had been known to "evaporate" all across the continent. Such metaphors were an integral part of the white image of the Indians of North America.

8. *San Francisco Alta California*, 5 Dec. 1850.

9. Ibid., 17 March 1851. See also William Perkins, *Three Years in California: William Perkins' Journal of Life at Sonora, 1849–1852*, ed. Dale L. Morgan and James R. Scobie, p. 310.

10. *Union City Times*, 14 Jan. 1875. See also *Humboldt Times*, 19 Nov. 1859; William I. Kip, "The Last of the Leatherstockings," *Overland Monthly* 2 (May, 1869): 401–402.

11. *San Francisco Alta California*, 3 June 1850, 10 May 1851, 6 Jan. 1859, 28 May 1868, 1 June 1868; *Marysville Herald*, 9 April 1854; Charles Edward Pancoast, *A Quaker Forty-Niner: The Adventures of Charles Edward Pancoast on the American Frontier*, ed. Anna Paschall Hannum, pp. 241, 265; John W. Caughey, ed., *The Indians of Southern California in 1852: The B. D. Wilson Report and a Selection of Contemporary Comments*, p. 20; W. E. Lovett, *Report of W. E. Lovett . . . to Austin Wiley, Superintendent of Indian Affairs in California*, p. 7; [Edwin F. Bean], *Bean's History and Directory of Nevada County, California*, p. 26; Edward E. Cheever, "The Indians of California," *American Naturalist* 4 (May, 1870): 142; Austin S. Clark, *Reminiscences of Travel, 1852–1865*, p. 38; Francis Marryat, *Mountains and Molehills: Or, Recollections of a Burnt Journal*, p. 81; Charles Loring Brace, *The New West: Or, California in 1867–1868*, p. 142; Ida Pfeiffer, *A Lady's Second Journey Round the World . . . and the United States*, p. 75.

12. Quoted in *San Francisco Alta California*, 6 Jan. 1859.

13. *Californian* (San Francisco), 8 Dec. 1847; *Los Angeles Star*, 12 Feb. 1853, 14 May 1853, 18 June 1853, 3 Dec. 1853; *San Francisco Alta California*, 9 Aug. 1873, 17 Oct. 1875; *Healdsburg Enterprise*, 27 June 1876, reprinted in *San Francisco Alta California*, 29 June 1876; *Marysville Herald*, reprinted in *San Francisco Alta California*, 9 April 1854; *Santa Barbara Press*, 27 April 1872; *New York Tribune*, 6 May 1872; *Alameda Independent*, 12 June 1875; Henry Vizetelly [J. Tyrwhitt Brooks, M.D.], *Four Months Among the Gold Finders in California: Being the Diary of an Expedition from San Francisco to the Gold Districts*, p. 26; John Doble, *John Doble's Journal and Letters from the Mines: Mokelumne Hill, Jackson, Volcano and San Francisco, 1851–1865*, ed. Charles L. Camp, pp. 45–46; Friedrich Gerstäcker, *Gerstäcker's Travels . . . and the Gold Fields*, p. 185; *Bean's History and Directory*, p. 26; Lovett, *Report*, p. 7. See also Nancy Oestreich Lurie, "The World's Oldest On-Going Protest Demonstration: North American Indian Drinking Patterns," in Norris Hundley, ed., *The American Indian*, pp. 55–76.

14. *Los Angeles Star*, 18 June 1853, cited in Caughey, ed., *Indians of Southern California*, p. 101.

15. Sandford Seymour, *Emigrant's Guide to the Gold Mines of Upper California*, p. 12. See also James Mason Hutchings, Diary, p. 179, Bancroft Library, University of California, Berkeley; Pfeiffer, *Lady's Second Journey*, p. 78; Pan-

coast, *Quaker Forty-Niner*, p. 343.

16. Cook, *Conflict: American Invasion*, pp. 14-20.

17. W. E. Roscoe, "A History of the Mattole Valley," p. 14, Bancroft Library, University of California, Berkeley; H. D. Richardson, "History of the Foundation of the City of Vallejo," p. 17, Bancroft Library, University of California, Berkeley; James Lawrence Tyson, *Diary of a Physician . . . and Observations on the Climate, Soil, Resources of the Country Etc.*, p. 68. See also Sherburne F. Cook, *The Epidemic of 1830-1833 in California and Oregon.*

18. Pancoast, *Quaker Forty-Niner*, p. 343.

19. Albert S. Evans, *Á La California: Sketches of Life in the Golden State*, pp. 207-208. For a full account of the Cahuillas see Lowell John Bean, *Mukat's People: The Cahuilla Indians of Southern California.*

20. Cook, *Conflict: American Invasion*, pp. 111, 115.

21. *San Francisco Alta California*, 10 May 1849, 5 June 1850, 28 and 31 Jan. 1860, 24 April 1867; *Yreka Herald*, 11 June 1873; *San Francisco Placer Times and Transcript*, 5 and 12 May, 1849.

22. *San Francisco Alta California*, 5 and 29 Dec. 1850. See also same newspaper, 22 Jan. 1860, 28 May 1868.

23. *Humboldt Times*, 2 Oct. 1858, 20 June 1860.

24. *Mendocino Herald*, 29 Nov. 1862.

25. *San Francisco Alta California*, 5 Dec. 1850, 21 Jan. 1851, 11 Feb. 1852, 13 Nov. 1852, 30 March 1853, 5 Sept. 1853, 22 Sept. 1853, 9 Jan. 1859, 22 Jan. 1860, 13 April 1862, 15 Nov. 1862, 24 Jan. 1863; *San Francisco Herald*, 3 May 1854; *San Francisco Bulletin*, 11 Sept. 1856; *San Francisco Chronicle*, 15 Nov. 1855; *Sacramento Union*, 2 Nov. 1857; *Los Angeles Star*, 30 Oct. 1852; *Humboldt Times*, 17 Dec. 1859; *Marysville Appeal*, 27 Oct. 1861; *San Joaquin Republican*, 22 Nov. 1852; *Mendocino Herald*, 29 Nov. 1862; *Trinity Journal*, 5 Oct. 1861; *Shasta Republican*, 14 March 1854; Caughey, ed., *Indians of Southern California*, p. 30; Doble, *Journal and Letters*, p. 129; Pancoast, *Quaker Forty-Niner*, pp. 313-14; Perkins, *Three Years*, pp. 123-27.

26. See Sherburne F. Cook, *The Mechanism and Extent of Dietary Adaptation Among Certain Groups of California and Nevada Indians.*

27. *San Francisco Alta California*, 21 Jan. 1851.

28. Ibid., 10 May 1849, 25 May 1860, 6 and 9 June 1860, 12 Sept. 1863; Melyer Casler, *A Journal Giving the Incidents of a Journey to California in the Summer of 1859 by the Overland Route*, p. 51.

29. *San Francisco Alta California*, 26 April 1849.

30. Ibid., 18 Jan. 1849, 10 and 17 May 1849, 30 April 1850, 9 May 1850, 12 and 16 Sept. 1850, 9 and 31 Oct. 1850, 11 and 29 Nov. 1850, 6 and 15 July 1851, 12 Nov. 1851, 1 Feb. 1852, 10 July 1852, 2 March 1853, 17 April 1863; *Visalia Delta*, 19 March 1863; *Aurora Times*, reprinted in *San Francisco Alta California*, 10 March 1863; James Delavan, *Notes on California and the Placers*, p. 53; Daniel B. Woods, *Sixteen Months at the Gold Diggings*, p. 111; William M. Stewart, *Reminiscences of Senator William M. Stewart of Nevada*, ed. George Rothwell Brown, pp. 73-74; Jasper S. Hill, *The Letters of a Young Miner: Covering the Adventures of Jasper S. Hill During the California Goldrush, 1849-1852*, ed. Doyce B. Nunis, Jr., p. 38; Richard L. Hale, *The Log of a*

Forty-Niner: Journal of a Voyage from Newburyport to San Francisco, ed. Carolyn Hale Russ, p. 106.

31. S[ilas] Weston, *Four Months in the Mines of California: Or, Life in the Mountains,* pp. 8–13.

32. *San Francisco Alta California,* 28 April 1862.

33. Correspondence to *San Francisco Alta California,* 17 April 1863, in Bancroft Scraps 36: 105. See also *Esmeralda Star,* 11 April 1863, in Bancroft Scraps, 36:53.

34. Correspondence, dated March 1863, to *San Francisco Alta California,* in Bancroft Scraps, 36:106–107.

35. James Beith to Dick Deighton, 5 June 1862, Beith Letterbooks, Bancroft Library, University of California, Berkeley. On Indian and white hostilities in Humboldt County see Jack Norton, *When Our Worlds Cried: Genocide in Northwestern California,* pp. 37–106.

36. James Beith to James McHary, 24 Sept. 1863, Beith Letterbooks. See also Beith to Dick Deighton, 20 Sept. 1863, and Beith to J. B. Prince, 14 Feb. 1864.

37. Correspondence to *San Francisco Alta California,* 19 Sept. 1863.

38. *Humboldt Times,* 20 Nov. 1858, 4 Feb. 1860, and 20 June 1860; *Humboldt Journal,* 6 Oct. 1865, in Bancroft Scraps, 36:27–28.

39. See chapter 6 above.

40. *Humboldt Times,* 20 and 27 Nov. 1858.

41. William C. Kibbe, *Report of the Expedition Against the Indians in the Northern Part of This State,* pp. 6, 8, 10.

42. *Humboldt Times,* 19 March 1859.

43. Lucius Fairchild, *California Letters of Lucius Fairchild,* ed. Joseph Schafer, p. 157.

44. Quoted in *San Francisco Alta California,* 15 Aug. 1853.

45. *Yreka Herald,* 7 Aug. 1853. See also same newspaper, 22 Dec. 1853, in Bancroft Scraps, 36:87; Hutchings, Diary, pp. 18–19.

46. Correspondence to *San Francisco Alta California,* 24 Feb. 1861. See also correspondence to *Sacramento Union,* in Bancroft Scraps, 36:53; *Petaluma Journal,* 15 April 1857; correspondence to *Sonoma Journal,* 1 Oct. 1859; *San Francisco Bulletin,* 21 Jan. 1860; *San Francisco Alta California,* 10 and 29 February 1860; *San Francisco Bulletin,* 2 March 1861.

47. See, for example, *San Francisco Alta California,* 8 March 1851, 10 and 31 May 1851, 30 June 1851, 27 July 1864, 12 Dec. 1872, 31 Jan. 1873; *San Francisco Herald,* 5 Oct. 1854; *San Francisco Bulletin,* 27 July 1864; *Sacramento Union,* 1 Jan. 1851; *Yreka Journal,* 1 Jan. 1873; *Humboldt Times,* 26 Aug. 1863; Walter Griffith Pigman, *The Journal of Walter Griffith Pigman,* ed. Ulla Staley Fawkes, pp. 45–46; Solomon Johnson, "The Gold Coast of California and Oregon," *Overland Monthly* 2 (June, 1869): 534–37; William Redmond Ryan, *Personal Adventures in Upper and Lower California, in 1848–49* 2:41–42.

48. *San Francisco Alta California,* 17 May 1849, 11 Nov. 1850, 4 May 1852, 21 and 23 Aug. 1853, 27 April 1868; *Placerville Herald,* 1 Oct. 1853; *Quincy Union,* in *San Francisco Alta California,* 1 Nov. 1862; *Esmeralda Star,* 11 April 1862; *Butte County Record,* 7 March 1863; *Oroville Union,* 1 Aug. 1863; *Oroville*

Appeal, 19 Sept. 1863; correspondence dated 12 Sept. 1863 to *San Francisco Alta California,* Bancroft Scraps, 36:118; correspondence to *Sacramento Union,* 14 Jan. 1865; *Los Angeles News,* 21 Jan. 1865; *Yreka Journal,* 11 June 1860.

49. William Jackson Barry, *Up and Down: Or, Fifty Years' Colonial Experiences in Australia, California . . . and the South Pacific,* pp. 123–24, 135–39.

50. Sim Moak, *The Last of the Mill Creeks and Early Life in Northern California,* pp. 11–12.

51. *Oroville Union,* 25 July 1863, in Bancroft Scraps, 36:115.

52. *Red Bluff Semi-Weekly Independent,* 5 Aug. 1862.

53. Moak, *Last of the Mill Creeks,* pp. 18, 22.

54. Robert A. Anderson, *Fighting the Mill Creeks: Being a Personal Account of Campaigns Against Indians of the Northern Sierras,* p. 80.

55. Moak, *Last of the Mill Creeks,* p. 23.

56. *Yreka Herald,* reprinted in *San Francisco Alta California,* 29 May 1854; *Humboldt Times,* 20 June 1860, 7 Dec. 1865.

57. Correspondence to *Sacramento Union,* 1 Jan. 185?, Bancroft Scraps, 36:53.

58. *Chico Courant,* 28 July 1866.

59. *Yreka Journal,* 12 and 19 March, 1873.

60. George R. Stewart, Jr., *Bret Harte: Argonaut and Exile,* pp. 83–90. For other evidence of protest see *San Francisco Alta California,* 11, 13, and 16 March 1850, 23 and 31 May 1850, 3 June 1850, 18 Jan. 1851, 5 Sept. 1853, 6 June 1859, 20 Jan. 1859, 31 Jan. 1860, 29 Feb. 1860, 27 Dec. 1873; *San Francisco Bulletin,* 1 June 1860; *San Francisco Herald,* 6 and 14 Feb. 1860; *Sacramento Union,* 26 Jan. 1860, 15 March 1860; *Plumas Argus,* reprinted in *San Francisco Alta California,* 6 Oct. 1859; *Yreka Journal,* 3 Jan. 1873; *Marysville Appeal,* 27 Oct. 1861; *Shasta Republican,* 14 March 1854; *Sacramento Union,* 25 Oct. 1859, 12 Nov. 1859, 17 Jan. 1860, 13 Feb. 1860, 15 March 1860.

61. *San Francisco Alta California,* 11 and 19 March 1850.

62. Ibid., 22 Feb. 1868, 28 Sept. 1871, 7 Oct. 1871.

63. Correspondence to *San Francisco Alta California,* 16 March 1850.

64. Moak, *Last of the Mill Creeks,* pp. 12–14.

65. *San Francisco Alta California,* 28 Jan. 1860.

66. Ibid., 25 May 1860.

67. Isaac Cox, *The Annals of Trinity County,* pp. 36, 114; "Reminiscences of Mendocino," *Hutchings' Illustrated California Magazine* 3 (Oct., 1858): 146–60; Cheever, "Indians of California," 146–48.

68. Quoted in *Sacramento Union,* 13 Feb. 1860. The controversy over state financing of the militia's operations may be traced in *San Francisco Alta California,* 23 May 1850, 27 Dec. 1850, 14 Jan. 1851, 10 Feb. 1851, 16 Jan. 1852, 1 Feb. 1852, 29 Feb. 1860, 15 Dec. 1872, 6 Jan. 1873, 27 Dec. 1873; *Sacramento Union,* 7 Feb. 1856, 31 May 1856, 2 Nov. 1857, 25 Oct. 1859, 17, 19 and 26 Jan. 1860, 13 Feb. 1860, 27 April 1860, 3 and 5 May 1860, 1 and 12 June 1861, 9 March 1863; *Yreka Herald,* 5 Feb. 1873, 26 March 1873; *Humboldt Times,* 4 and 11 Feb. 1860.

69. Carl Meyer, *Bound for Sacramento: Travel Pictures of a Returned Wanderer,* p. 279; *Marysville Express,* 16 April 1859; *Sacramento Union,* 13 May 1861; *Marysville Appeal,* 20 February 1863.

70. Walton Bean and James J. Rawls, *California: An Interpretive History*, p. 141. See also Edward D. Castillo, "The Impact of Euro-American Exploration and Settlement," in Robert F. Heizer, ed., *California* (*Handbook of North American Indians*, vol. 8), p. 108.

71. *San Francisco Alta California*, 22 Aug. 1868; *San Francisco Bulletin*, 29 June 1857; "Scenes Among the Indians of California," *Hutchings' Illustrated California Magazine* 3 (April, 1859): 433–46; Horace Bushnell, *California: Its Characteristics and Prospects*, p. 28; Theodore T. Johnson, *California and Oregon: Or, Sights in the Gold Region and Scenes by the Way*, pp. 142–43; Felix Paul Wierzbicki, *California As It Is, and As It May Be: Or, a Guide to the Gold Region*, p. 16; Mrs. D. B. Bates, *Incidents on Land and Water: Or Four Years on the Pacific Coast*, pp. 150–51; Philip T. Tyson, *Geology and Industrial Resources of California*, p. 97; Delavan, *Notes on California*, p. 55; Perkins, *Three Years*, p. 123; Pigman, *Journal*, p. 47.

72. See, for example, Franklin Langworthy, *Scenery of the Plains, Mountains and Mines*, ed. Paul C. Phillips, pp. 189–90; J. D. Borthwick, *Three Years in California*, p. 129; Frank Soulé, John H. Gihon, and James Nisbet, *The Annals of San Francisco: Containing . . . Prominent Citizens*, p. 51; R. N. Willcox, *Reminiscences of California Life . . . and Other Lands*, p. 185; Brace, *New West*, p. 137.

73. B. Schmölder, *The Emigrant's Guide to California, Describing its Geography, Agricultural and Commercial Resources*, pp. 12–13.

74. Cronise, *Natural Wealth*, p. 21.

75. *San Francisco Alta California*, 15 Jan. 1852, 28 July 1853; Leonard Kip, *California Sketches with Recollections of the Gold Mines*, p. 43. See also Isabel Truesdell Kelly, *The Carver's Art of the Indians of Northwestern California;* Adan E. Treganza, *Californian Clay Artifacts;* Robert F. Heizer and C. W. Clewlow, Jr., *Prehistoric Rock Art of California;* and the references in Alfred L. Kroeber, *Handbook of the California Indians*, p. 970.

76. Brace, *New West*, pp. 146–47. See Anna Hardwick Gayton, *Yokuts and Western Mono Pottery-Making;* Stuart L. Peck, *Some Pottery from the Sand Hills, Imperial County, California, Site 4-Im-11;* Sherburne F. Cook and Robert F. Heizer, *The Physical Analysis of Nine Indian Mounds of the Lower Sacramento Valley*.

77. *San Francisco Alta California*, 29 July 1853; Étienne Derbec, *A French Journalist in the California Gold Rush: The Letters of Étienne Derbec*, ed. A. P. Nasatir, pp. 155–56; Woods, *Sixteen Months*, p. 49; Borthwick, *Three Years*, pp. 130–33.

78. [Louise Amelia Knapp Smith Clappe], *The Shirley Letters From the California Mines, 1851–1852*, ed. Carl I. Wheat, pp. 8, 135. Albert Elsasser, "Basketry," in Heizer, ed., *California*, p. 626. See also Roland Burrage Dixon, *Basketry Designs of the Indians of Northern California;* and Alfred L. Kroeber, *Basket Designs of the Mission Indians of California*.

79. Alfred Barstow, "Statement of Alfred Barstow, a Pioneer of 1849," p. 5, Bancroft Library, University of California, Berkeley; Samuel C. Upham, *Notes on a Voyage to California . . . in the Years 1849–50*, pp. 240–48; Adolphus Windeler, *The California Gold Rush Diary of a German Sailor*, ed. W. Turrentine

Jackson, p. 51; Benjamin Butler Harris, *The Gila Trail: The Texas Argonauts and the California Gold Rush*, ed. Richard H. Dillon, pp. 102–103; Heinrich Schliemann, *Schliemann's First Visit to America, 1850–1851*, ed. Shirley H. Weber, p. 58; Langworthy, *Scenery of the Plains*, pp. 189–90; Clark, *Reminiscences of Travel*, p. 33; Doble, *Journal and Letters*, p. 43. See also Kroeber on the dress of the Yuroks and Pomos (Kroeber, *Handbook*, pp. 76, 240) and on the variety of garments (*Handbook*, p. 969).

80. *San Francisco Bulletin*, 29 June 1857.

81. Luther M. Schaeffer, *Sketches of Travels in South America, Mexico and California*, pp. 162–63; Doble, *Journal and Letters*, p. 113; Bates, *Incidents on Land and Water*, pp. 154–55; Pfeiffer, *Lady's Second Journey*, p. 76; Weston, *Four Months*, p. 22; Borthwick, *Three Years*, p. 312; Buck, *Yankee Trader*, p. 109. See also Robert F. Heizer, ed., *The Destruction of California Indians: A Collection of Documents . . . of Some of the Things that Happened to Some of the Indians of California*, pp. 309–13.

82. *San Francisco Alta California*, 29 July 1853; W[illiam] L[awrence] Humanson, *From the Atlantic Surf to the Golden Gate*, p. 50; Tyson, *Diary of a Physician*, p. 86; Johnson, *California and Oregon*, pp. 142–43; Woods, *Sixteen Months*, p. 122; *Bean's History and Directory*, p. 26. Mrs. D. B. Bates concluded, "From their burrowing propensities, these Indians have derived the name of 'Diggers'" (Bates, *Incidents on Land and Water*, p. 154).

83. Langworthy, *Scenery of the Plains*, pp. 189–90.

84. *San Francisco Bulletin*, 29 June 1857; Schliemann, *First Visit*, p. 58; Schmölder, *Emigrant's Guide to California*, p. 38.

85. Rufus B. Sage, *Rocky Mountain Life: Or, Startling Scenes and Perilous Adventures in the Far West*, p. 229. See also Borthwick, *Three Years*, p. 128.

86. Upham, *Notes on a Voyage*, p. 240.

87. Soulé, Gihon, and Nisbet, *Annals of San Francisco*, p. 51. See also Brace, *New West*, pp. 142, 146–47; for the range of religious culture—creation stories, mythology, prayers, altars, ceremonial structures, cults, and rituals—of the California Indians, see Alfred L. Kroeber, *The Religion of the California Indians*.

88. *San Francisco Alta California*, 31 Oct. 1853, 3 Feb. 1857; *San Francisco Herald*, 19 June 1857; *San Francisco Bulletin*, 17 April 1864, 14 Sept. 1864; "The Way the Digger Indians Bury Their Dead," *Hutchings' Illustrated California Magazine* 3 (Jan., 1859): 322; Barstow, "Statement of . . . a Pioneer," pp. 4–5; Pancoast, *Quaker Forty-Niner*, p. 344; Willcox, *Reminiscences*, pp. 85–87; Clark, *Reminiscences of Travel*, pp. 36–37; Pigman, *Journal*, p. 30; *Bean's History and Directory*, p. 26.

89. [Alfred T. Jackson], *The Diary of a Forty-Niner*, ed. Chauncey L. Canfield, pp. 10–11. The true identity or existence of "Alfred T. Jackson" is uncertain. Alfred L. Kroeber confirms that cremation was standard practice among hill and southern Maidus, while burial was more common elsewhere. (*Handbook of the Indians of California*, p. 403).

90. John A. Perry, *Thrilling Adventures of a New Englander: Travels, Scenes and Sufferings in Cuba, Mexico and California*, p. 165; Langworthy, *Scenery of the Plains*, p. 191; Schaeffer, *Sketches of Travel*, p. 118; *Bean's History and Directory*, p. 26; Buffum, *Gold Rush*, p. 55; Moak, *Last of the Mill Creeks*, p. 9.

91. Windeler, *Gold Rush Diary*, p. 191. Kroeber comments on the mourning customs of the Maidu: "A widow cut or burned her hair off close and covered it with pitch, which was never deliberately removed" (*Handbook*, p. 404).

92. Soulé, Gihon, and Nisbet, *Annals of San Francisco*, p. 51; Pfeiffer, *Lady's Second Journey*, p. 77; Willcox, *Reminiscences of California Life*, pp. 85–86; Humanson, *From the Atlantic Surf,* p. 50; Perkins, *Three Years*, p. 123.

93. Kroeber comments: "Observers have mentioned what appealed to their sense of novelty or ingenuity, what they happened to see at a given moment, or what their native informants were interested in" (*Handbook*, p. 525).

94. King, "Report on California," in *Message from the Pesident* [*sic*], pp. 8–9.

95. "Scenes Among the Indians of California," pp. 433–46; Upham, *Notes on a Voyage to California*, p. 240; Tyson, *Geology and Industrial Resources*, p. 97; Pancoast, *Quaker Forty-Niner*, p. 342; Bushnell, *Characteristics and Prospects*, p. 29.

96. *San Francisco Bulletin*, 29 June 1857. See also Kroeber, *Handbook*, pp. 597, 722, 735, 797, 803, 815.

97. Edward Washington McIlhany, *Recollections of a '49er: A Quaint and Thrilling Narrative of . . . the Far West*, p. 46. Pancoast, *Quaker Forty-Niner*, p. 342; Borthwick, *Three Years*, p. 131. On the acorn diet of the California Indians, see Kroeber, *Handbook*, p. 87.

98. Perkins, *Three Years*, p. 124. See the excellent discussion of "The Problem of Taste," in Cook, *Dietary Adaptation*, pp. 40–49.

99. Clark, *Reminiscences of Travel*, p. 35.

100. Windeler, *Gold Rush Diary*, p. 191.

101. Moak, *Last of the Mill Creeks*, p. 12; Clark, *Reminiscences*, pp. 35–36; Bates, *Incidents on Land and Water*, p. 152; Leeper, *Argonauts of 'Forty-Nine*, p. 57; Tyson, *Diary of a Physician*, p. 86; Woods, *Sixteen Months*, p. 49; Schaeffer, *Sketches of Travels*, p. 118; Johnson, *California and Oregon*, pp. 142–43; Cheever, "Indians of California," pp. 129–30; Dr. Dietrich, *The German Emigrants: Or, Frederich Wohlgemuth's Voyage to California*, p. 40. Among California Indians there was a great variety of food preferences; some groups preferred foods that were specifically rejected by other tribes (Kroeber, *Handbook*, 526).

102. Derbec, *French Journalist*, p. 157.

103. Ibid., p. 156; Moak, *Last of the Mill Creeks*, pp. 12–14.

104. Dietrich, *German Emigrants*, p. 41.

105. Perry, *Thrilling Adventures*, p. 72.

106. Cook, *Conflict: American Invasion*, pp. 45–46.

107. Bates, *Incidents on Land and Water*, p. 155; Cox, *Annals of Trinity County*, p. 35; Langworthy, *Scenery of the Plains*, p. 190.

108. Hinton Rowan Helper, *Dreadful California: Being a True and Scandalous Account of . . . the Golden State*, ed. Lucius Beebe and Charles M. Clegg, p. 152 (originally published in 1855 as *The Land of Gold: Reality Versus Fiction*).

109. Winthrop Jordan has probed the historical and psychological roots of the association by whites of a dark complexion with dirt and inferiority (Jordan, *White Over Black: American Attitudes Toward the Negro, 1550–1812*, pp. 255–57). Joel Kovel has described the "dirt fantasy" that he believes is at the root of the repulsion that some whites feel for dark-skinned people. The his-

torically crucial aspects of white racism "are grounded somehow in a bodily fantasy about dirt, which rests in turn upon the equation of dirt with excrement: the insides of the body turned out and threatening to return within. And within this nuclear fantasy, black people have come to be represented as the personification of dirt, an equation that stays locked in the deeper recesses of the unconscious, and so pervades the course of social action between the races beyond any need of awareness" (Kovel, *White Racism: A Psychohistory*, pp. 89–90).

110. Leeper, *Argonauts of 'Forty-Nine*, p. 57; *San Francisco Bulletin*, 29 June 1857.

111. Helper, *Dreadful California*, pp. 152–54.

112. John Woodhouse Audubon, *Audubon's Western Journal: 1849–1850*, ed. Frank Heywood Hodder, p. 213; William Shaw, *Golden Dreams and Waking Realities*, p. 16; King, "Report on California," in *Message from the Pesident [sic]*, p. 8; Marryat, *Mountains and Molehills*, p. 41; Tyson, *Diary of a Physician*, p. 68; [Clappe,] *Shirley Letters*, p. 133.

113. Brace, *New West*, p. 138. See also Jackson, *Diary of a Forty-Niner*, p. 9; Schaeffer, *Sketches of Travels*, p. 171. These images of "filthy" Indians also reflected the great cultural shock and disintegration suffered by the natives during the gold rush. In precontact times personal cleanliness was ensured by ritual use of sweathouses and by bathing in streams and lakes.

114. William M'Collum, *California As I Saw It: Pencillings by the Way of Its Gold and Gold Diggers*, ed. Dale L. Morgan, pp. 168–69; Delavan, *Notes on California*, p. 55; Upham, *Notes on a Voyage to California*, p. 240; Perry, *Thrilling Adventures*, p. 72; Brace, *New West*, pp. 137, 144; Ryan, *Personal Adventures* 2:42; [Clappe], *Shirley Letters*, p. 72.

115. Pfeiffer, *Lady's Second Journey*, pp. 75–76. See also Perry, *Thrilling Adventures*, p. 72.

116. George Payson [Ralph Raven], *Golden Dreams and Leaden Realities*, p. 256.

117. Audubon, *Western Journal*, p. 213.

118. Borthwick, *Three Years*, p. 132.

119. "Black dominates among the Indians," wrote Etienne Derbec from Mariposa County in 1850, "only the children are bronze-colored and they become darker as they grow older" (Derbec, *French Journalist*, p. 154). See also Pfeiffer, *Lady's Second Journey*, pp. 75–77; Woods, *Sixteen Months*, p. 49; Harris, *Gila Trail*, pp. 102–103.

120. Ernest de Massey, *A Frenchman in the Gold Rush: The Journal of Ernest de Massey, Argonaut of 1849*, trans. Marguerite Eyer Wilbur, pp. 59–60.

121. Johnson, *California and Oregon*, pp. 142–43. See also Brace, *New West*, p. 137; Bates, *Incidents on Land and Water*, p. 150.

122. Ryan, *Personal Adventures* 1:73, 92–93, 159.

123. *California Star* (San Francisco), 29 Jan. 1848, 26 Feb. 1848; *San Francisco Alta California*, 25 March 1851, 31 Sept. 1872, 15 April 1873; *Yreka Journal*, 11 June 1873; "A Digger in the Chimney," *Hutchings' Illustrated California Magazine* 2 (June, 1858): 560–61; J. A. Veach, "About Clear Lake: Its Scenery,

&c. &c.," *Hesperian* 2 (March, 1859): 21–26; Kip, "The Last of the Leatherstockings," pp. 401–402; Jessie Benton Frémont, *Mother Lode Narratives*, ed. Shirley Sargent, p. 151; Bates, *Incidents on Land and Water*, pp. 150–51; Marryat, *Mountains and Molehills*, p. 41; Pigman, *Journal*, pp. 35, 39, 47; Kelly, *Excursion to California*, p. 114; Schaeffer, *Sketches of Travels*, pp. 161–64; Willcox, *Reminiscences of California Life*, pp. 88–94; [Clappe], *Shirley Letters*, pp. 1–13, 132–36.

124. Jordan, *White Over Black*, pp. 27, 239–51.

125. *San Francisco Alta California*, 29 June 1850; Marryat, *Mountains and Molehills*, p. 57; Payson, *Golden Dreams and Leaden Realities*, p. 256; Perry, *Thrilling Adventures*, p. 72; M'Cullom, *California As I Saw It*, p. 169.

126. Langworthy, *Scenery of the Plains*, pp. 189–90.

127. Upham, *Notes on a Voyage*, p. 240.

128. Massey, *Frenchman in the Gold Rush*, p. 60. See also Joseph Sedgley, *Overland to California in 1849*, p. 61.

129. *San Francisco Bulletin*, 29 June 1857.

130. Ibid.; Bates, *Incidents on Land and Water*, p. 151; Waugh, *Autobiography of Lorenzo Waugh*, p. 195.

131. Schaeffer, *Sketches of Travels*, p. 161; Perry, *Thrilling Adventures*, p. 72; Helper, *Dreadful California*, pp. 152–54; Derbec, *French Journalist*, p. 156.

132. Clark, *Reminiscences of Travel*, p. 36; Bates, *Incidents on Land and Water*, pp. 155–56; Cox, *Annals of Trinity County*, p. 35; *Humboldt Times*, 20 Feb. 1858.

133. M'Collum, *California As I Saw It*, p. 169; Derbec, *French Journalist*, p. 159; Dietrich, *German Emigrants*, p. 41.

134. Perry, *Thrilling Adventures*, p. 86.

135. Massey, *Frenchman in the Gold Rush*, p. 60.

136. See Jordan's comments on "The Apes of Africa" in *White Over Black*, pp. 28–32. While the comparison of Negroes to apes was not uncommon, the likening of Indians to simians was very unusual.

137. Correspondence to *San Francisco Alta California*, 17 March 1851. See also Weston, *Four Months*, p. 22.

138. Johnson, *Sights in the Gold Region*, p. 198.

139. Audubon, *Western Journal*, p. 213.

140. Upham, *Notes on a Voyage*, p. 240.

141. Peter Decker, *The Diaries of Peter Decker: Overland to California in 1849 and Life in the Mines, 1850–1851*, ed. Helen S. Giffen, p. 173. See also Willcox, *Reminiscences of California Life*, p. 94.

142. Correspondence to *California Star* (San Francisco), 26 Feb. 1848. See also Soulé, Gihon, and Nisbet, *Annals of San Francisco*, pp. 50–51.

143. Clark, *Reminiscences of Travel*, p. 39.

144. Brace, *New West*, pp. 140–41, 149.

145. Correspondence to *Sacramento Union*, 1 Jan. 1851, in Bancroft Scraps, 36:53; *Yreka Herald*, 26 Dec. 1853, in Bancroft Scraps, 36:87; *Yreka Journal*, 11 June 1873.

146. M'Collum, *California As I Saw It*, p. 147. See also Helper, *Dreadful California*, p. 119; Buck, *Yankee Trader*, pp. 109–111; Letts, *California Illustrated*,

p. 111; Robert Anderson recalled that the Mill Creek Indians were a difficult quarry: "They are just like ground squirrels, hard to kill" (quoted in Moak, *Last of the Mill Creeks*, p. 26).

Epilogue

1. Stephen Powers, "The Northern California Indians," *Overland Monthly* 8 (April, 1872): 325.

2. Robert F. Heizer, "Stephen Powers as Anthropologist," in Powers, *California Indian Characteristics & Centennial Mission to the Indians of Western Nevada and California*, pp. 39–53.

3. *Yreka Journal*, 19 March 1873.

4. Richard Dillon, *Burnt-Out Fires: California's Modoc Indian War*, p. viii. The story of the Modoc War has been told many times. In addition to Dillon's comprehensive account see Doris Palmer Payne, *Captain Jack, Modoc Renegade;* Keith Murray, *The Modocs and Their War;* Erwin N. Thomas, *Modoc War: Its Military History and Topography;* and Jeff C. Riddle, *The Indian History of the Modoc War.*

5. Frances W. Watkins, "Charles F. Lummis and the Sequoya League," *Quarterly of the Historical Society of Southern California* 26 (June–Sept., 1944): 99–109; Edward D. Castillo, "Twentieth-Century Secular Movements," in Robert F. Heizer, ed., *California* (*Handbook of North American Indians*, vol. 8), pp. 713–15; Jack D. Forbes, *Native Americans of California and Nevada*, pp. 93–94.

6. Castillo, "Twentieth-Century Secular Movements," in Heizer, ed., *California*, pp. 713–16; Forbes, *Native Americans*, p. 93. See also Rubert Costo's comments on Collett in *The Indian Historian* 3 (Winter, 1970): 62.

7. Kenneth M. Johnson, *K-344: Or, The Indians of California vs. the United States;* Omer C. Stewart, "Litigation and its Effects," in Heizer, ed., *California*, p. 706; Castillo, "Twentieth-Century Secular Movements," in Heizer, ed., *California*, p. 716; Forbes, *Native Americans*, pp. 104–106; Sherburne F. Cook, *The Population of the California Indians, 1769–1970*, pp. 71–73.

8. "As of June 30, 1971, the 1964 award of $29,100,000 had been reduced by payment of attorneys' fees to $26,491,000 but had been increased by interest less costs by $9,643,543.66 to a total of $36,134,534.66 to be added to the $1,496,246.08 remaining from the Act of 1928. Thus as of June 30, 1971, $37,630,781.74 was available for per capita distribution" (Stewart, "Litigation and Its Effects," in Heizer, ed., *California*, p. 708). See also Cook, *Population of the California Indians*, p. 72; Castillo, "Twentieth-Century Secular Movements," in Heizer, ed., *California*, pp. 716–18.

9. Cook, *Population of the California Indians*, pp. 61ff.; Edward D. Castillo, "The Impact of Euro-American Exploration and Settlement," in Heizer, ed., *California*, p. 118.

10. S. Lyman Tyler, *A History of Indian Policy*, pp. 95–149; Florence C. Shipek, "History of Southern California Mission Indians," in Heizer, ed., *California*, p. 613; Lowell John Bean and Florence C. Shipek, "Luiseño," in

Heizer, ed., *California*, pp. 558-59; Castillo, "Euro-American Exploration and Settlement," in Heizer, ed., *California*, pp. 119-22; Stewart, "Litigation and Its Effects," in Heizer, ed., *California*, pp. 705-706.

11. Tyler, *History of Indian Policy*, pp. 151-247; Castillo, "Euro-American Exploration and Settlement," in Heizer, ed., *California*, p. 122; Shipek, "Southern California Mission Indians," in Heizer, ed., *California*, pp. 614-15; Forbes, *Native Americans*, pp. 114-15.

12. Lowell John Bean and Sylvia Brakke Vane, "Cults and Their Transformations," in Heizer, ed., *California*, pp. 670-71; Norman L. Wilson and Arlean H. Towne, "Nisenan," in Heizer, ed., *California*, p. 396; William J. Wallace, "Southern Valley Yokuts," in Heizer, ed., *California*, p. 460. The later 1890 Ghost Dance had little impact on the California Indians (see James J. Rawls, ed., *Dan De Quille of the Big Bonanza*, pp. 107-121).

13. See Theodora Kroeber's masterful account, *Ishi in Two Worlds: A Biography of the Last Wild Indian in North America*.

14. See, for example, Campbell Grant, "Chumash: Introduction," in Heizer, ed., *California*, p. 507; Katharine Luomala, "Tipai and Ipai," in Heizer, ed. *California*, pp. 594-95; Lowell John Bean and Dorothea Theodoratus, "Western Pomo and Northeastern Pomo," in Heizer, ed., *California*, p. 302; Castillo, "Euro-American Exploration and Settlement," in Heizer, ed., *California*, p. 118; Shipek, "Southern California Mission Indians," in Heizer, ed., *California*, p. 611.

15. William J. Wallace, "Hupa, Chilula, and Whilkut," in Heizer, ed., *California*, p. 176; Castillo, "Euro-American Exploration and Settlement," in Heizer, ed., *California*, pp. 124-27.

16. Cook, *Population of the California Indians*, pp. 71, 113-17, 139-40, 200-202.

17. Ibid., pp. 73-77, 174, 202; Cook, "Historical Demography," in Heizer, ed., *California*, pp. 93-94, 97; Castillo, "Euro-American Exploration and Settlement," in Heizer, ed., *California*, p. 123.

18. Lowell John Bean, *Mukat's People: The Cahuilla Indians of Southern California;* Bean, "Cahuilla," in Heizer, ed., *California*, pp. 585-86; Katherine Siva Sauvel and Pamela Monroe, *Chem'ivillu': Let's Speak Cahuilla.* See also Bean and Shipek, "Luiseño," in Heizer, ed., *California*, pp. 560-61; Shipek, "Southern California Mission Indians," in Heizer, ed., *California*, pp. 610-18.

19. Wallace, "Hupa, Chilula, and Whilkut," in Heizer, ed., *California*, p. 167.

20. Byron Nelson, Jr., *Our Home Forever: A Hupa Tribal History*.

21. Bean and Theodoratus, "Western Pomo and Northeastern Pomo," in Heizer, ed., *California*, pp. 299-304; *Santa Rosa Press-Democrat*, 22 April 1979.

22. D. L. Olmsted and Omer C. Stewart, "Achumawi," in Heizer, ed., *California*, pp. 234-35; George H. Phillips, *The Enduring Struggle: Indians in California History*, pp. 75-76.

Bibliography

I. MANUSCRIPTS

All the manuscripts listed below are in the Bancroft Library, University of California, Berkeley. Their location and a brief description of their contents are listed in the library's manuscript catalog.

Bailey, Henry Clay. "California in '53. From the Reminiscences of H. C. Bailey." N.d.

Barstow, Alfred. "Statement of Alfred Barstow, a Pioneer of 1849." 1877.

Beith, James. Letterbooks, 1854–67. Diaries and Journals. 1862–88.

Belden, Josiah. "Statement of Historical Facts on California." 1878.

Bidwell, John. "California, 1841–1848. An Immigrant's Recollections of a Trip Across the Plains and of Men and Events in Early Days." 1877.

Bigler, John. Correspondence and Papers. 1850–69.

Booth, Joseph W. Diary. 1852–53.

Bowen, Ben. "Record of Life. Commenced at Fort John, California, September 1851." 1854–59.

Brown, Charles F. "Statement of Recollections of Early Events in California." 1878.

Brown, H. S. "Statement of Early Days of California." 1878.

Chamberlain, John. "Memoirs of California Since 1840." 1877.

Clark, Galen. "Reminiscences of Galen Clark, Guardian of Yosemite Valley." 1880.

Coronel, Antonio Francisco. "Cosas de California." 1877.

Dally, Henry J. "Narrative of His Life and Events in California Since 1843." 1878.

Davidson, William A. "Indian Adventures in California and Mining in Colorado." 1886.

Dixon, H. S. G. Letter to Hubert Howe Bancroft. 1 May 1875.

Engbeck, Joseph. *La Purisima Mission State Historic Park.* Sacramento, Calif.: n.d.

Flournoy, H. C. "Digger Indians in Plumas County." [1865?].

Hayes, Benjamin Ignatius. "Emigrant Notes." 1875.

Hutchings, James Mason. Diary. 1848–49 and 1855.

Logbooks of the *Eagle*, 1820–22; *Arab*, 1821–25; *Rover*, 1822–26; *Mentor*, 1824–25; *Courier*, 1825–29; *Waverly*, 1828–29.

McKinstry, George. "Papers on the History of California." 1846–65.

Maltby, Charles. Letter to Hubert Howe Bancroft. 10 Aug. 1872.

Martin, Thomas S. "Narrative of John C. Frémont's Expedition to California in 1845–46." 1878.

Phelps, William Dane. "Solid Men of Boston in the Northwest." [1872?].

Potter, Elijah Renshaw. "Reminiscences of the Early History of Northern California and of the Indian Troubles." N.d.

Richardson, H. D. "History of the Foundation of the City of Vallejo." 1874.

Roscoe, W. E. "A History of the Mattole Valley." N.d.

Ross, John E. "Narrative of an Indian Fighter." 1878.

Warner, Jonathan Trumbull. "Biographical Sketch." 1872.

―――. "Reminiscences of Early California." 1873–77.

Weeks, James W. Francis. "Reminiscences." 1877.

Wozencraft, Oliver M. "Indian Affairs, 1849–1850." N.d.

II. GOVERNMENT DOCUMENTS

A.　California

Constitution of the State of California. 1849.

Joint Committee on the Mendocino War. *Majority and Minority Reports*. 1860.

Journal of the Assembly. 1st sess., 1850. 3d sess., 1852. 5th sess., 1854. 8th sess., 1857. 11th sess., 1860.

Journal of the Senate. 1st sess., 1850. 3d sess., 1852. 11th sess., 1860.

Statutes of California. 1st sess., chap. 133, 1850. 11th sess., chap. 221, 1860.

B.　United States

House of Representatives. *Executive Documents*. 30th Cong., 2d sess., 1848–49, doc. 1. 31st Cong., 1st sess., 1849–50, doc. 59. 34th Cong., 3d sess., 1856–57, doc. 76.

Interior Department. Office of Indian Affairs. *Report of the Commissioner of Indian Affairs, Accompanying the Annual Report of the Secretary of the Interior for the Year 1856*. California Superintendency, docs. 100–106.

―――. *Report of the Commissioner of Indian Affairs, Accompanying the Annual Report of the Secretary of the Interior for the Year 1858*. California Superintendency, docs. 102–109.

―――. *Report of the Commissioner of Indian Affairs, Accompanying the Annual Report of the Secretary of the Interior for the Year 1861*. California Superintendency, docs. 54–56½.

―――. *Report of the Commissioner of Indian Affairs for the Year 1862*. California Superintendency, docs. 62–67.

―――. *Report of the Commissioner of Indian Affairs for the Year 1863.* California Superintendency, docs. 28–40.

―――. *Report of the Commissioner of Indian Affairs for the Year 1864.* California Superintendency, docs. 35–45½.

―――. *Report of the Commissioner of Indian Affairs for the Year 1865.* California Superintendency, docs. 14–19.

―――. *Report of the Commissioner of Indian Affairs for the Year 1866.* California Superintendency, docs. 16–24.

―――. *Report on Indian Affairs by the Acting Commissioner for the Year 1867.* California Superintendency, docs. 26–31.

―――. *Annual Report of the Commissioner of Indian Affairs for the Year 1868.* California Superintendency, docs. 19–23.

―――. *Report of the Commissioner of Indian Affairs Made to the Secretary of the Interior on the Year 1869.* California Superintendency, docs. 27–35.

―――. *Annual Report of the Commissioner of Indian Affairs to the Secretary of the Interior for the Year 1870.* California Superintendency, docs. 21–28.

―――. *Report of the Commissioner of Indian Affairs to the Secretary of the Interior for the Year 1871.* California Superintendency, docs. 19–28.

―――. *Annual Report of the Commissioner of Indian Affairs to the Secretary of the Interior for the Year 1875.* California Reports, pp. 220–30.

Senate. *Congressional Globe.* 32d Cong., 1st sess., 1851–52, pt. 3. 36th Cong., 1st sess., 1859–60, pts. 2 and 3.

―――. *Executive Documents.* 31st Cong., 1st sess., 1849–50, doc. 18. 32d Cong., 2d sess., 1850–53, doc. 57. 33d Cong., spec. sess., 1853, doc. 4. 36th Cong., 1st sess., 1859–60, doc. 46.

Statutes at Large. Vol. 10. 1851–55.

III. NEWSPAPERS

A. *California*

Alameda Independent
Aurora Times
Butte County Appeal
Butte County Record
California Star (Yerba Buena and San Francisco)
Californian (Monterey and San Francisco)
Chico Courant
Columbia Times
Colusa Sun
Esmeralda Star
Eureka Times

Grass Valley Telegraph
Healdsburg Enterprise
Humboldt Times
Inyo Independent
Los Angeles News
Los Angeles Times
Los Angeles Southern Californian
Los Angeles Star
Mariposa Republican
Marysville Appeal
Marysville Herald
Mendocino Herald
Nevada County Democrat

Nevada County Journal
Oroville Union
Petaluma Journal
Placerville Herald
Plumas Standard
Quincy Union
Red Bluff Beacon
Red Bluff Semi-Weekly Independent
Red Bluff Sentinel
Sacramento Bee
Sacramento Standard
Sacramento Union
San Bernardino Guardian
San Diego Union
San Francisco Alta California
San Francisco Daily Chronicle
San Francisco Daily Evening Bulletin
San Francisco Daily Herald

San Francisco Monitor
San Francisco Placer Times and
   Transcript
San Joaquin Republican
Santa Barbara Press
Santa Rosa Press-Democrat
Shasta Courier
Shasta Republican
Sonoma Journal
Stanislaus Index
Stockton Times
Trinity Journal
Ukiah Herald
Visalia Delta
Weaverville Journal
Yreka Herald
Yreka Journal

B. Other

New York Times

New York Tribune

IV. THESES AND DISSERTATIONS

Azevedo, Cecilia Imelda. "Description of California Indians by Early Voyagers." Master's thesis, University of California, Berkeley, 1946.

Bailey, Lois Ruth. "The Indian Problem in California, 1848–1860." Master's thesis, Stanford University, 1933.

Ellison, William Henry. "The Federal Indian Policy in California, 1846–1860." Ph.D. diss., University of California, Berkeley, 1918.

Holliday, Jaquelin Smith. "The California Gold Rush in Myth and Reality." Ph.D. diss., University of California, Berkeley, 1959.

Knoop, Anna Marie. "The Federal Indian Policy in the Sacramento Valley, 1846–1860." Master's thesis, University of California, Berkeley, 1941.

Leonard, Charles Berdan. "The Federal Indian Policy in the San Joaquin Valley: Its Application and Results." Ph.D. diss., University of California, Berkeley, 1928.

V. BOOKS AND ARTICLES

Alexander, Charles. *The Life and Times of Cyrus Alexander.* Edited by George Shochat. Los Angeles: Dawson's Bookshop, 1967.

Anderson, George E.; W. H. Ellison; and Robert F. Heizer. *Treaty Making and Treaty Rejection by the Federal Government in California, 1850–1852.*

Ballena Press Publications in Archaeology, Ethnology, and History, no. 9. Socorro, N. Mex.: Ballena Press, 1978.

Anderson, Robert A. *Fighting the Mill Creeks: Being a Personal Account of Campaigns Against Indians of the Northern Sierras.* Chico, Calif.: 1909.

Andrews, Thomas F. "Lansford W. Hastings and the Promotion of the Salt Lake Desert Cutoff: A Reappraisal." *Western Historical Quarterly* 4 (April, 1973): 133–55.

Ansted, David T. *The Gold-Seeker's Manual: Being a Practical and Instructive Guide to All Persons Emigrating to the Newly-Discovered Gold Regions of California.* New York: D. Appleton, 1849.

Archibald, Robert. *The Economic Aspects of the California Missions.* Academy of American Franciscan History, vol. 12. Washington, D.C.: Academy of American Franciscan History, 1978.

Atherton, Faxon Dean. *The California Diary of Faxon Dean Atherton, 1836–1839.* Edited by Doyce B. Nunis, Jr. San Francisco: California Historical Society, 1964.

Audubon, John Woodhouse. *Audubon's Western Journal: 1849–1850.* Edited by Frank Heywood Hodder. Cleveland: Arthur H. Clark, 1906.

Bailey, Henry Clay. "Indian Life in the Sacramento Valley." *Quarterly of San Bernardino County Museum Association* 7 (Fall, 1959): 1–18.

Bancroft, Hubert Howe. *California Pastoral, 1769–1848.* San Francisco: History Co., 1888.

———. *History of California.* 7 vols. San Francisco: History Co., 1884–89.

———. *The Native Races of the Pacific States of North America.* 5 vols. New York: D. Appleton, 1874–76.

Bandini, José. *A Description of California in 1828.* Translated by Doris Marion Wright. Berkeley, Calif.: Friends of the Bancroft Library, 1951.

Bannon, John Francis, ed. *Bolton and the Spanish Borderlands.* Norman: University of Oklahoma Press, 1964.

Bannon, John Francis; Robert Ryal Miller; and Peter Masten Dunne. *Latin America.* 4th ed. Encino, Calif.: Glencoe Press, 1977.

Bard, James C.; Edward Castillo; and Karen Nissen. *A Bibliography of California Indians: Archaeology, Ethnology, Indian History.* New York and London: Garland Publishing Co., 1977.

Barry, William Jackson. *Up and Down: Or, Fifty Years' Colonial Experiences in Australia, California, New Zealand, India, China, and the South Pacific.* London: S. Low, Marston, Searle, and Rivington, 1879.

[Bartlett, Washington Allon.] "Letters from California (1846)." *Magazine of History with Notes and Queries* 24 (1923): 59–78.

Bates, Mrs. D. B. *Incidents on Land and Water: Or Four Years on the Pacific Coast.* Boston: E. O. Libby, 1858.

[Bean, Edwin F.] *Bean's History and Directory of Nevada County, California.* Nevada City, Calif.: Daily Gazette Book and Job Office, 1867.

Bean, Lowell John. *Mukat's People: The Cahuilla Indians of Southern Cali-*

fornia. Berkeley: University of California Press, 1972.

Bean, Lowell John, and Thomas C. Blackburn, eds. *Native Californians: A Theoretical Retrospective.* Ramona, Calif.: Ballena Press, 1976.

Bean, Lowell John, and Sylvia Brakke Vance. *California Indians: Primary Resources.* Socorro, N. Mex.: Ballena Press, 1977.

Bean, Walton and James J. Rawls. *California: An Interpretive History.* 4th ed. New York: McGraw-Hill, 1983.

Beechey, Frederick William. *Narrative of a Voyage to the Pacific and Beering* [*sic*] *Strait, to Cooperate with the Polar Expeditions: Performed in His Majesty's Ship Blossom Under the Command of Captain F. W. Beechey in the Years 1825, 26, 27, 28.* 2 vols. London: H. Colburn and R. Bentley, 1831.

Belden, Josiah. *Josiah Belden, 1841 California Overland Pioneer: His Memoir and Early Letters.* Edited by Doyce B. Nunis, Jr. Georgetown, Calif.: Talisman Press, 1962.

Bell, Horace. *Reminiscences of a Ranger: Or, Early Times in Southern California.* Foreword by Arthur M. Ellis. Santa Barbara, Calif.: Wallace Hebberd, 1927.

Benson, William Ralganal. "The Stone and Kelsey 'Massacre' on the Shores of Clear Lake in 1849." *California Historical Society Quarterly* 7 (Sept., 1932): 266–73.

Berkhofer, Robert F., Jr. *Salvation and the Savage: An Analysis of Protestant Missions and American Indian Response, 1787–1862.* Lexington: University of Kentucky Press, 1965.

———. *The White Man's Indian: Images of the American Indian from Columbus to the Present.* New York: Alfred A. Knopf, 1978.

Bidwell, John. *A Journey to California.* [Missouri: 1842?].

Bieber, Ralph P. "California Gold Mania." *Mississippi Valley Historical Review* 35 (June, 1948): 3–28.

Bledsoe, Anthony Jennings. *Indian Wars of the Northwest: A California Sketch.* Foreword by Joseph A. Sullivan. Oakland, Calif.: Biobooks, 1956.

Blue, George Verne, ed. "The Report of Captain La Place on his Voyage to the Northwest Coast and California in 1839." *California Historical Society Quarterly* 18 (Dec., 1939): 315–28.

Bonsal, Stephen. *Edward Fitzgerald Beale: A Pioneer in the Path of Empire, 1822–1903.* New York: G. P. Putnam's Sons, 1912.

Borah, Woodrow. *New Spain's Century of Depression.* Ibero-Americana, no. 35. Berkeley: University of California Press, 1951.

Borthwick, J. D. *Three Years in California.* Edinburgh and London: W. Blackwood and Sons, 1857.

Brace, Charles Loring. *The New West: Or, California in 1867–1868.* New York: G. P. Putnam and Son, 1869.

Brewer, William H. *Up and Down California in 1860–1864: The Journal of William H. Brewer.* Edited by Francis P. Farquhar. New Haven, Conn.: Yale University Press, 1931.

Browne, J. Ross. "The Coast Rangers: A Chronicle of Events in California." *Harpers' New Monthly Magazine* 23 (Aug., 1861): 309–15.

――――. *Report of the Debates in the Convention of California on the Formation of the State Constitution in September and October, 1849.* Washington, D.C.: J. T. Towers, 1850.

Bruff, J. Goldsborough. *The Journals, Drawings, and Other Papers of J. Goldsborough Bruff, April 6, 1849–July 20, 1851.* Edited by Georgia Willis Read and Ruth Gaines. New York: Columbia University Press, 1949.

Bryant, Edwin. *What I Saw in California: Being the Journal of a Tour by the Emigrant Route and South Pass of the Rocky Mountains, Across the Rocky Mountains, Across the Continent of North America, the Great Desert Baisin, and Through California, in the Years 1846, 1847.* 2d ed. New York: D. Appleton, 1848.

Buck, Franklin A. *A Yankee Trader in the Gold Rush: The Letters of Franklin A. Buck.* Edited by Katherine A. White. Boston: Houghton Mifflin, 1930.

Buffum, E. Gould. *The Gold Rush: An Account of Six Months in the California Diggings.* 1850. [London ?]: Folio Society, 1959.

Burnett, Peter H. *Recollections and Opinions of an Old Pioneer.* New York: D. Appleton, 1880.

Bushnell, Horace. *California: Its Characteristics and Prospects.* San Francisco: Whitton, Towne and Co., 1858.

Carranco, Lynwood, and Estle Beard. *Genocide and Vendetta: The Round Valley Wars of Northern California.* Norman: University of Oklahoma Press, 1981.

Carson, James II. *Recollections of the California Mines: An Account of the Early Discoveries of Gold, with Anecdotes and Sketches of California Miners' Life, and a Description of the Great Tulare Valley.* Foreword by Joseph A. Sullivan. Oakland, Calif.: Biobooks, 1950.

Carson, Thankful A. *Captured by the Mill Creek Indians.* Chico, Calif.: privately printed by the author, 1915.

Casler, Melyer. *A Journal Giving the Incidents of a Journey to California in the Summer of 1859 by the Overland Route.* Fairfield, Wash.: Ye Galleon Press, 1969.

Caughey, John W. *Don Benito Wilson: An Average Southern Californian.* San Marino, Calif.: Huntington Library, 1939.

――――. ed. *The Indians of Southern California in 1852: The B. D. Wilson Report and a Selection of Contemporary Comment.* San Marino, Calif.: Huntington Library, 1952.

Cheever, Edward E. "The Indians of California." *American Naturalist* 4 (May, 1870): 129–48.

Chiles, Joseph B. *A Visit to California in 1841 as Recorded for Hubert Howe Bancroft in an Interview with Joseph B. Chiles.* Foreword by George R. Stewart. Berkeley, Calif.: Friends of the Bancroft Library, 1970.

Chittenden, Hiram M. *The American Fur Trade of the Far West: A History of the Pioneer Trading Posts and Early Fur Companies of the Missouri Valley and the Rocky Mountains and of the Overland Commerce with Santa Fe.* 3 vols. New York: Francis P. Harper, 1902.

[Clappe, Louise Amelia Knapp Smith.] *The Shirley Letters from the California Mines, 1851-1852.* Edited by Carl I. Wheat. New York: Ballantine Books, 1971.

Clark, Austin S. *Reminiscences of Travel, 1852-1865.* Middletown, Conn.: J. S. Stewart, n.d.

"Clear Lake." *Hutchings' Illustrated California Magazine* 4 (Feb., 1860): 349-50.

Cleland, Robert Glass. *The Early Sentiment for the Annexation of California: An Account of the Growth of American Interest in California from 1835 to 1846.* Austin: Texas State Historical Association, 1915.

Cleland, Robert Glass, and Osgood Hardy. *March of Industry.* Los Angeles: Powell Publishing Co., 1929.

Cleveland, Richard J. *A Narrative of Voyages and Commercial Enterprises.* 2 vols. Cambridge, Mass.: John Owen, 1842.

Clyman, James. "James Clyman: His Diaries and Reminiscences." Edited by Charles L. Camp. *California Historical Society Quarterly* 6 (March, 1927): 58-68.

Colton, Walter. *Three Years in California.* Cincinatti: H. W. Derby & Co., 1850.

Colvocresses, George M. *Four Years in a Government Exploring Expedition.* New York: Cornish, Lamport and Co., 1852.

Cook, James. *A Voyage to the Pacific Ocean, Undertaken by the Command of His Majesty, for Making Discoveries in the Northern Hemisphere in the Years 1776, 1777, 1778, 1779 and 1780.* 3 vols. London: G. Nicol and T. Cadell, 1784.

Cook, Sherburne F. *The Conflict Between the California Indian and White Civilization: The Indian Versus the Spanish Mission.* Ibero-Americana, no. 21. Berkeley: University of California Press, 1943.

————. *The Conflict Between the California Indian and White Civilization: The American Invasion, 1848-1870.* Ibero-Americana, no. 23. Berkeley: University of California Press, 1943.

————. *The Epidemic of 1830-1833 in California and Oregon.* University of California Publications in American Archaeology and Ethnology, vol. 43. Berkeley: University of California Press, 1955.

————. *Expeditions to the Interior of California: Central Valley, 1820-1840.* University of California Anthropological Records, no. 20. Berkeley: University of California Press, 1962.

————. *The Mechanism and Extent of Dietary Adaptation Among Certain Groups of California and Nevada Indians.* Ibero-Americana, no. 18. Berkeley: University of California Press, 1941.

————. *The Population of the California Indians, 1769-1970.* Berkeley: University of California Press, 1976.

Cook, Sherburne F., and Robert F. Heizer. *The Physical Analysis of Nine Indian Mounds of the Lower Sacramento Valley.* University of California Publications in American Archaeology and Ethnology, vol. 40. Berkeley: University of California Press, 1951.

Cossley-Batt, Jill L. *The Last of the California Rangers.* New York: Funk and Wagnalls, 1928.

Costo, Rubert. Review of Jack D. Forbes, *Native Americans of California and Nevada. Indian Historian* 3 (Winter, 1970): 62–63.

Coulter, John. *Adventures on the Western Coast of South America and in the Interior of California.* 2 vols. London: Longman, Brown, Green, and Longmans, 1847.

Coulter, Thomas. *Notes on Upper California: A Journey from Monterey to the Colorado River in 1832.* Early California Travels Series, no. 1. Introduction by Glen Dawson. Los Angeles: Glen Dawson, 1951.

Cowan, Robert Ernest. "Alexander S. Taylor, 1817–1876." *California Historical Society Quarterly* 8 (March, 1933): 18–24.

Cox, Isaac. *The Annals of Trinity County.* Preface by Caroline Wenzel. Introduction by Owen C. Coy. Foreword by James W. Bartlett. Eugene, Oreg.: John Henry Nash of the University of Oregon, 1940.

Coy, Owen C. *The Humboldt Bay Region, 1850–1875: A Study in the American Colonization of California.* Los Angeles: California State Historical Association, 1929.

Coyner, David H. *The Lost Trappers.* 1847. Edited by David J. Weber. Albuquerque: University of New Mexico Press, 1970.

Cronise, Titus Fey. *The Natural Wealth of California.* San Francisco: H. H. Bancroft and Co., 1868.

Crosby, Elisha Oscar. *Memoirs of Elisha Oscar Crosby: Reminiscences of California and Guatamala from 1849 to 1864.* San Marino, Calif.: Huntington Library, 1945.

Cross, Ira B. *A History of the Labor Movement in California.* University of California Publications in Economics, no. 14. Berkeley: University of California Press, 1935.

Dakin, Susanna Bryant. *The Lives of William Hartnell.* Stanford: Stanford University Press, 1949.

――――. *A Scotch Paisano: Hugo Reid's Life in California, 1832–1852, Derived from his Correspondence.* Berkeley: University of California Press, 1939.

Dale, Edward Everett. *Indians of the Southwest: A Century of Development Under the United States.* Civilization of the American Indian Series, no. 28. Norman: University of Oklahoma Press for the Huntington Library, 1949.

Dale, Harrison Clifford, ed. *The Ashley-Smith Explorations and the Discovery of a Central Route to the Pacific, 1822–1829.* Rev. ed. Glendale, Calif.: Arthur H. Clark, 1941.

Damon, Samuel C. "A Trip from the Sandwich Islands to Lower Oregon and Upper California." *Magazine of History with Notes and Queries* 25 (1923): 1.

Dana, Richard Henry, Jr. *The Journal of Richard Henry Dana.* Edited by Robert F. Lucid. Cambridge, Mass.: Harvard University Press, Belknap Press, 1968.

———. *Two Years Before the Mast: A Personal Narrative of Life at Sea.* Edited by John Haskell Kemble. 2 vols. Los Angeles: Ward Ritchie, 1964.

Davis, William Heath. *Sixty Years in California: A History of Events and Life in California: Personal, Political and Military, under the Mexican Regime; During the Quasi-Military Government of the Territory by the United States, and After the Admission of the State into the Union, Being a Compilation by a Witness of the Events Described.* San Franciso: A. J. Leary, 1889.

Dawson, Nicholas. *California in '41. Texas in '51.* Brasada Series, vol. 9. Edited by John H. Jenkins. Austin, Texas: Pemberton Press, 1969.

Decker, Peter. *The Diaries of Peter Decker: Overland to California in 1849 and Life in the Mines, 1850–1851.* Edited by Helen S. Giffen. Georgetown, Calif.: Talisman Press, 1966.

De Groot, Henry P. *Recollections of California Mining Life.* San Francisco: Dewey and Co., 1884.

Delavan, James. *Notes on California and the Placers: How to Get There and What to Do Afterwards.* Foreword by Joseph A. Sullivan. Oakland, Calif.: Biobooks, 1956.

Derbec, Étienne. *A French Journalist in the California Gold Rush: The Letters of Étienne Derbec.* Edited by A. P. Nasatir. Georgetown, Calif.: 1964.

Dietrich, Dr. *The German Emigrants: Or, Frederich Wohlgemuth's Voyage to California.* Translated by Leopold Wray. Stanford: Stanford University Press, 1949.

Dillon, Richard. *Burnt-Out Fires: California's Modoc Indian War.* Englewood Cliffs, N.J.: Prentice-Hall, 1973.

———. *Fool's Gold: The Decline and Fall of Captain John Sutter of California.* New York: Coward-McCann, 1967.

———. *J. Ross Browne: Confidential Agent in Old California.* Norman: University of Oklahoma Press, 1965.

Dixon, Roland Burrage. *Basketry Designs of the Indians of Northern California.* New York: Museum of Natural History, 1902.

Doble, John. *John Doble's Journal and Letters from the Mines: Mokelumne Hill, Jackson, Volcano and San Francisco, 1851–1865.* Edited by Charles L. Camp. Denver: Old West Publishing Co., 1962.

Duchell, Margaret. "Bret Harte and the Indians of Northern California." *Huntington Library Quarterly* 18 (Nov., 1954): 59–63.

Duhaut-Cilly, August Bernard. "Duhaut-Cilly's Account of California in the Years 1827–1828." Translated by Charles F. Carter. *California Historical Society Quarterly* 8 (Dec., 1929): 305–356.

266

Dunbar, Edward E. *The Romance of the Age: Or, the Discovery of Gold in California.* New York: D. Appleton, 1867.

Duniway, Clyde A. "Slavery in California after 1848." In *Annual Report of the American Historical Association for the Year 1905.* Washington, D.C.: American Historical Association, 1906.

Du Petit-Thouars, Abel. *Voyage of the Venus: Sojourn in California.* Early California Travels Series, no. 35. Translated by Charles N. Rudkin. Los Angeles: Glen Dawson, 1956.

Dye, Job F. "Recollections of a Pioneer of California," *Santa Cruz Sentinel,* 15 May 1869.

Eccleston, Robert. *The Mariposa Indian War, 1850–1851: Diaries of Robert Eccleston.* Edited by C. Gregory Crampton. Salt Lake City: University of Utah Press, 1957.

Ellison, William Henry. *A Self-Governing Dominion: California, 1849–1860.* Berkeley: University of California Press, 1950.

Evans, Albert S. *Á La California: Sketches of Life in the Golden State.* San Francisco: A. L. Bancroft, 1873.

Fairchild, Lucius. *California Letters of Lucius Fairchild.* Wisconsin Historical Publications Collections, vol. 31. Edited by Joseph Schafer. Madison: State Historical Society of Wisconsin, 1931.

Farnham, Thomas Jefferson. *Life and Adventures in California and Scenes in the Pacific Ocean.* New York: W. H. Graham, 1846.

———. *Travels in the Californias and Scenes in the Pacific Ocean.* New York: Saxton and Miles, 1844.

Forbes, Alexander. *California: A History of Upper and Lower California.* 1839. Introduction by Herbert Ingram Priestley. San Francisco: John Henry Nash, 1937.

Forbes, Jack D., ed., *The Indian in America's Past.* Englewood Cliffs, N.J.: Prentice-Hall, 1964.

———. "The Native American Experience in California History." *California Historical Society Quarterly* 50 (Sept., 1971): 234–42.

———. *Native Americans of California and Nevada.* Healdsburg, Calif.: Naturegraph, 1969.

———. *Warriors of the Colorado: The Yumas of the Quechan Nation and Their Neighbors.* Civilization of the American Indian Series, no. 76. Norman: University of Oklahoma Press, 1965.

Forbes, Robert B. *Personal Reminiscences.* Boston: Little, Brown and Co., 1878.

Foreman, Grant. *Indian Removal: The Emigration of the Five Civilized Tribes of Indians.* Civilization of the American Indian Series, no. 2. Norman: University of Oklahoma Press, 1953.

Foster, G. G., ed. *The Gold Regions of California: Being a Succinct Description of the Geography, History, Topography, and General Features of California.* 3d ed. New York: DeWitt and Davenport, 1849.

Franklin, John Hope. *Reconstruction after the Civil War.* Chicago: University of Chicago Press, 1961.

Frémont, Jessie Benton, *Mother Lode Narratives.* Edited by Shirley Sargent. Ashland, Oreg.: Lewis Osborne, 1970.

———. *A Year of American Travel: Narrative of Personal Experience.* Introduction by Patrice Mahan. San Francisco: Book Club of California, 1960.

Frémont, John Charles. *Narrative of the Exploring Expedition to the Rocky Mountains, in the Year 1842, and to Oregon and North California in the Years 1843–1844.* London: Wiley and Putnam, 1846.

Fritz, Henry E. *The Movement for Indian Assimilation, 1860–1890.* Philadelphia: University of Pennsylvania Press, 1963.

Gardiner, Howard C. *In Pursuit of the Golden Dream: Reminiscences of San Francisco and the Northern and Southern Mines, 1849–1857.* Edited by Dale L. Morgan. Stoughton, Mass.: Western Hemisphere, 1970.

Garner, William Robert. *Letters from California, 1846–1847.* Edited by Donald Munro Craig. Berkeley: University of California Press, 1970.

Gayton, Anna Hardwick. *Yokuts and Western Mono Pottery-Making.* University of California Publications in American Archaeology and Ethnology, vol. 24. Berkeley: University of California Press, 1929.

Geiger, Maynard. *The History of California's Santa Barbara Mission from 1786 to the Present.* Santa Barbara, Calif.: Franciscan Fathers, 1959.

Geiger, Maynard, and Clement W. Meighan, eds. *As the Padres Saw Them: California Indian Life and Customs as Reported by the Franciscan Missionaries, 1813–1815.* Santa Barbara, Calif.: Santa Barbara Mission Archive Library, 1976.

Gerstäcker, Friedrich. *Gerstacker's Travels: Rio de Janeiro–Buenos Ayres–Ride Through the Pampas—Winter Journey Across the Cordilleras—Chile—Valpariso—California and the Gold Fields.* London: T. Nelson and Sons, 1854.

Gibson, Charles. *The Aztecs Under Spanish Rule: A History of the Indians of the Valley of Mexico.* Stanford: Stanford University Press, 1964.

———. *The Black Legend: Anti-Spanish Attitudes in the Old World and New.* New York: Alfred A. Knopf, 1971.

———. *Spain in America.* The New American Nation Series. New York: Harper & Row, 1966.

Gifford, Edward Winslow, and Gwendolyn Harris Block, comps. *California Indian Nights Entertainments: Stories of the Creation of the World, of Man, of Fire, of the Sun, of Thunder, etc.* Glendale, Calif.: Arthur H. Clark, 1930.

Gilliam, Albert M. *Travels in Mexico During the Years 1843 and 44: Including a Description of California, the Principal Cities and Mining Districts of that Republic.* Aberdeen: G. Clark & Son, 1847.

Glassley, Ray Howard. *Indian Wars of the Pacific Northwest.* 2d ed. Portland, Oreg.: Binfords and Mort, 1972.

Green, Jonathan S. *Journal of a Tour on the North West Coast of America in the Year 1829.* Heartman's Historical Series, no. 10. New York: Charles Heartman, 1915.

Griffin, John Strother. *A Doctor Comes to California: The Diary of John S. Griffin, Assistant Surgeon with Kearny's Dragoons, 1846–1847.* Introduction by George Walcott Ames, Jr. Foreword by George D. Lyman. San Francisco: California Historical Society, 1943.

Gudde, Erwin G. *California Place Names: The Origin and Etymology of Current Geographical Names.* 3d rev. ed. Berkeley: University of California Press, 1969.

Guest, Francis F. "An Examination of the Thesis of S. F. Cook on the Forced Conversion of Indians in the California Missions." *Southern California Quarterly* 61 (Spring, 1979): 1–78.

Hackett, Charles W., et al., eds. *New Spain and the Anglo-American West: Historical Contributions Presented to Herbert Eugene Bolton.* 2 vols. Los Angeles: privately printed, 1932.

Hagan, William T. *American Indians.* Chicago: University of Chicago Press, 1961.

Hale, Richard L. *The Log of a Forty-Niner: Journal of a Voyage from Newburyport to San Francisco.* Edited by Carolyn Hale Russ. Boston: B. J. Brimmer, 1923.

Hallowell, A. Irving. "The Impact of the Indian on American Culture." *American Anthropologist* 59 (April, 1957).

Hammond, George P. *The Weber Era in Stockton History.* Berkeley, Calif.: Friends of the Bancroft Library, 1982.

Hanke, Lewis, ed., *Do the Americas Have a Common History? A Critique of the Bolton Theory.* New York: Alfred A. Knopf, 1964.

Haring, Clarence Henry. *The Spanish Empire in America.* New York: Oxford University Press, 1947.

Harlan, Jacob Wright. *California '46 to '48.* San Francisco: Bancroft Co., 1888.

Harris, Benjamin Butler. *The Gila Trail: The Texas Argonauts and the California Gold Rush.* Edited by Richard H. Dillon. Norman: University of Oklahoma Press, 1960.

Hart, James D. *American Images of Spanish California.* Berkeley, Calif.: Friends of the Bancroft Library, 1960.

———. "The Education of Richard Henry Dana, Jr." *New England Quarterly* 9 (March, 1936): 3–25.

Hastings, Lansford W. *The Emigrants' Guide to Oregon and California: Containing Scenes and Incidents of a Party of Oregon Emigrants; a Description of Oregon; Scenes and Incidents of a Party of California Emigrants; and a Description of California; with a Description of the Different Routes to those Countries; and All Necessary Information Relative to the Equipment, Supplies, and the Methods of Travelling.* Cincinnati: George Conclin, 1845.

Hawgood, John A. "The Pattern of Yankee Infiltration in Mexican California, 1821–1848." *Pacific Historical Review* 28 (Feb., 1958): 27–38.

Heckendorn, J. *Miners and Business Men's Directory.* Columbia, Calif.: Heckendorn and Wilson, 1856.

Heizer, Robert F. "The California Indians: Archaeology, Varieties of Culture, Arts of Life." *California Historical Society Quarterly* 41 (March, 1962): 1–28.

――――, ed. *The Destruction of California Indians: A Collection of Documents from the Period 1847 to 1865 in which Are Described Some of the Things that Happened to Some of the Indians of California.* Santa Barbara, Calif.: Peregrine Smith, 1974.

――――. *The Eighteen Unratified Treaties of 1851–1852 between the California Indians and the United States Government.* Berkeley: University of California Archaeological Research Facility, 1972.

――――. *Elizabethan California: A Brief and Sometimes Critical Review of Opinions on the Location of Francis Drake's Five Weeks' Visit with the Indians of Ships Land in 1579.* Ramona, Calif.: Ballena Press, 1974.

――――, ed. *Federal Concern About Conditions of California Indians, 1853–1913.* Socorro, N. Mex.: Ballena Press, 1979.

Heizer, Robert F., ed. *California. Handbook of North American Indians,* edited by William C. Sturtevant, vol. 8. Washington, D.C.: 1978.

――――. *The Indians of California: A Critical Bibliography.* Bloomington: Indiana University Press, 1976.

――――, ed. *They Were Only Diggers: A Collection of Articles from California Newspapers, 1851–1866, on Indian and White Relations.* Ramona, Calif.: Ballena Press, 1974.

Heizer, Robert F., and Alan J. Almquist. *The Other Californians: Prejudice and Discrimination Under Spain, Mexico, and the United States to 1920.* Berkeley: University of California Press, 1971.

Heizer, Robert F., and C. W. Clewlow, Jr. *Prehistoric Rock Art of California.* Ramona, Calif.: Ballena Press, 1973.

Heizer, Robert F., and Albert B. Elsasser. *The Natural World of the California Indians.* Berkeley: University of California Press, 1980.

Heizer, Robert F., Karen M. Nissen, and Edward D. Castillo. *California Indian History: A Classified and Annotated Guide to Source Materials.* Socorro, N. Mex.: Ballena Press, 1976.

Heizer, Robert F., and M. A. Whipple, eds. *The California Indians: A Source Book.* 2d rev. ed. Berkeley: University of California Press, 1971.

Helper, Hinton Rowan. *Dreadful California: Being a True and Scandalous Account of the Barbarous Civilization, Licentious Morals, Crude Manners and Depravities, Inclement Climate and Niggling Resources, Together with Various Other Offensive and Calamitous Details of Life in the Golden State.* 1855. Edited by Lucius Beebe and Charles M. Clegg. New York: Bobbs-Merrill, 1948.

Hill, Dorothy J. *The Indians of Chico Rancheria.* Sacramento, Calif.: n.d.

Hill, Edward E. *The Office of Indian Affairs, 1824-1880: Historical Sketches.* New York: Clearwater Publishing Co., 1974.

Hill, Jasper S. *The Letters of a Young Miner: Covering the Adventures of Jasper S. Hill During the California Goldrush, 1849-1852.* Edited by Doyce B. Nunis, Jr. San Francisco: John Howell, 1964.

Hill, Joseph J. *The History of Warner's Ranch and its Environs.* Edited and with a preface by Herbert E. Bolton. Los Angeles: Young and McCallister, 1927.

————. "Ewing Young in the Fur Trade of the Far Southwest, 1822-1834." *Oregon Historical Society Quarterly* 24 (March, 1923): 1-35.

Hilsop, Donald L. *The Nome Lackee Indian Reservation, 1854-1870.* Chico, Calif.: Association for Northern Records and Research, 1978.

History of Contra Costa County, California, Including its Geography, Geology, Topography and Biographical Sketches of Early Prominent Settlers and Representative Men. San Francisco: W. A. Slocum, 1882.

Hittel, Theodore H. *History of California, 1830-1917.* 4 vols. San Francisco: N. J. Stone, 1885-97.

Holliday, J[aquelin] S[mith]. *The World Rushed In: The California Gold Rush Experience.* New York: Simon and Schuster, 1981.

Hoopes, Alban. *Indian Affairs and Their Administration: With Special Reference to the Far West, 1849-1860.* Philadelphia: University of Pennsylvania Press, 1932.

Horsman, Reginald. "American Indian Policy and the Origins of Manifest Destiny." *University of Birmingham Historical Journal* 11 (Dec., 1968): 128-40.

Hughes, John T. *California: Its History, Population, Climate, Soil, Productions, and Harbors.* Cincinnati: J. A. and U. P. James, 1848.

Humanson, W[illiam] L[awrence]. *From the Atlantic Surf to the Golden Gate.* Hartford, Conn.: William C. Hutchings, 1869.

Hundley, Norris, ed. *The American Indian.* Santa Barbara, Calif.: Clio Press, 1974.

Hunt, Roxwell D. *John Bidwell: Prince of California Pioneers.* Caldwell, Idaho: Caxton Printers, 1942.

Hutchings, James Mason. *Scenes of Wonder and Curiosity in California: Illustrated with Over One Hundred Engravings; A Tourist's Guide to the Yosemite Valley Etc.* New York: A. Roman, 1876.

Hutchison, Claude B., ed. *California Agriculture.* Berkeley: University of California Press, 1946.

An Illustrated History of San Joaquin County, California, Together with Glimpses of its Future Prospects. Chicago: Lewis Publishing Co., 1890.

Irving, Washington. *The Adventures of Captain Bonneville, U.S.A., in the Rocky Mountains and the Far West.* American Exploration and Travel Series, no. 34. Edited by Edgeley W. Todd. Norman: University of Oklahoma Press, 1961.

[Jackson, Alfred T.] *The Diary of a Forty-Niner.* Edited by Chauncey L. Canfield. Boston: Houston Mifflin, 1920.

Jackson, Helen Hunt. *A Century of Dishonor: A Sketch of the United States Government's Dealings with Some of the Indian Tribes:* Rev. ed. Boston: Roberts Brothers, 1885.

————. *Ramona: A Story.* Boston: Roberts Brothers, 1884.

Jacobs, Wilbur R. "The Fatal Confrontation: Early Native-White Relations on the Frontiers of Australia, New Guinea, and America—A Comparative Study." *Pacific Historical Review* 40 (Sept., 1971): 283–310.

Johnson, Kenneth M. *K-344: Or, The Indians of California vs. the United States.* Foreword by Homer D. Crotty. Los Angeles: Dawson's Book Shop, 1966.

Johnson, Richard R. "The Search for a Usable Indian: An Aspect of the Defense of Colonial New England." *Journal of American History* 64 (Dec., 1977): 623–51.

Johnson, Solomon. "The Gold Coast of California and Oregon." *Overland Monthly* 2 (June, 1869): 534–37.

Johnson, Theodore T. *California and Oregon: Or, Sights in the Gold Region and Scenes by the Way.* 4th ed. Philadelphia: J. B. Lippincott, 1857.

————. *Sights in the Gold Region, and Scenes by the Way.* New York: Baker and Scribner, 1849.

Johnston, William G. *Experiences of a Forty-Niner.* Pittsburgh: 1892.

Jordan, Winthrop D. *White Over Black: American Attitudes Toward the Negro, 1550–1812.* Baltimore: Penguin Books, 1969.

Josephy, Alvin M., Jr. "By Fayre and Gentle Means: The Hudson's Bay Company and the American Indian." *American West* 9 (Sept., 1972): 4–12.

Kelly, Isabel Truesdell. *The Carver's Art of the Indians of Northwestern California.* University of California Publications in American Archaeology and Ethnology, no. 24. Berkeley: University of California, 1930.

Kelly. William. *An Excursion to California Over the Prairie, Rocky Mountains, and Great Sierra Nevada.* London: Chapman and Hall, 1851.

Kelsey, Harry. "The California Indian Treaty Myth." *Southern California Quarterly* 55 (Fall, 1973): 225–35.

Khlebnikov, Kirill Timofeevich. "Memoirs of California." 1829. Translated by Anatole G. Mazour. *Pacific Historical Review* 9 (Sept., 1940): 307–60.

Kibbe, William C. *Report of the Expedition Against the Indians in the Northern Part of this State.* Sacramento, Calif.: 1860.

King, Thomas Butler. "Report on California." In *Message from the Pesident [sic] of the United States, Transmitting the Report of T. Butler King.* Washington, D.C.: 1850.

Kip, Leonard. *California Sketches with Recollections of the Gold Mines.* Introductions by Lyle H. Wright. California Centennial Series, no. 1. Los

Angeles: N. A. Kovach, 1946.

Kip, William I. "The Last of the Leatherstockings." *Overland Monthly* 2 (May, 1869): 401–12.

Kovel, Joel. *White Racism: A Psychohistory.* New York: Vintage Books, 1971.

Kroeber, Alfred L. *Basket Designs of the Mission Indians of California.* Anthropological Papers of the American Museum of Natural History, no. 20. New York: Trustees of the American Museum of Natural History, 1922.

———. *Elements of Culture in Native California.* University of California Publications in American Archaeology and Ethnology, no. 13. Berkeley: University of California Press, 1922.

———. *Handbook of the Indians of California.* Bureau of American Ethnology Bulletin no. 78. Washington, D.C.: Government Printing Office, 1925.

———. *The Religion of the Indians of California.* University of California Publications in American Archaeology and Ethnology, no. 4. Berkeley: University of California Press, 1907.

Kroeber, Theodora. *Ishi in Two Worlds: A Biography of the Last Wild Indian in North America.* Berkeley: University of California, 1961.

Kroeber, Theodora, Albert B. Elsasser, and Robert F. Heizer. *Drawn from Life: California Indians in Pen and Brush.* Socorro, N. Mex.: Ballena Press, 1977.

Kroeber, Theodora, and Robert F. Heizer. *Almost Ancestors: The First Californians.* Edited by David Hales. San Francisco: Sierra Club, 1968.

Künzel, Heinrich. *Upper California.* 1848. Translated by Anthony and Max Knight. Introduction by Carrol D. Hall. San Francisco: Book Club of California, 1967.

Lambert, Richard, comp., *Homographic Chart of the State Officers, Senators, Representatives of the Eleventh Session of the California Legislature.* Sacramento, Calif.: 1860.

Lambert, Claude François. *Curious Observations Upon the Manners, Customs, Usages . . . of the Several Nations of Asia, Africa, and America.* 2 vols. London: G. Woodfall, 1751.

Lang, James. *Conquest and Commerce: Spain and England in the Americas.* New York: Academic Press, 1975.

Langsdorff, Georg Heinrich von. *Langsdorff's Narrative of the Rezanov Voyage to Nueva California in 1806.* Edited and translated by Thomas C. Russell. San Francisco: Thomas C. Russell, 1927.

Langworthy, Franklin. *Scenery of the Plains, Mountains and Mines.* Edited by Paul C. Phillips. Princeton: Princeton University Press, 1932.

La Pérouse, Jean François Galaup de. *A Voyage Round the World, in the Years 1785, 1786, 1787, and 1788.* Edited by M. L. A. Milet-Mureau. 3 vols. London: J. Johnson, 1798.

Lapp, Rudolph M. *Blacks in the California Gold Rush.* New Haven: Yale University Press, 1977.

————. "Negro Rights Activities in Gold Rush California." *California Historical Society Quarterly* 45 (March, 1966): 3–20.

Larkin, Thomas Oliver. *The Larkin Papers: Personal, Business and Official Correspondence of Thomas Oliver Larkin.* Edited by George P. Hammond. 10 vols. Berkeley: University of California Press, 1951–64.

Lauber, Almon Wheeler. *Indian Slavery in Colonial Times Within the Present Limits of the United States.* Studies in History, Economics, and Public Law, no. 134. New York: Columbia University Press, 1913.

Leeper, David Rohrer. *The Argonauts of 'Forty-Nine: Some Recollections of the Plains and the Diggings.* South Bend, Ind.: J. B. Stoll, 1894.

Le Netrel, Edmond. *Voyage of the Héros Around the World with Duhaut-Cilly in the Years 1826, 1827, 1828 & 1829.* Early California Travels Series, no. 3. Translated by Blanche Collet Wagner. Los Angeles: Glen Dawson, 1951.

Leonard, Zenas. *Narrative of the Adventures of Zenas Leonard.* 1839. Lakeside Classics Series, no. 32. Edited by Milo Milton Quaife. Chicago: Lakeside Press, 1934.

[Letts, John M.] *California Illustrated: Including a Description of the Panama and Nicaragua Routes.* New York: William Holdredge, 1852.

Lienhard, Heinrich. *From St. Louis to Sutter's Fort, 1846.* Translated and edited by Erwin G. and Elisabeth K. Gudde. Norman: University of Oklahoma Press, 1961.

Lovett, W. E. *Report of W. E. Lovett, Special Indian Agent to Austin Wiley, Superintendent of Indian Affairs in California.* San Francisco: Mining and Scientific Press, 1865.

Lyman, Albert. *Journal of a Voyage to California and Life in the Gold Diggings, and Also of a Voyage from California to the Sandwich Islands.* Hartford, Conn.: E. T. Pease, 1852.

Lyman, George D. *John Marsh, Pioneer: The Life Story of a Trailblazer on Six Frontiers.* New York: Charles Scribner's Sons, 1931.

M'Collum, William. *California As I Saw It: Pencillings by the Way of Its Gold and Gold Diggers.* Edited by Dale L. Morgan. Los Gatos, Calif.: Talisman Press, 1960.

McGowan, Joseph A. *History of the Sacramento Valley.* New York: Lewis Historical Publishing Co., 1961.

McIlhany, Edward Washington. *Recollections of a '49er: A Quaint and Thrilling Narrative of a Trip Across the Plains, and Life in the California Gold Fields During the Stirring Days Following the Discovery of Gold in the Far West.* Kansas City, Mo.: Haliman, 1908.

McWilliams, Carey. *Factories in the Field: The Story of Migratory Farm Labor in California.* Boston: Little, Brown and Co., 1939.

Mahr, August C., ed. *The Visit of the "Rurik" to San Francisco in 1816.* Stanford, Calif.: Stanford University Press, 1932.

Malaspina, Alejandro. *Malaspina in California.* 1791. Edited by Donald C.

Cutter. San Francisco: John Howell, 1960.

Markoff, Alexander. *The Russians on the Pacific Coast.* 1845. Early California Travels Series, no. 27. Translated by Ivan Petroff. Foreword by Arthur Woodward. Los Angeles: Glen Dawson, 1955.

Marryat, Francis. *Mountains and Molehills: Or Recollections of a Burnt Journal.* 1855. Introduction by Robin W. Winks. Philadelphia: J. B. Lippincott, 1962.

Marsh, John. "Letter of Dr. John Marsh to Hon. Lewis Cass." *California Historical Society Quarterly* 22 (Dec., 1943): 315–22.

Massey, Ernest de. *A Frenchman in the Gold Rush: The Journal of Ernest de Massey, Argonaut of 1849.* Translated by Marguerite Eyer Wilbur. San Francisco: California Historical Society, 1927.

Meyer, Carl. *Bound for Sacramento: Travel-Pictures of a Returned Wanderer.* Translated by Ruth Frey Axe. Introduction by Henry R. Wagner. Claremont, Calif.: Sauders Studio Press, 1938.

Mitchell, Annie R. "Major James D. Savage and the Tulareños." *California Historical Society Quarterly* 28 (Dec. 1949): 323–41.

Moak, Sim. *The Last of the Mill Creeks and Early Life in Northern California.* Chico, Calif., 1923.

Mofras, Eugene Duflot de. *Duflot de Mofras' Travels on the Pacific Coast.* Edited and translated by Marguerite Eyer Wilbur. 2 vols. Santa Ana, Calif.: Fine Art Press, 1937.

Morgan, Dale L. *Jedediah Smith and the Opening of the West.* Lincoln: University of Nebraska Press, 1971.

Morris, Albert Ferdinand. "The Journal of a 'Crazy Man.' Travels and Scenes in California from the Year 1834 to the American Conquest: The Narrative of Albert Ferdinand Morris." Edited by Charles L. Camp. *California Historical Society Quarterly* 15 (June and Sept., 1936): 103–38, 224–41.

Murray, Keith. *The Modocs and Their War.* Civilization of the American Indian Series, no. 52. Norman: University of Oklahoma Press, 1959.

Nasatir, Abraham P. *French Activities in California: An Archival Calendar Guide.* Stanford: Stanford University Press, 1945.

Nash, Gary B. *Red, White and Black: The Peoples of Early America.* Englewood Cliffs, N.J.: Prentice Hall, 1974.

Nash, Roderick. *Wilderness and the American Mind.* New Haven: Yale University Press, 1967.

Nelson, Byron, Jr. *Our Home Forever: A Hupa Tribal History.* Edited by Laura Bayer. Hoopa, Calif.: Hupa Tribe, 1978.

Nidever, George. *The Life and Adventures of George Nidever.* Edited by William Henry Ellison. Berkeley: University of California Press, 1937.

Nordhoff, Charles. *California for Health, Pleasure, and Residence: A Book for Travellers and Settlers.* New York: Harper and Brothers, 1872.

Norton, Jack. *When Our Worlds Cried; Genocide in Northwestern California.*

San Francisco: Indian Historical Press, 1979.

Ogden, Adele. "Alfred Robinson, New England Merchant in Mexican California." *California Historical Society Quarterly* 23 (Sept., 1944): 193–18.

————. "Boston Hide Droghers Along California Shores." *California Historical Society Quarterly* 8 (Dec., 1929): 289–305.

————. *The California Sea Otter Trade, 1784–1848.* University of California Publications in History, vol. 26. Berkeley: University of California Press, 1941.

————. "Hides and Tallow: McCulloch, Hartnell and Company, 1822–1828." *California Historical Society Quarterly* 4 (Sept. 1927): 254–64.

Pancoast, Charles Edward. *A Quaker Forty-Niner: The Adventures of Charles Edward Pancoast on the American Frontier.* Edited by Anna Paschall Hannum. Foreword by John Bach McMaster. Philadelphia: University of Pennsylvania Press, 1930.

Parsons, George Frederic. *The Life and Adventures of James W. Marshall: The Discoverer of Gold in California.* Sacramento, Calif.: James W. Marshall and W. Burke, 1870.

Pattie, James Ohio. *Personal Narrative of James O. Pattie.* 1831. Edited by William Goetzmann. Philadelphia: J. B. Lippincott, 1962.

Paul, Rodman. *California Gold: The Beginning of Mining in the Far West.* Cambridge, Mass.: Harvard University Press, 1947.

Payne, Doris Palmer. *Captain Jack, Modoc Renegade.* Portland, Oreg.: Binford & Mort, 1938.

Payson, George [Ralph Raven]. *Golden Dreams and Leaden Realities.* Introduction by Francis Fogie. New York: G. P. Putnam, 1853.

Peale, Titian Ramsey. *Titian Ramsey Peale 1799–1885 and His Journals of the Wilkes Expedition.* Edited by Jessie Poesch. Philadelphia: American Philosophical Society, 1961.

Pearce, Roy Harvey. *The Savages of America: A Study of the Indian and the Idea of Civilization.* Baltimore: Johns Hopkins University Press, 1965.

————. "The Metaphysics of Indian Hating." *Ethnohistory* 4 (1957): 27–37.

Peckham, Howard, and Charles Gibson, eds. *Attitudes of Colonial Powers Toward the American Indian.* Publications in the American West, no. 2. Salt Lake City: University of Utah Press, 1969.

Perkins, Elisha Douglass. *Gold Rush Diary.* Edited by Thomas D. Clark. Lexington: University of Kentucky Press, 1967.

Perkins, William. *Three Years in California: William Perkins' Journal of Life at Sonora, 1849–1852.* Edited by Dale L. Morgan and James R. Scobie. Berkeley: University of California Press, 1964.

Pfeiffer, Ida. *A Lady's Second Journey Round the World: From London to the Cape of Good Hope, Borneo, Java, Sumatra, Celebes, Ceram, the Moluccas, etc., California, Panama, Peru, Ecuador, and the United States.* London: Longman, Brown, Green and Longmans, 1855.

Phillips, George Harwood. *Chiefs and Challengers: Indian Resistance and Co-*

operation in Southern California. Berkeley: University of California Press, 1975.

———. *The Enduring Struggle: Indians in California History.* San Francisco: Boyd and Fraser, 1981.

———. "Indians in Los Angeles, 1781–1875: Economic Integration, Social Disintegration," *Pacific Historical Review* 49 (August, 1980): 427–51.

Pigman, Walter Griffith. *The Journal of Walter Griffith Pigman.* Edited by Ulla Staley Fawkes. Mexico, Mo.: Walter G. Staley, 1942.

Pitt, Leonard. *The Decline of the Californios: A Social History of the Spanish-Speaking Californians, 1846–1890.* Berkeley: University of California Press, 1970.

Powell, Philip Wayne. *Tree of Hate: Propaganda and Prejudice Affecting United States Relations with the Hispanic World.* New York: Basic Books, 1971.

Powers, Stephen. "California Indian Characteristics." *Overland Monthly* 14 (April, 1875): 297–309.

———. *California Indian Characteristics & Centennial Mission to the Indians of Western Nevada and California.* Introduction by Robert F. Heizer. Preface by N. Scott Momaday. Berkeley, Calif.: Friends of the Bancroft Library, 1975.

———. "The Northern California Indians." *Overland Monthly* 8 (April, 1872): 325–35.

———. *Tribes of California.* 1877. Introduction and notes by Robert F. Heizer. Berkeley: University of California Press, 1976.

Priest, Loring Benson. *Uncle Sam's Stepchildren: The Reformation of United States Indian Policy, 1865–1887.* New Brunswick, N.J.: Rutgers University Press, 1942.

Prucha, Francis Paul. *America's Indian Policy in the Formative Years: The Indian Trade and Intercourse Acts, 1780–1834.* Cambridge: Harvard University Press, 1962.

———. "Andrew Jackson's Indian Policy: A Reassessment." *Journal of American History* 56 (Dec., 1969): 527–39.

Rawls, James J., ed. *Dan De Quille of the Big Bonanza.* San Francisco: Book Club of California, 1980.

Reid, Hugo. *The Indians of Los Angeles County: Hugo Reid's Letters of 1852.* Southwest Museum Papers, no. 21. Edited by Robert F. Heizer. Los Angeles: Southwest Museum, 1968.

"Reminiscences of Mendocino." *Hutchings' Illustrated California Magazine* 3 (Oct. 1858): 146–60.

Revere, Joseph Warren. *Naval Duty in California.* Foreword by Joseph A. Sullivan. Oakland, Calif.: Biobooks, 1947.

———. *A Tour of Duty in California: Including a Description of the Gold Region.* Edited by Joseph N. Balestier. New York: C. S. Francis, 1849.

Rezanov, Nikolai Petrovich. *The Rezanov Voyage to Nueva California in 1806.* Edited and translated by Thomas C. Russell. San Francisco: Thomas C.

Russell, 1926.

Richardson, James D., comp. *A Compilation of the Messages and Papers of the Presidents*, vol. 2. Washington, D.C.: 1900.

Riddle, Jeff C. *The Indian History of the Modoc War.* San Francisco: Marnell & Co., 1914.

Robinson, Alfred. "Business Letters of Alfred Robinson." Edited by Adele Ogden. *California Historical Society Quarterly* 23 (Dec., 1944): 305–310.

———. "Journal on the Coast of California, on Board the Ship Brookline, Year 1829." *California Historical Society Quarterly* 23 (Sept., 1944): 203–208.

———. *Life in California: During a Residence of Several Years in that Territory, Comprising a Description of the Country and the Missionary Establishments.* 1846. Edited by Doyce B. Nunis, Jr. New York: DaCapo Press, 1969.

Robinson, William W. *The Indians of Los Angeles: Story of the Liquidation of a People.* Early California Travels Series, no. 8. Los Angeles: G. Dawson, 1952.

———. *Land in California: The Story of Mission Lands, Ranchos, Squatters, Mining Claims, Railroad Grants, Land Scrip Homesteads.* Berkeley: University of California Press, 1948.

Rochester. "A Digger in the Chimney." *Hutchings' Illustrated California Magazine* 2 (June, 1858): 560–61.

Rolle, Andrew F. *An American in California: The Biography of William Heath Davis, 1822–1909.* San Marino, Calif.: Huntington Library, 1956.

Roosevelt, Theodore. *The Winning of the West.* Vol. 1. New York: G. P. Putnam's Sons, 1899.

Roquefeuil, Camille de. *Camille de Roquefeuil in San Francisco, 1817–1818.* Early California Travels Series, no. 23. Edited and translated by Charles N. Rudkin. Los Angeles: Glen Dawson, 1954.

Ryan, William Redmond. *Personal Adventures in Upper and Lower California, in 1848–49.* 2 vols. London: William Shoberl, 1850.

Rydell, Raymond A. *Cape Horn to the Pacific: The Rise and Decline of an Ocean Highway.* Berkeley: University of California Press, 1952.

Sage, Rufus B. *Rocky Mountain Life: Or, Startling Scenes and Perilous Adventures in the Far West.* Boston: Wentworth and Co., 1857.

Saum, Lewis O. "Frenchmen, Englishmen, and the Indian." *American West* 1 (Fall, 1964): 4–11.

———. "The Fur Trader and the Noble Savage." *American Quarterly* 15 (Winter, 1963): 554–71.

———. *The Fur Trader and the Indian.* Seattle: University of Washington Press, 1965.

Sauvel, Katherine Siva, and Pamela Monroe. *Chem'ivillu': Let's Speak Cahuilla.* Banning, Calif.: Malki Museum, 1982.

"Scenes Among the Indians of California." *Hutchings' Illustrated California*

Magazine 3 (April, 1859): 433–46.

Schaeffer, Luther M. *Sketches of Travels in South America, Mexico and California.* New York: James Egbert, 1860.

Schliemann, Heinrich. *Schliemann's First Visit to America, 1850–1851.* Edited by Shirley H. Weber. Cambridge, Mass.: Harvard University Press for the American School of Classical Studies, 1942.

Schmeckebier, Laurence F. *The Office of Indian Affairs: Its History, Activities and Organization.* Baltimore: Johns Hopkins University, 1927.

Schmölder, B. *The Emigrant's Guide to California: Describing its Geography, Agricultural and Commercial Resources.* London: Pelham Richardson, 1849.

Schoolcraft, Henry Rowe. *Archives of Aboriginal Knowledge: Containing All the Original Papers Laid before Congress Respecting the History, Antiquities, Language, Ethnology, Pictography, Rites, Superstitions, and Mythology, of the Indian Tribes of the United States.* Vol. 3. Philadelphia: J. B. Lippincott, 1860.

Sedgley, Joseph. *Overland to California in 1849.* Oakland, Calif.: Butler and Bowman, 1877.

Seyd, Ernest. *California and its Resources: A Work for the Merchant, the Capitalist, and the Emigrant.* London: Trubner and Co., 1858.

Seymour, Sandford. *Emigrant's Guide to the Gold Mines of Upper California.* Chicago: R. L. Wilson, 1849.

Shaler, William. *Journal of a Voyage Between China and the Northwestern Coast of America, Made in 1804 by William Shaler.* Introduction by Lindley Bynum. Claremont, Calif.: Sauders Studio Press, 1935.

Shaw, William. *Golden Dreams and Waking Realities: Being the Adventures of a Gold-Seeker in California and the Pacific Islands.* London: Smith, Elder and Co., 1851.

Sheehan, Bernard W. *Seeds of Extinction: Jeffersonian Philanthropy and the American Indian.* Chapel Hill: University of North Carolina Press, Institute of Early American History and Culture, 1973.

Shepard, William Finley, ed. "California Prior to Conquest: A Frenchman's Views." *California Historical Society Quarterly* 37 (March, 1958): 63–77.

Sherwood, J. Ely. *California: And the Way to Get There; with the Official Documents, Relating to the Gold Region, Including Col. Mason's Report, and Other Authentic Information Connected with the Subject.* New York: George F. Nesbitt, 1848.

———. *The Pocket Guide to California: A Sea and Land Route Book. Containing a Full Description of the El Dorado, its Agricultural Resources, Commercial Advantages, and Mineral Wealth. To Which is Added Practical Advice to Voyagers.* New York: J. E. Sherwood, 1849.

Shiveley, J. M. *Route and Distances to Oregon and California: With a Description of Watering-places, Crossings, Dangerous Indians, &c. &c.* Washington, D.C.: William Greer, 1846.

Simpkinson, Francis Guillemard, and Edward Belcher. *H. M. S. Sulphur at California, 1837 and 1839.* Edited by Richard A. Pierce and John W. Winslow. San Francisco: Book Club of California, 1969.

Simpson, George. *Narrative of a Voyage to California Ports in 1841–42.* San Francisco: Thomas C. Russell, 1930.

Simpson, Henry I. *Three Weeks in the Gold Mines: Or Adventures with the Gold Diggers of California in August, 1848, Together with Advice to Emigrants, with Full Instructions upon the Best Method of Getting There, Living Expenses, etc., etc., and a Complete Description of the Country, with a Map and Illustrations.* New York: Joyce and Co., 1848.

Simpson, Lesley Byrd. *The Repartimiento System of Native Labor In New Spain and Guatamala.* Studies in the Administration of the Indians in New Spain, vol. 3. Berkeley: University of California Press, 1938.

Soulé, Frank, John H. Gihon, and James Nisbet. *The Annals of San Francisco: Containing a Summary of the History of the First Discovery, Settlement, Progress, and Present Condition of California, and a Complete History of All the Important Events Connected with its Great City. To Which Are Added, Biographical Memoirs of Some Prominent Citizens.* New York: D. Appleton, 1854.

Stampp, Kenneth M. *The Era of Reconstruction, 1865–1877.* New York: Vintage, 1965.

Starr, Kevin. *Americans and the California Dream, 1850–1915.* New York: Oxford University Press, 1973.

Stewart, George R., Jr. *Bret Harte: Argonaut and Exile.* Boston and New York: Houghton Mifflin, 1931.

——. *Take Your Bible in One Hand: The Life of William Henry Thomes.* San Francisco: Colt Press, 1939.

Stewart, William M. *Reminiscences of Senator William M. Stewart of Nevada.* Edited by George Rothwell Brown. New York: Neale, 1908.

Stillman, Jacob D. B. *The Gold Rush Letters of J. D. B. Stillman.* Introduction by Kenneth Johnson. Palo Alto, Calif.: Lewis Osborne, 1967.

——. *Seeking the Golden Fleece: A Record of Pioneer Life in California.* San Francisco: A. Roman, 1877.

Stratton, R. B. *Captivity of the Oatman Girls: Being an Interesting Narrative of Life Among the Apache and Mohave Indians.* San Francisco: Whitton, Towne and Co., 1857.

Sullivan, Maurice S., ed. *The Travels of Jedediah Smith: A Documentary Outline Including the Journal of the Great American Pathfinder.* Santa Ana, Calif.: Fine Arts Press, 1934.

Sutter, John A. "The Discovery of Gold in California." *Hutchings' Illustrated California Magazine* 2 (Nov., 1857): 194–202.

——. *Sutter's Own Story: The Life of General Johann August Sutter and the History of New Helvetia in the Sacramento Valley.* Edited by Erwin G. Gudde. New York: G. P. Putnam's Sons, 1936.

Swan, John A. *A Trip to the Gold Mines of California in 1848.* Edited by

John A. Hussey. San Francisco: Book Club of California, 1960.

Swartzlow, Ruby Johnson. "Peter Lassen, Northern California's Trail-Blazer." *California Historical Society Quarterly* 18 (Dec., 1939): 291-314.

Tac, Pablo. *Indian Life and Customs at Mission San Luis Rey.* San Luis Rey, Calif.: Old Mission, 1958.

Tarakanoff, Vassilli Petrovitch. *Statement of My Captivity Among the Californians.* Early California Travels Series, no. 14. Translated by Ivan Petroff. Notes by Arthur Woodward. Los Angeles: Glen Dawson, 1953.

Taylor, Alexander Smith. "The Indianology of California." *California Farmer and Journal of Useful Sciences,* vols. 8-20 (Feb., 1860-Oct., 1863).

Taylor, Bayard. *Eldorado: Or, Adventures in the Path of Empire. Comprising a Voyage to California, via Panama; Life in San Francisco and Monterey; Pictures of the Gold Region, and Experiences of Mexican Travel.* 2 vols. 18th ed. New York: G. P. Putnam, 1859.

TePaske, John J. *Three American Empires.* New York: Harper and Row, 1967.

Thomas, Erwin N. *Modoc War: Its Military History and Topography.* Preface by Keith A. Murray. Sacramento, Calif.: Argus Books, 1971.

Thomes, William H. *On Land and Sea: Or, California in the Years 1843, '44, and '45.* Boston: DeWolfe, Fiske, 1884.

Treganza, Adan E. *Californian Clay Artifacts.* Robert E. Schenk Archives of California Archaeology, no. 22. San Francisco: Society for California Archaeology, 1946.

Trenholm, Virginia Cole, and Maurine Carley. *The Shoshonis: Sentinels of the Rockies.* Civilization of the American Indian Series, no. 74. Norman: University of Oklahoma Press, 1964.

Trennert, Robert A., Jr. *Alternative to Extinction: Federal Indian Policy and the Beginnings of the Reservation System, 1846-1851.* Philadelphia: Temple University Press, 1975.

Tyler, S. Lyman. *A History of Indian Policy.* Washington, D.C.: 1973.

Tyson, James L. *Diary of a Physician in California: Being the Results of Actual Experience Including Notes of the Journey by Land and Water and Observations on the Climate, Soil, Resources of the Country, Etc.* 1850. Index and foreword by Joseph A. Sullivan. Oakland, Calif.: Biobooks, 1955.

Tyson, Philip T. *Geology and Industrial Resources of California.* Baltimore: William Minifie, 1851.

Underhill, Reuben L. *From Cowhides to Golden Fleece: A Narrative of California, 1832-1858, Based upon Unpublished Correspondence of Thomas Oliver Larkin, Trader, Developer, Promoter, and California's Only American Consul.* Stanford: Stanford University Press, 1939.

Upham, Samuel C. *Notes on a Voyage to California, Via Cape Horn, Together with Scenes in El Dorado, in the Years 1849-50.* Philadelphia: printed by the author, 1878.

Vancouver, George. *Vancouver in California, 1792-1794: The Original Ac-*

count of George Vancouver. Early California Travels Series, nos. 9, 10, and 22. Edited by Marguerite Eyer Wilbur. Los Angeles: Glen Dawson, 1953–54.

Vandor, Paul E. *History of Fresno County, California, with Biographical Sketches of the Leading Men and Women of the County Who Have Been Identified with its Growth and Development from the Early Days to the Present.* Los Angeles: Historic Record Co., 1919.

Van Every, Dale. *Disinherited: The Lost Birthright of the American Indian.* New York: Morrow, 1966.

Veach, J. A. "About Clear Lake: Its Scenery &c. &c." *Hesperian* 2 (March, 1859): 21–26.

Victor, Frances Auretta Fuller Barrett. *The River of the West: Life and Adventure in the Rocky Mountains and Oregon; Embracing Events in the Lifetime of a Mountainman and Pioneer; with an Early History of the Northwestern Slope, Including an Account of the Fur Traders.* Hartford, Conn.: Columbian Book Co.; San Francisco: R. J. Trumbull and Co., 1870.

Vizetelly, Henry [J. Tyrwhitt Brooks]. *Four Months Among the Gold Finders in California: Being the Diary of an Expedition from San Francisco to the Gold Districts.* New York: D. Appleton, 1849.

Vogel-Jorgensen. T. "Peter Lassen of California." Translated by Helge Norrung. Mimeographed. Red Bluff, Calif.: Red Bluff Union High School, 1966.

Walker, Franklin. *A Literary History of Southern California.* Berkeley: University of California Press, 1950.

[Wallace, W. F.], ed. *History of Napa County: Comprising an Account of Its Topography, Geology, and Biography of Its Pioneers and Principal Inhabitants.* Oakland, Calif.: Enquirer Printing, 1901.

Ward, Sam. *Sam Ward in the Gold Rush.* Edited by Carvel Collins. Stanford: Stanford University Press, 1949.

Ware, Joseph E. *The Emigrants' Guide to California.* Introduction and notes by John Caughey. Princeton: Princeton University Press, 1932.

Washburn, Wilcomb E., ed. *The American Indian and the United States: A Documentary History.* Vol. 2. New York: Random House, 1973.

———. *The Indian and the White Man.* New York: New York University Press, 1964.

———. *The Indian in America.* The New American Nation Series. New York: Harper & Row, 1975.

Watkins, Frances W. "Charles F. Lummis and the Sequoya League." *Quarterly of the Historical Society of Southern California* 26 (June–Sept., 1944): 99–114.

Watson, Douglas S. "Spurious Californiana." *California Historical Society Quarterly* 11 (March, 1932): 65–68.

Waugh, Lorenzo. *Autobiography of Lorenzo Waugh.* 2d ed. San Francisco: S. P. Taylor, 1884.

"The Way the Digger Indians Bury Their Dead." *Hutchings' Illustrated California Magazine* 3 (Jan., 1859): 322.

Webb, Edith Buckland. *Indian Life at the Old Missions.* Foreword by F. W. Hodge. Los Angeles: W. F. Lewis, 1952.

Weber, David J., ed., *New Spain's Far Northern Frontier: Essays on Spain in the American West, 1540–1821.* Albuquerque: University of New Mexico Press, 1979.

Weinberg, Albert K. *Manifest Destiny: A Study of Nationalist Expansionism in American History.* Baltimore: Johns Hopkins University Press, 1935.

Weston S[ilas]. *Four Months in the Mines of California: Or, Life in the Mountains.* 2d ed. Providence, R.I.: Benjamin T. Albro, 1854.

Wheat, Carl I. *Books of the California Gold Rush: A Centennial Selection.* San Francisco: Colt Press, 1949.

Wilkes, Charles. *Narrative of the United States Exploring Expedition During the Years 1838, 1839, 1840, 1841, 1842.* Philadelphia: C. Sherman, 1844.

Willcox, R. N. *Reminiscences of California Life: Being an Abridged Description of Scenes Which the Author Has Passed Through in California and Other Lands.* Avery, Ohio: Willcox, 1897.

Willys, Rufus Kay. "French Imperialists in California." *California Historical Society Quarterly* 8 (June, 1929): 116–29.

Wilson, Benjamin David. "Observations on Early Days in California and New Mexico." *Annual Publication of the Historical Society of Southern California.* (1934): 74–150.

Windeler, Adolphus. *The California Gold Rush Diary of a German Sailor.* Edited by W. Turrentine Jackson. Berkeley: Howell-North Books, 1969.

Woods, Daniel B. *Sixteen Months at the Gold Diggings.* New York: Harper and Brothers, 1851.

"The World in California," *Hutchings' Illustrated California Magazine* 1 (Feb., 1857): 338–46.

Wyld, James. *A Guide to the Gold Country of California: An Authentic and Descriptive Narrative of the Latest Discoveries in that Country.* London: W. Strange, 1849.

Yates, John. *A Sailor's Sketch of the Sacramento Valley in 1842.* Edited by Ferol Egan. Berkeley, Calif.: Friends of the Bancroft Library, 1971.

Yount, George C. "The Chronicles of George C. Yount." Edited by Charles L. Camp. *California Historical Society Quarterly* 2 (April, 1923): 3–66.

Zollinger, James P. *Sutter: The Man and His Empire.* New York: Oxford University Press, 1939.

Index

285

De la Guerra, Pablo: 86
Delevan, James: 94
Diegueño Indians: 13
Diet of California Indians: 6, 8, 11, 12, 18, 33, 49, 50, 51, 176, 177, 190–95, 198, 201, 214–16
"Diggers": 49, 51, 59, 97, 99, 155, 172, 187, 190, 195, 199
Dillon, Edward: 103
Dirt, associated with California Indians: 190, 191, 193, 195, 197
Disease among California Indians: at Spanish missions, 18, 39, 55, 61–62; in American period, 171, 175, 176; resistance to, 214; *see also* population; smallpox; venereal disease
Domestic servants, California Indians as: 67, 75, 81, 90, 93, 99, 105, 109, 111, 114–15, 213
Douglas, David F.: 89
Drake, Francis: 25
Dress of California Indians: 6, 8, 11, 14, 25, 33, 53, 187, 188, 190–95, 201; *see also* nudity
Drug use by California Indians: 8
Duhaut-Cilly, Auguste Bernard: 37, 38
Dunbar, Edward: 127
Du Petit-Thouars, Abel: 29, 34, 39
Duran, Narciso: 56

Echeandía, José María: 56
Education of California Indians: 209–14; on reservations, 159–60, 212, 216
Eel River: 100, 164
El Dorado, legend of: 3
Ellison, William Henry: 141, 147
Elsasser, Albert D.: 7, 187
Encomienda: 3, 85, 105
Estudillo, María de Jesus: 70
Evans, Albert S.: 175–76
Extermination of California Indians: 55, 132, 141, 162, 170; advocated and attempted, 171, 176–84, 200, 206; protest against, 183–85; sup-

ported by policy, 185–86; related to alleged primitiveness, 186, 200–201

Farnham, Thomas Jefferson: 23, 63, 64, 70
Feather River: 120, 122, 123, 187
Federal Indian policy: *see* removal policy; reservations for California Indians; termination policy; treaties
Federated Women's Clubs: 210
Forbes, Alexander: 10
Forbes, Robert B.: 61–62
Fort Humboldt: 100, 103
Franciscans: 3, 5–6, 13–14, 19–21, 25–26, 55, 60, 64; *see also* missionaries; missions
Frémont, Jessie Benton: 115
Frémont, John Charles: 78, 79, 188
Fresno county: 163
Fresno reservation: 152, 163, 164
Fresno River: 124
Fur trade: *see* beaver trappers

Gabrielino Indians: 8, 47–48, 52, 215
Gálvez, José de: 13
Ghost Dance: 212–13
Gibbs, George: 110
Gibson, Hugh: 159–60
Gila River: 48, 196
Gold: discovery of, 116–17, 121, 123, 140; mining of, 117–33; *see also* miners
Good, Hiram: 100, 182
Grant, Campbell: 8
Grant, Ulysses S.: 158, 211
Great Basin: 6, 12, 49
Green, Jonathan: 62–63
Green, Thomas J.: 117
Guadalupe Hidalgo, Treaty of: 81, 82, 86

Hacienda: 3–4, 20–21, 85, 107
Halleck, Henry W.: 85
Hanson, George M.: 95, 96, 102, 103, 163, 167

287